LOUISIANA IN THE
CONFEDERACY

LOUISIANA
IN THE
CONFEDERACY

BY

JEFFERSON DAVIS BRAGG

LOUISIANA STATE UNIVERSITY PRESS
BATON ROUGE, LOUISIANA

Copyright © 1941, 1969 by Louisiana State University Press
Manufactured in the United States of America

Louisiana Paperback Edition, 1997
06   05   04   03   02   01   00   99   98   97   5   4   3   2   1

Library of Congress Cataloging-in-Publication Data

Bragg, Jefferson Davis.
    Louisiana in the Confederacy / by Jefferson Davis Bragg. –
Louisiana pbk. ed.
        p.   cm.
    Originally published: 1941.
    Includes bibliographical references (p.   ) and index.
    ISBN 0-8071-2179-7 (pbk.   : alk. paper)
    1. Louisiana–History–Civil War, 1861–1865.   I. Title.
E565.B73   1997
973.7'463–dc21   96-49698
                                                         CIP
The paper in this book meets the guidelines for permanence and durabil-
ity of the Committee on Production Guidelines for Book Longevity of the
Council on Library Resources. ∞

TO
MILDRED, MARY OWENS, AND DAVIS

Preface

THE STORY OF the Civil War and the history of the Confederacy have been written around the campaigns in Virginia, Tennessee, and North Georgia, and from the viewpoint of Richmond. The Lower South and the Southwest have not received the attention which they deserve. Likewise, the history of Louisiana has too often been the record of New Orleans. This study is an attempt to tip the scales, howsoever lightly, in favor of a neglected section and people.

A pleasant task was made a delightful experience by the universal spirit of co-operation and helpfulness which the writer met in every direction in which he happened to turn in search of material. I can mention here only a few of those to whom I am indebted for assistance. For courteous, efficient, and helpful services, I wish to express my gratitude to the staffs of the Library of the University of Texas, Baylor University Library, Louisiana State University Library, Howard Memorial Library, the Library of the Louisiana Historical Society, and the Confederate Memorial Museum in New Orleans. To Mr. W. R. Hogan, assistant archivist at the Louisiana State University, and his staff I am grateful for many courtesies. I am especially indebted to Miss Lavinia Egan of Mt. Lebanon, Mrs. H. T. Gladney of Shreveport, and Mrs. Shirley Staples of Alexandria for permission to use valuable manuscript source material, and to the late Mrs. J. D. Lindsay of Shreveport for the privilege of examining the files of the Shreveport *News,* now possessed by Louisiana State University.

I wish to thank Professors Walter Prichard and Fred C. Cole of Louisiana State University for reading the manuscript

Preface

and suggesting changes that have been most helpful. Professor Charles W. Ramsdell of the University of Texas was my counselor during the period of research and at the time of the preparation of the original manuscript. His broad and accurate knowledge of the subject and of the sources, his unfailing sympathetic interest in the problems involved, and his many helpful criticisms of both content and style contributed immeasurably to bring this study to a conclusion. To Professor Ramsdell and to my wife, for her encouragement and assistance in proofreading, I am indebted most.

Thanks are due also to Mr. Louis P. Carr and to my brother, Hilton S. Bragg, both of Houston, Texas, for the map that is reproduced on the end leaves. Finally, the writer is indebted to Dr. Marcus M. Wilkerson, Director of the Louisiana State University Press, for counsel and for his interest in this volume, and to Mrs. Leta B. Triche, also of the Press, for her many helpful suggestions and for her expert assistance in preparing the manuscript for the printer.

J. D. B.

Contents

Chapter I

Secession of Louisiana

NATIONAL POLITICS HAD become of supreme importance in Louisiana by 1860. Interest in the approaching presidential election was manifested very early in the year, for many Louisianians were apprehensive of the future of their economic and social institutions. Naturally, they had not remained indifferent to the sectional controversies of the past decade but had watched the actors on the national stage with more than ordinary interest. Northern hostility to the Fugitive Slave Law, the debates in Congress over the Kansas-Nebraska Bill, the troubles in Kansas, and the founding and phenomenal growth of the Republican party, with its belief in the restriction of slave territory and with its abolitionist wing, had greatly disturbed many Louisianians. Retiring Governor Paul O. Hébert and the incoming Governor Robert C. Wickliffe considered the situation serious enough to devote attention to the question of the Union in their public messages in 1856. Governor Hébert said in his last message to the Legislature that the wild spirit of fanaticism had disturbed the peace of the country for many years and had steadily increased in power and influence. This spirit nullified the laws of Congress and "now aspires to control the Federal Legislature." The slaveholding states had been warned and should be prepared for the issue. The time for concession and compromise on the part of the South had passed. "If the Union cannot be maintained upon the just

1

and wholesome principles of the Constitution," he said, "concessions and compromise will only retard its dissolution, spoke ominously of the Union. "Next to the liberty of the citizens and the sovereignty of the States," he regarded the not save it."[1] In his inaugural address Governor Wickliffe Union as the "primary object of patriotic desire." It was very evident, he said, "that the hold which the Union once had upon the affection of the South had been materially weakened, and that its dissolution is now frequently spoken of, if not with absolute levity, yet with positive indifference, and, occasionally, as desirable."[2]

The uneasy state of the public mind in Louisiana experienced an extension which with many grew to alarm with the John Brown Raid of October, 1859, and the sympathy with which Brown's plan was received in the North. The bitter contest in the United States House of Representatives over the election of the speaker, involving as it did Hinton R. Helper's indictment of slavery in *The Impending Crisis,* added to the excitement among slaveholders. William Tecumseh Sherman, newly elected superintendent of the Louisiana State Seminary of Learning, wrote from New Orleans on December 12, 1859: "As long as the abolitionists and the Republicans seem to threaten the safety of slave property so long will this excitement last, and no one can foresee its result; but all here talk as if a dissolution of the Union were not only a possibility but a probability of easy execution."[3] Sherman was embarrassed in his new position in Louisiana by the fact that his brother John, prominent Republican

[1] New Orleans *Daily Crescent,* January 24, 1856; Charles Gayarré, *History of Louisiana* (New York, 1854–1866), IV, 680.

[2] New Orleans *Daily Crescent,* January 31, 1856; Gayarré, *History of Louisiana,* IV, 681.

[3] William T. Sherman to Mrs. William T. Sherman. Reprinted by permission of the publishers, Arthur H. Clark Company, from Walter L. Fleming (ed.), *General W. T. Sherman As College President* (Cleveland, 1912), 77.

candidate for the speakership, had endorsed Helper's attack on slavery. Writing from the Seminary near Alexandria, December 23, Sherman said: "You can readily imagine the delicate position I now hold at the head of a seminary to open January 1 next, for the instruction and training of young men to science and arms, at the same time that John Sherman's name is bandied about as the representative of all that is held here murderous and detestable." [4]

Doubtless many Louisianians agreed in substance with the New Orleans *Daily Crescent* when on January 5, 1860, it said, editorially·

A modern Black Republican is but a political chrysalis that the first ray of political sunshine must inevitably worm into an Abolitionist. . . . So far, therefore, as the South is concerned, it makes little difference whether Garrison, Fred Douglass, or Abby Kelly are selected as the leaders of the Republicans, or that party chooses to follow the counsels of Seward, Greeley, Grow or the Washburnes. The end of both classes of these men is the same. . . . One wishes to knock you down and take away your slaves by force; the other desires the privilege of persuading your slave to knock you down himself and escape—or, failing in that, to . . . compel you, in self-defence, to send him away yourself.

The Louisiana Legislature convened at Baton Rouge on January 17, 1860. The subject of "Federal Relations" consumed about one fourth of the message of the retiring governor, Robert C. Wickliffe. In introducing the subject, the governor said:

I had hoped to retire from the exalted position with which the people of the Commonwealth have honored me without extended reference to national affairs or national politics. I had fondly wished that I might bring my administration to a close with a simple, yet favorable allusion to those subjects. It is, however, with profound regret that I feel constrained to announce to you

[4] Sherman to Thomas Ewing, Jr. Reprinted by permission of the publishers, Arthur H. Clark Company, from *ibid.*, 88. See also William T. Sherman, *Memoirs of General W. T. Sherman* (New York, 1891), I, 175–76.

my hopes in this respect have been blighted, and that I deem it my solemn duty, as your Chief Magistrate and representative of the people, to enlarge upon a disagreeable topic. Its importance demands my best attention and commands your closest consideration.[5]

Governor Wickliffe then referred to the "quarter-century sectional warfare waged by the North against the South," beginning with a small band of "fanatics" whose promulgations were deemed "fit subjects for mirth." But the small band had grown into a powerful organization; and the cloud, "once a mere speck upon the horizon, has attained such dimensions that it blackens the skies of the majority section of the Confederacy." States, he said, had passed laws which set at defiance the Constitution of the United States and nullified laws of Congress. The message insisted that the fanaticism which afflicted the North must be "confronted and beaten back." As a constructive suggestion, the governor recommended a complete reorganization of the militia. "The state," he said, "should provide for the equipment of her own men, in all respects, within herself, so as to be independent should the hour of trial come, of all outside assistance." Governor Wickliffe recommended that Louisiana be represented in case a congress or convention of the slave states should be called for consultation regarding means of mutual safety.

The retiring governor shared the popular alarm and indignation over the John Brown affair at Harper's Ferry, and he included the following recommendations in his message:

To assure her [Virginia], as well as the other border slave States of the active cooperation of Louisiana; to show them that we recognize their cause as our cause, I recommend the immediate appropriation by the Legislature of $25,000, as Louisiana's quota toward these expenses, accompanied by a solemn pledge that our State will stand by her sister Southern States to the utmost extent

[5] The message is quoted in full in the New Orleans *Daily Crescent,* January 19, 1860.

4

of the men and means she can command, in any course they may see proper to adopt to secure our Constitutional rights.

In line with the governor's recommendations, on January 18, Henry W. Allen of West Baton Rouge Parish, chairman of the House Committee on Federal Relations, introduced a resolution which declared that the Harper's Ferry affair was an attack by the North upon the rights of the entire South; that Louisiana would stand by Virginia in case of another invasion of her territory; that Northern sympathy for John Brown was evidence of a deep-seated hostility in the North toward the constitutional rights of the South; and that the election of a "Black Republican President" in November would be sufficient cause for a dissolution of the Union. Therefore, he recommended the appropriation of $25,000 to be given to Virginia to aid in defraying the expenses of the state in fighting the battles of the South. The resolution also provided that in the event of the election of a "Black Republican President," the "Governor shall order an election of delegates to represent Louisiana in a Southern Convention, and to cooperate with other states in taking such steps as the circumstances of the case and honor of the country may require." [6]

The inauguration of Governor Thomas Overton Moore occurred on January 23. The new governor devoted much time in his inaugural address to the subject of Federal relations. Louisiana, he said, had always been moderate and conservative in her sentiments; and her citizens had been loyal lovers of the Union. But Louisiana, proclaimed the new governor, was something more than a mere state of the Union; she was a Southern slaveholding state, and Louisiana's duty to herself and to her sister slaveholding states might be

[6] *Ibid.* The *Crescent*, January 21, 1860, reported that the resolution was "laid over" and two days later editorially recommended adoption. The resolution seems to have died in committee, as the Louisiana *Acts*, 1860, contain no joint resolution of such a nature.

brought into painful conflict with her devotion to the Union. A great party, he continued, had grown up in the North and West based on animosity to the institutions of fifteen states; unless every state be permitted to determine her own social institutions and enjoy them in peace, the Union could not last.[7]

This inaugural address was delivered nearly ten months before Lincoln's election and several months before the national party conventions convened. Louisiana's chief executive, who was to serve in that capacity for the greater part of the Civil War, correctly stated the one great issue which was the crux of the whole question of sectional conflict. The territories, he said, must be freely opened for settlement; and the demand that there be no more slave states must be abandoned.[8]

The Louisiana Democratic party did not, however, enjoy complete harmony. A wing of the party, known as New Liners, supported Stephen A. Douglas and was distinctly hostile to the Buchanan Administration and to John Slidell, United States senator and the leader of the "Southern rights" group of Louisiana Democrats. When the state Democratic convention met at Baton Rouge on March 5 to select delegates to the national convention at Charleston, the Old Liners, as the Slidell Democrats were called, were in a decided majority. The New Orleans *Daily Picayune* correspondent seems to have gauged the situation correctly on the first day when he wrote:

Squatter sovereignty and the popular sovereignty doctrines of Mr. Douglas will receive their final quietus at the hands of the convention, as far as Louisiana is concerned. The Douglas men, who come principally from Lafourche, Assumption, Ascension, and that section of the State will be found in a sad minority, and it is thought they will not attempt to bring Douglas forward.

[7] New Orleans *Daily Crescent*, January 24, 1860.
[8] *Ibid.*

Secession of Louisiana

So far as I can learn, Mr. Breckenridge [*sic*] is the favorite of the convention; but, as I telegraphed this morning; no expression of opinion will be made in his favor, over any other man who favors the Administration—at least that is the expectation at this moment.[9]

The convention adopted a series of resolutions in which "undiminished confidence" in the administration of Buchanan and belief in the ability and statesmanship of John Slidell were expressed.[10] With reference to Slidell, the resolution stated also that Louisiana Democrats "consider him eminently qualified for the office of President of the United States." A motion to strike out the resolution expressing confidence in Slidell was defeated 206 to 34. The convention refused to instruct the delegates to the Charleston convention on the question of a presidential nominee. A motion to instruct delegates to cast their votes for John C. Breckinridge was defeated 233 to 29.[11]

The sixth resolution stated that in the event of the election of a President on the principles of the Republican party, "we concur in the opinion that Louisiana should meet in council her sister slaveholding States to consult as to the means of future protection." On the question of slavery the convention adopted the following resolution:

That the territories of the United States belong to the several States as their common property, and not to the individuals

[9] New Orleans *Daily Picayune*, March 7, 1860. Apparently, not every Douglas supporter in Louisiana endorsed the Senator's popular sovereignty doctrine. Alexander F. Pugh, a sugar planter of Assumption Parish, while in New Orleans on March 12, 1860, wrote in his diary, "I have met Dr. Ballard, and I find he is a strong advocate for Mr. Douglas for the Presidency. Like all other Southern supporters I discover he is nonetheless opposed to his squatter sovereignty principles." Alexander Franklin Pugh Diary (MS. in Louisiana State University Department of Archives). Cited hereafter as Alexander F. Pugh Diary.

[10] New Orleans *Daily Picayune*, March 7, 1860.

[11] *Ibid.*

7

thereof. That the federal constitution recognized property in slaves, and, as such, the owner thereof is entitled to carry his slaves into any of the Territories of the United States, and hold them there as property; and in case the people of the Territories, by inaction, unfriendly legislation, or otherwise should endanger the tenure of such property, or discriminate against it, by withholding that protection given to other species of property in the Territories, it is the duty of the General Government to interpose by active exertion of its constitutional powers to secure the rights of slaveholders.[12]

The delegates elected to the Charleston convention were F. H. Hatch, Effingham Lawrence, John Tarleton, D. D. Withers, James A. McHatton, Charles Jones, Benjamin W. Pearce, Alexander Mouton, Emile La Sere, Augustus G. Talbot, Robert A. Hunter, and Richard Taylor.[13] Professor Dwight L. Dumond says of these delegates: "The Louisiana delegation was composed almost entirely of large property holders, there being but one lawyer and one officeholder. It represented several million dollars in sugar and cotton plantation property, eight of its members having average incomes in excess of $25,000, and more than sixty slaves each." [14] The Louisiana delegation to the convention at Charleston, therefore, represented the ultra-Southern doctrines. It was definitely opposed to the views of Douglas and firmly committed to the principle of Congressional protection of slavery in the territories. The vote of Louisiana at Charleston was to be cast as a unit by a majority of the delegates present.[15]

The proceedings of the Democratic convention at Charleston are too well known to require an extended discussion. The convention assembled on April 21. On the twenty-sixth

[12] *Ibid.*   [13] *Ibid.*

[14] Reprinted by permission of the publishers, The Macmillan Company, from Dwight L. Dumond, *The Secession Movement, 1860–1861* (New York, 1931), 52 n. See also editorial in New Orleans *Daily Delta,* May 5, 1860.

[15] Fifth Resolution of the Louisiana Convention, in New Orleans *Daily Picayune,* March 7, 1860.

Secession of Louisiana

the special correspondent of the New Orleans *Crescent* wrote from Charleston:

Senator Slidell keeps himself in the background. He is rarely seen in the streets and never in the Convention Hall. He is quietly engaged in endeavoring so to stock [*sic*] the cards as that Douglas will be defeated and some one nominated whom he can be intimately associated with, politically, of course, as well as personally. . . .

The Louisiana delegation, as a body compares favorably with that from any other State in point of solid attainments, make whatever use of the word you may choose. They are firm and decided in their expression of views, and are not generally regarded as being of the ultra stripe, though two or three of them are as much so as Yancey himself.[16]

Alexander Mouton of the Louisiana delegation presented the resolution of the Louisiana convention providing for Congressional protection of slavery in the territories. The correspondent of the New York *Tribune* was of the opinion on April 25 that the "Louisiana resolutions" would be adopted by the convention.[17] But that body rejected the majority report of its platform committee and adopted the minority report, sustaining the views of Stephen A. Douglas. The *Picayune*'s special correspondent describes the seriousness of the situation on Sunday, April 29:

Charleston presents today a novel scene. If the city was besieged and its people called upon to surrender, there could not be more earnestness depicted on men's countenances, or a more serious attitude maintained, giving expression to the alarming agitation of the times. . . . The excitment is very great, greater than it has been yet, and the breach in the party wider than it was before, with hardly a hope of reconciliation.[18]

On Monday, April 30, the Louisiana delegation, following those of Alabama and Mississippi, withdrew from the Charles-

16 New Orleans *Daily Crescent,* May 2, 1860.
17 New Orleans *Daily Picayune,* April 25, 1860.
18 *Ibid.,* May 4, 1860.

ton convention. Mouton, in announcing their departure, stated that two members of the delegation—Jones and Mc-Hatton—, although acting with the majority, did so under protest.[19] On the next day, the delegation addressed a communication to Caleb Cushing, president of the convention, stating that their withdrawal was due to the rejection of the resolution on slavery in the territories, since the convention "refused to recognize the fundamental principles of the Democracy of the State we have the honor to represent." [20]

Opinion in Louisiana concerning the action of the Charleston convention delegates was divided. On May 2 the New Orleans *Delta* justified the withdrawal of the delegates as the "logical culmination of the principles of Southern Democracy," and characterized the disruption of the Charleston convention as "the natural and justifiable consequences of the arrogant pretensions set up by the Northern delegations to govern the Convention in its choice of a nominee, and to impose upon it a platform of principles which would be rejected by every Southern State." In Northwest Louisiana the *Bossier Banner* commended the delegates in the following language:

We can lay no blame at the hands of those of our delegates that seceded when they saw that our rights were not to be respected. . . . We sent them there to elect a Democrat with Southern sentiments, and to defeat, and show no favor to the Illinois Traitor, and to the best of their ability they did so. Rather than submit to his odious doctrine of slavery in the territories they withdrew from the convention, and who can blame them? We do not for one. The men who are now opposed and derided by some, as being secessionists, fire-eaters, etc., are the very men that have fought bravely and manfully for the Constitutional rights of the South. They would not submit calmly to doctrines antagonistic to our future good welfare, and for this they are cried down by

[19] Dumond, *Secession Movement,* 52.

[20] James K. Greer, "Louisiana Politics, 1845–1860," in *Louisiana Historical Quarterly* (New Orleans), XIII (1930), 468.

their fellow Democrats. Well and good. We are truly proud to know that there are at least a few pure-minded patriots who will not trust their honor in the keeping of the Abolition fanatics at the North. . . .

Stephen Arnold Douglas! the Abolition traitor, whose vaulting ambition of "Rule or Ruin" has succeeded in creating a breach in the Democratic ranks that will take time to repair. To him and his followers may we attribute the causes of the late disruption. Traitors to the heart—corrupt as the foul demons of the damned are the treacherous hearts of the incarnate wretches who planned the overthrow and defeat of the friends of the South. Well does Shakespeare say:

> "I will be hang'd if some eternal villain,
> Some busy and insinuating rogue,
> Some cogging cozzening slave, to get some office,
> Have not devised this plot." [21]

Meanwhile, the Douglas Democrats were expressing their disapproval of the Charleston "seceders." On May 7 the following announcement, to which were attached the names of 107 citizens,[22] appeared in the New Orleans *Crescent:*

All citizens opposed to the secession movements of the Louisiana and other State delegations at the Charleston Convention, and who approve the course pursued by Stephen A. Douglas, are invited to meet in LaFayette Square, at 7 o'clock, to take counsel together, and to protest against any action of any citizens of this State, which, at Charleston or elsewhere, would commit the people of Louisiana to any measure or scheme destructive of the Union.

Citizens of East Baton Rouge Parish met in Baton Rouge on May 9, condemned the Louisiana delegation for withdrawing at Charleston, and recommended that a state convention be called to elect representatives to Baltimore to replace the seceding delegates.[23]

[21] Bellevue *Bossier Banner,* May 25, 1860.

[22] One of the names was that of Michael Hahn, destined to be governor of the New Orleans area of Louisiana in 1864–1865.

[23] Baton Rouge *Weekly Gazette and Comet,* May 10, 1860.

Louisiana in the Confederacy

The New Orleans *Daily True Delta* condemned the bolters in no uncertain terms and charged that the destruction of the Union was "the grand aim of the Yanceys and the Moutons." [24] The *Picayune*, whose attitude may be described as neutral rather than "Douglas," said, "Few men, with a full conviction of its expediency, advocate the holding of a convention at Richmond," and added, "Louisiana will not sustain disunionism." [25] The Alexandria *American* of May 17, 1860, made the following remarks concerning one of the Charleston delegates:

We learn that R. A. Hunter, late delegate to the Charleston Convention, arrived in town last night. The query is, what did he come for? By some it is supposed that he came for the purpose of stirring up the Slidellians to get up a ratification meeting to endorse his bullying course at the Charleston Convention. It is also said that he has been dispatched by John Slidell as a missionary to enlighten the heathen of Rapides, and to confer with Governor Moore in relation to the troubles in the camp of the faithful.[26]

More than six hundred names were attached to an announcement in the *Crescent* of May 11 calling a mass meeting in New Orleans for the following evening. The purpose of the meeting was declared to be to sustain the Louisiana delegates to the Charleston convention "in their manly defense of the interests and honor of the slaveholding States." The meeting was held in Odd Fellows Hall, and resolutions were adopted endorsing and commending the action of the Charleston delegates from Louisiana and urging the reassembling of the state Democratic convention "for the purpose of deter-

[24] Dwight L. Dumond (ed.), *Southern Editorials on Secession* (New York, 1931), 86–89.

[25] New Orleans *Daily Picayune*, May 15, 1860.

[26] Quoted in the Bellevue *Bossier Banner*, May 25, 1860. The editor of the *Banner* replied that no matter what Colonel Hunter's business was "he will be sure to act the straightforward gentleman, which is more than the editor of the *American* can do, to save his gizzard."

mining the course to be pursued by the State in reference to the Presidency." [27]

Supporters of Douglas held a "National Democratic" meeting in New Orleans on May 19 and elected delegates to the state convention scheduled to convene at Donaldsonville, June 6. Pierre Soulé, former United States minister to Spain, addressed the audience at length, asserting that the coming issue was one of the greatest importance; for it might result in the "ruin and consummation of that glorious fabric, the Constitution." [28]

Meanwhile, Bell and Everett had been nominated; and there was considerable enthusiasm for them in Louisiana, especially among slaveholders, merchants, and other businessmen. A meeting of their supporters was held in Odd Fellows Hall, New Orleans, on May 30. According to the *Picayune*, the building was filled to capacity; and the *Crescent* asserted that the hall was "jammed," adding that "a more crowded or respectable meeting never, on any occasion, assembled within its walls." [29] Christian Roselius, a German immigrant who had risen to a place of eminence in the Louisiana bar and who occupied at this time the chair of civil law in the University of Louisiana; and Randell Hunt, also a distinguished New Orleans attorney and a professor of common law, were the principal speakers. Roselius alluded to the disturbing element that menaced the Union and referred to "secession," "nullification," and "abolition" as "demagogueism." Resolutions were adopted endorsing and ratifying the nomination of Bell and Everett and asserting that "we admit of no other platform than the Constitution." [30]

The state Democratic convention reconvened at Baton Rouge on June 4. The action of the delegates in withdraw-

[27] New Orleans *Daily Crescent*, May 14, 1860.
[28] *Ibid.*, May 21, 1860.   [29] *Ibid.*, May 31, 1860.
[30] *Ibid.*; Willie M. Caskey, *Secession and Restoration of Louisiana* (University, La., 1938), 6–7.

13

ing from the Charleston convention was sustained; the right of the delegates to seats in the Baltimore convention was affirmed; the Richmond convention was approved; and the delegates were authorized to withdraw from Baltimore, if they saw fit, and to join the Richmond convention in nominating candidates.[31]   A minority report was submitted, which, while upholding the position that the South was entitled to protection of property of every description at all times in the territories and sustaining the delegates to Charleston, called for the Louisiana delegation to the Baltimore convention to remain in that convention, though protesting if guarantees to slavery in territories were not included in the platform.[32]   The purpose of the instruction to remain in Baltimore was stated to be unwillingness to "hazard the existence of the only party to which the country looks to defeat the avowed enemies of our equality in the Union."   The minority report received the support of the delegates of the parishes of Bossier, Caddo, Claiborne, Rapides, and Sabine— a total of thirty-three votes.[33]

The Soulé faction of Louisiana Democrats held a state convention on June 6, at Donaldsonville, with 141 delegates from twenty-one of the forty-eight parishes.[34]   The convention, by resolutions, declared that the Louisiana delegates at Charleston had vacated their seats and had "severed themselves from the great National Democratic family."   The delegates expressed themselves concerning the position of the Charleston bolters on the question of Congressional protection of slavery in the territories by asserting "that the attempt to call for the interference of Congress in questions concerning slavery in the Territories can only be productive of a conflict between

[31] New Orleans *Daily Picayune,* June 5, 1860.

[32] New Orleans *Daily Delta,* June 7, 1860.

[33] *Ibid.*

[34] Greer, "Louisiana Politics, 1845–1860," in *loc. cit.,* 472.   Greer, however, says there were forty-nine parishes.   The *United States Census* for 1860 and the official election returns list forty-eight parishes.

the North and the South, which must inevitably end in the disruption of this great confederacy of ours." Delegates to the Baltimore convention were elected; and, although Stephen A. Douglas was endorsed, support was pledged to the Baltimore nominee.[35]

Two sets of delegates from Louisiana, therefore, appeared at the Democratic convention in Baltimore. One delegation was that which had withdrawn from the Charleston meeting, and the other delegates were those elected by the Donaldsonville convention, June 6. On June 19 the former Charleston delegates from Louisiana were refused admission at Baltimore, and two days later the Soulé delegation was seated.[36] A member of this delegation, former Governor Wickliffe, had a share in framing the "Douglas" platform.[37]

The anti-Douglas delegates met as the Southern Constitutional Democratic convention in Baltimore, with twenty-one states represented, and nominated John C. Breckinridge for the presidency. Richard Taylor of Louisiana was one of the vice-presidents of this convention, and Robert A. Hunter took an active part in the convention proceedings.[38]

The campaign was waged in Louisiana with increasing enthusiasm in the months of July, August, September, October, and November. Parades, music, fireworks, torches, cannon, bells, mottoes, banners, and flags were all used in the effort to win the voters. The "Breckinridge Guards," "Lane Dragoons," "Young Bell Ringers," "Young Men's Douglas and Johnson Clubs," and the "Minute Men of '60" added life and color to the contest.

It appeared from the first that the contest in Louisiana was between Bell and Breckinridge, although Douglas possessed considerable strength in New Orleans. As early as June 28,

[35] New Orleans *Daily Picayune*, June 7, 1860.

[36] Greer, "Louisiana Politics, 1845–1860," in *loc. cit.*, 474.

[37] Emerson D. Fite, *The Presidential Campaign of 1860* (New York, 1911), 185.

[38] Greer, "Louisiana Politics, 1845–1860," in *loc. cit.*, 474.

the *Crescent* declared its "unqualified preference" for Bell and Everett and on the following day said:

The times demand that some one should be at the head of affairs whose administration, while securing justice to all, would have a tendency to repress and destroy the fell spirit of sectionalism that bids fair to overthrow the Government if stimulated and kept up a few years longer. We believe that, of all the candidates before the people, the election of Mr. Bell would have the happiest effect in restoring the whole Union to those feelings of nationality that pervaded the people everywhere when the Presidency was so ably administered by Mr. Fillmore.

Later the *Crescent* urged the South to unite upon Bell and Everett as the only way to prevent a "Black Republican" triumph.[39] In answering the criticism that the Constitutional Union platform was vague and indefinite, the *Crescent* said that platforms were a modern invention; and that a platform, "like many other modern inventions, . . . is a humbug." Washington, Adams, Jefferson, and Madison were not elected upon any prescribed platforms. The editor concluded by saying: "We would sooner have an honest and reliable man for President without any platform whatever, than a tricky and time-serving politician with the best platform in the world." [40]

The *Crescent* announced that the *Courrier du Teche* of St. Martinsville, the Opelousas *Patriot,* the *Morehouse Advocate* of Bastrop, and the Thibodaux *Gazette* had come out for Bell and Everett.[41] The Shreveport *South-Western* carried on an active campaign for the Constitutional Union candidates. At the head of its editorial column appeared a likeness of the United States flag with the words "Our country and our Party" written across the flag. Underneath were the words "Forever Float That Standard Sheet." In August a new

[39] New Orleans *Daily Crescent,* July 2, 1860.
[40] *Ibid.,* July 24, 1860.
[41] *Ibid.,* July 25, August 2, 23, 1860.

16

paper, the *Constitutional,* edited by C. W. Boyce and devoted to the cause of Bell, appeared at Alexandria.[42]

The New Orleans *Delta* championed the cause of Breckinridge and Lane. It waged a campaign more of satire and sarcasm than of calm rationalism, frequently ridiculing the candidates and the campaign of the opposition. Bell was described as a "quaint, homely, sleepy old gentleman"; Everett, though "greatly inferior to Bell," was his superior in "frigidity"—his best statue was erected by Boston boys "out of January snow." Campaign methods of the Bell followers were characterized as "tomfoolery." [43]

The Baton Rouge *Weekly Gazette and Comet* supported Douglas. Actually, the editor confessed that he favored Bell and Everett, but he saw no chance of their election. Could it be shown that they had a fair chance of success, "we would go in for them and do our handsomest. But as this cannot be done, the next best thing, will be to go for Douglas. We do not like his 'squatter' doctrine any better than you do; but admire him for his bold, consistent and fearless course." [44]

The *Picayune* seemed to be more concerned over the future of the country than with the prospects of any particular candidates. Its editorials were characterized by dignity, seriousness, and penetrating thought. It sought to harmonize the Southern factions and to warn the South of the danger in the

[42] Shreveport *South-Western,* August 15, 1860.

[43] New Orleans *Daily Delta,* May 31, September 20, 1860. Alexander F. Pugh was impressed most unfavorably by the oratory of a Bell and Everett meeting in New Orleans on August 1. Writing in his diary on that date, he said: "I attended and such stuff as I heard was enough to disgust any decent man. It was a fair sized meeting, but if I am to judge of the position of the members of the party from the talks of the speakers I heard I should say they were the lowest dregs of society." Alexander F. Pugh Diary.

[44] Baton Rouge *Weekly Gazette and Comet,* June 3, 1860. This paper said on May 27 that Douglas could be elected "because he is just the blunt, outspoken man, demanded by the largest and best half of the people, to run against the army of hungry office seekers—State and Federal stipendiaries, who would have a quarrel and fight in order to rob the public exchequer."

"talk" of secession. The *Picayune*'s nonpartisan attitude was rebuked by the *Delta* when it said, "The *Picayune,* rivaling the phlegm of old Archimedes studying a mathematical proposition in his tower whilst the enemy was thundering at the gates of Syracuse, presents us with the statistics of Railroads in America and Great Britain." [45]

Three weeks before the election, the *Picayune* urged that each board of electors for Louisiana be instructed to vote for the candidate who, having the largest number of electoral votes, "can, by a union of all opponents of Lincoln, secure his defeat." [46] A week later in an editorial, "What of the Future," the *Picayune* said:

Every man should understand the position in which this election is likely to place him. He should have decided before he casts his ballot, that, result as it may, so far as the election of the President is concerned, neither public safety, nor State honor, nor business interests, nor individual patriotism, calls upon him to entertain the idea of immediately resorting to revolution. We say revolution advisedly, for there is no possible dismemberment of the Union but by the sword. There is no State secession, peacefully. There is no reorganization of the South but through a baptism of blood. Then, there is no certainty that Republican institutions will succeed in the destruction of the present relations of the States.

With such a prospect before us, the public mind cannot be unexcited, but it need not be bewildered with uncertainty. A plain duty lies before every voter in all the States, to labor for the safety of the Government which has been so beneficent, and to which all we have of national character, of general prosperity, of individual happiness and of future hope, are so clearly due.[47]

In an editorial of November 1 entitled "Secession—Attempted Dictation," the *Picayune* concluded:

[45] New Orleans *Daily Delta,* September 26, 1860.
[46] New Orleans *Daily Picayune,* October 17, 1860.
[47] *Ibid.,* October 24, 1860.

Secession of Louisiana

Louisiana, we venture to affirm, will neither lead nor follow in any secession movement. She acknowledges a fealty to the Constitution, and regards her own honor too highly to favor extreme measures before they become the last alternatives. In the words of the illustrious Jackson, whose memory she reveres, she believes that compared to disunion, all other evils yet experienced are light, because that brings with it an accumulation of all.

The popular vote in the election in Louisiana was Breckinridge, 22,681; Bell, 20,204; Douglas, 7,625. Bell led in the parishes of East Baton Rouge, Jefferson, Madison, Orleans, Ouachita, St. James, St. John the Baptist, St. Tammany, and West Baton Rouge. Douglas carried Ascension, Assumption, and Lafourche, and was second in Jefferson, Orleans, and Plaquemines.[48] The fact that Breckinridge received less than 45 per cent of the vote would seem to indicate a strong conservative element in the state. The Bell-Douglas majorities were principally from Southeast Louisiana, the home of the great planter and the site of the industrial and commercial city of New Orleans. The central and northern portions of the state, on the other hand, were carried by Breckinridge, who received a majority of the votes in sixteen of the twenty parishes in those sections. The Douglas vote in Central and North Louisiana, with the exception of Ouachita and Winn parishes, was negligible. For instance, Senator Douglas received 7 votes out of a total of 1,047 in Avoyelles and 2 votes out of 1,000 in De Soto.[49]

There were the usual divisions of opinion in Louisiana in the weeks succeeding the election. One group of leaders counseled delay in acting and hoped for a compromise on the critical issues. Some believed that, whatever action might be necessary, the South should at least wait until after Lincoln's

---

[48] *Ibid.,* December 5, 1860 (official election returns). For a map of Louisiana illustrating the election of 1860, see Caskey, *Secession and Restoration of Louisiana,* 14.

[49] New Orleans *Daily Picayune,* December 5, 1860.

inauguration.[50] On the other hand, those who thought that the time for secession had arrived were divided between those who favored separate state action and those who urged a convention of Southern states to act.

The New Orleans *Bee,* on November 8, announced the election of Lincoln and advised a policy of waiting, asserting that "Our wrongs are prospective rather than real, nor can they be inflicted so long as Abraham Lincoln is rendered practically powerless by an adverse Congress." [51] Three weeks later the *Bee* was speaking in quite another vein, asserting in an editorial entitled "Are They Blind?" that the people of the North were failing to realize the seriousness of the secession movement in the South, and issuing the warning that the entire weight of preserving the Union lay with the North, which was the "aggressor" while the South was the "aggrieved." Continuing, the editor said:

There is no remedy for the evils complained of, save an entire change in Northern policy. The South does not look upon the triumph of Lincoln, *per se,* with any special apprehension, but simply regards it as the crown and capstone of grievance, the last straw on the camel's back, the drop that causes the cup of bitterness to overflow.[52]

On December 14 the *Bee* asserted that "The Union is broken in two" and that one might as well expect "to breathe life into a corpse . . . as imagine that the Union may yet be preserved." The editor concluded by expressing the opinion that while the South remained a part of the Union nothing could prevent "her progressive degradation, humiliation and

[50] Greer, "Louisiana Politics, 1845–1860," in *loc. cit.,* 620. See also Caskey, *Secession and Restoration of Louisiana,* 12–13.

[51] Dumond (ed.), *Southern Editorials on Secession,* 222. The Baton Rouge *Weekly Gazette and Comet* advised its readers on November 9 to wait and see "what the first sectional President of the Union will do, when inaugurated into authority."

[52] Dumond (ed.), *Southern Editorials on Secession,* 276.

spoliation" by the victorious North. "We are doomed," he said, "if we proclaim not our political independence." [53]

The change of attitude on the part of the *Bee* was typical of the growth of secession sentiment in Louisiana. An eminent authority states that another Bell paper, the New Orleans *Crescent,* was an advocate of immediate secession before the end of 1860 and that by January 8, 1861, the only paper of importance in the Gulf States still opposed to secession was the New Orleans *True Delta;* and "it was wavering." [54]

Professor Dumond gives us an admirable discussion of the causes of the growth of secession sentiment after the November election. He says in this connection that the refusal of Republican majorities to countenance the Southern demands for additional guarantees, the refusal of Republican congressmen to enter into the spirit of conciliation, and the speeches of Senators Hale, Wade, and Seward were "important elements in the shaping of majority sentiment in the South." "The inflexible opposition of Republican congressmen to the several proposals designed to prevent civil war," Dumond adds, "broke down differences of opinion and united the two great parties in the lower South." [55]

A special session of the Legislature called by Governor Moore met on December 10. The *Picayune* of that date seems to have sensed the changing public opinion in Louisiana. An editorial entitled "Public Opinion" read:

Since the announcement of the election of the chief of sectionalism to the office of the Presidency, public opinion in Louisiana has undergone a very important change. The movement in other Southern States, as well as the haughty, threatening, overbearing attitude of the North, has had a marked influence in hurrying forward what may truly be denominated a revolutionary sentiment in this State.

[53] *Ibid.,* 334–36.

[54] *Ibid.,* xviii, xx. On November 18, 1860, Alexander F. Pugh recorded that "all the talk now is disunion." Alexander F. Pugh Diary.

[55] Dumond (ed.), *Southern Editorials on Secession,* xix, xx.

Louisiana in the Confederacy

A few weeks earlier, on November 20, the *True Delta* severely criticized the action of the governor in calling a special session of the Legislature, charging that he had yielded "before the pressure of Slidell and his rump retinue." The governor was condemned as a "weak, irresolute and easily persuaded executive," and his action in calling the Legislature was deplored as an unwise act and an expensive proceeding likely to "add to the excitement, distrust and alarm already pervading the community." [56]

The purpose of the special session, as explained by Governor Moore in his message to the Legislature, was the consideration of the present and future relations of Louisiana to the Federal Government "before the control of that Government is lodged in the hands of a party whose avowed principles are in antagonism to the interests, the dignity, and the well being of Louisiana." [57] In the opinion of the governor, Southerners had been driven to the thoughts of secession by the unreasonable and fanatical opposition to slavery by the Republican party, by Northern nullification of the Fugitive Slave Law, and by the election of Lincoln, who had said the country could not remain part slave and part free. He recommended that the Legislature provide for the election of members to a convention which should decide on the policy of Louisiana in relation to the Federal Government. In concluding, the governor said:

I have earnestly desired that a Conference or Convention of the slaveholding States should be held in order that they might counsel together, and act unitedly in this grave crisis. I still desire that such a Conference shall be had, if practicable in point of time. Louisiana ought not to refuse to meet her sister slaveholding States in council, and there unitedly determine upon a firm demand to be made of the Northern States for the repeal of their obnoxious legislation, and the guarantee and security of those rights, which have so long been persistently refused. Still,

[56] *Ibid.*, 255–58.
[57] New Orleans *Daily Picayune*, December 11, 1860.

Secession of Louisiana

although such a course has seemed to my mind desirable, and I had hoped that a practical and practicable plan might ere this have been suggested to accomplish this object, I do not think the action of Louisiana should be unreasonably postponed under the mere hope or expectation that such a Body would be at some distant time convened. It should meet at once, and determine at once, before the day arrives for the inauguration of a Black Republican President.

I do not think that it comports with the honor and self-respect of Louisiana, as a slaveholding State, to live under the Government of a Black Republican President.[58]

In response to a recommendation of the governor, the Legislature created a military board to be composed of the governor and four others to be named by him. The duty of this military board was to purchase arms and ammunition and to distribute these to volunteers. A company of thirty-two men in each parish, either cavalry or infantry, was to be equipped.[59]

A "Convention Bill" passed by the Legislature required the governor to call for January 7, 1861, an election of delegates to a state convention which was to meet January 23. Representation in the convention was placed upon the same basis as representation in the Legislature, and all persons qualified to vote for members of the Legislature were entitled to vote for delegates to the convention. This meant that every free white male, twenty-one years old, a resident of the state twelve months and of the parish six months, and a citizen of the United States, was eligible to vote and to be elected to the convention.[60]

[58] Governor's message, *Documents of the Second Session of the Fifth Legislature of Louisiana, 1861* (Baton Rouge, 1861). Cited hereafter as *Louisiana Legislature Documents*.

[59] *Acts Passed by the Fifth Legislature of the State of Louisiana, Second Session*, 1861 (Baton Rouge, 1861), 3–4. The *Acts* of the special session are printed with those of the regular session. Cited hereafter as Louisiana *Acts*. New Orleans *Daily Picayune*, December 11, 12, 1860.

[60] Louisiana *Acts*, 1861, pp. 6–7. For "Convention Bill," see New Orleans *Daily Picayune*, December 13, 1860.

Louisiana in the Confederacy

A joint resolution requested the governor to communicate to the governors of the slaveholding states the action of this session of the Legislature and to request them "to communicate to him the action and views of their respective states in regard to the present critical condition of the country." [61]

A regular political campaign was waged in Louisiana over the election of delegates to the convention. Rallies were held throughout the state, and speechmaking and resolutions were the order of the day.[62] The advocates of secession were very active. When the news of the secession of South Carolina reached New Orleans on December 21, the event was celebrated with demonstrations of joy. The *Picayune* of that date reported that:

At 12 o'clock to-day a salute of 800 guns, 200 per district, was fired in honor of South Carolina. As the first gun was heard, the flag of Louisiana was hoisted from the third story window of the rooms of the Southern Rights Association, No. 72 Camp street, amid the cheers of the assembled multitude. A brass band placed beneath the windows struck up the "Marseillaise," which was encored.

The flag is, like the original flag of Louisiana, of spotless white, with the addition in the centre of a red star, containing in its centre the emblematic pelican.

On the second story window could be seen a fine bust of John C. Calhoun, with a blue badge passed around the neck.

After the flag had unfolded itself to the breeze, Gen. Miles, in response to loud calls, addressed the crowd which had blocked up Camp street from side to side. He alluded to the importance of the event made the occasion for the hoisting of the flag of Louisiana, and appealed to Louisiana, having common wrongs with South Carolina, to range themselves under the banner of the revolution. He was frequently interrupted by cheers. . . . While we write the crowd is still in the street, and loud acclaims

61 Louisiana *Acts*, 1861, pp. 5–6.

62 The New Orleans *Picayune* of December 29 and January 1 reports such meetings in the parishes of Plaquemines, East Baton Rouge, Natchitoches, Claiborne, Concordia, and Point Coupee.

24

greet the remarks which are made by the speakers called and by the excited crowd. It is a stormy event in the history of the Southern movement.

Newspapers took an active part in the campaign. As stated above, the New Orleans *True Delta* was the only paper of importance opposed to secession, at least after the election of January 7; and its opposition was weakening. The *Picayune* advocated united Southern action as a means of convincing the North of the strength of the Southern-rights movement, and, in case of failure of compromise, of assuring to the South its share in the public property and domain of the country.[63] The *Daily Crescent,* December 20, 1860, held that the only proper method of secession was the separate action of each state in its capacity as an independent political sovereign. "The States must go out of the Union if they go out at all," said the *Crescent,* "precisely as they went in—one by one." [64] The *Bee,* December 24, 1860, opposed united Southern action before separate state secession as impracticable; South Carolina was already out of the Union, and Louisiana could not enter into agreements with her as long as Louisiana was still in the Union.[65]

On the other hand, at the state capital the Baton Rouge *Weekly Gazette and Comet* remained in the fight against secession. On January 5, 1861, the editor reminded his readers of the approaching convention election and declared:

This convention is called in violation of all former precedent —outside of our own Constitution and the laws—in an inflamed state of public mind, made so by the vilest fabrications to this end, and when assembled, will claim the right to dispose of the lives and property of our citizens as may best suit the purpose of the leaders in this matter, who place no value on the Union

[63] See New Orleans *Picayune* editorials for December 17, 18, 20, 21, 1860. See also Dumond (ed.), *Southern Editorials on Secession,* 351–54.
[64] Dumond (ed.), *Southern Editorials on Secession,* 357.
[65] *Ibid.,* 365–68.

or anything else that stands in the way to the attainment of their desperate ends. . . .

. . . The issue, good people, is this: Shall Louisiana be degraded into the humiliating position of South Carolina? Shall she be unconstitutionally withdrawn and trust to Providence and poltroons for the consequences? Shall the credit of the State be stained by such a violent course? If you agree to it, for heaven's sake do not do so without calculating what is to follow immediately after.

The election of January 7, 1861, resulted in the election of eighty "secessionists," forty-four "co-operationists," and six "doubtful" delegates. Only nineteen of the forty-eight parishes went "co-operationist." The popular vote of the state, however, was 20,448 for secessionist delegates and 17,296 for co-operationists.[66]

The fact should not be overlooked that the vote for delegates to the convention was 12,766 less than the total number of votes cast in Louisiana in the presidential election in November. Presumably, there are no records or sources available to account for this reduction in the state's vote, and any effort at explanation will be speculation to a certain degree. It seems reasonable to conclude, however, that the failure of a considerable percentage of the qualified voters to exercise the privilege in this case was not due, to any great extent, to a lack of interest. The issues were too well defined; and the

[66] Greer, "Louisiana Politics, 1845–1860," in *loc. cit.*, 634–35, 638. Most of the co-operationists, no doubt, were in favor of secession but thought that the slaveholding states should take some form of united action and withdraw from the Union as a group, whereas the secessionists were for immediate, separate state action. Some of those who called themselves co-operationists were secessionists in view, in that they believed in the right of secession; but they denied that there was sufficient cause, or at least questioned the expediency of such action. In this connection it should be remembered that, when the Louisiana election of January 7 was held, only one state, South Carolina, had seceded; but by January 23, when the Louisiana convention met, four more states—Mississippi, Florida, Alabama, and Georgia—had left the Union. Doubtless these actions influenced public opinion and convention delegates in Louisiana.

campaign, including the press, was too heated to result in indifference or apathy. Somehow, the writer cannot escape the opinion that these twelve thousand nonvoting citizens represent in a large degree an opposition to the whole movement of secession, that they were Union men who stayed away from the polls as a means of protest against the seemingly inevitable withdrawal of Louisiana from the Union, either separately or in a united Southern movement. There is evidence to show that Union men, unless they were men of position and influence, were extremely unpopular and were sometimes victims of harsh treatment. In St. Charles Parish, for instance, two people were ordered out of the parish because they had "tampered" with slaves, "hurrahed" for Lincoln, and expressed "sentiments at the present hostile to the interests of the parish." [67] This occurred early in December. On January 9, 1861, the Shreveport *South-Western* contained the following item of interest:

Warned Off—Last Friday, January 4 our vigilance committee notified Lemuel Gilbert, the piano manufacturer of Boston, to depart from this place, and he took his leave on Saturday. The principle [*sic*] cause of their so doing was that Gilbert had avowed himself a supporter of Mr. Lincoln. We are pleased to see the prompt action of the committee, and hope that action will be taken to rid the community of all suspicious persons.

The state convention met on January 23 at Baton Rouge (until January 29, when it adjourned to meet in New Orleans) with 127 delegates present. On January 24 Governor Moore submitted to the convention a copy of his annual message to the Legislature, which he had addressed January 22, "this being," as he said, "the only communication I am at present prepared to make." The governor referred to his opinions "on the momentous question" expressed in his message to the Legislature in December, and added:

[67] New Orleans *Daily Picayune,* December 15, 1860.

27

Louisiana in the Confederacy

The vote of the people has since confirmed the faith of their Representatives, in legislative and executive station, that the undivided sentiment of the State is for immediate and effective resistance, and that there is not found within her limits any difference of sentiment, except as to minor points of expediency in regard to the manner and time of making such resistance, so as to give it the most imposing form for dignity and success. Our enemies, who have driven on their conflict with the slaveholding States to this extremity, will have found that throughout the borders of Louisiana we are one people—a people with one heart and one mind—who will not be cajoled into an abandonment of their rights, and who cannot be subdued.[68]

Hopes of healing the dissensions had, in the governor's opinion, disappeared "under the accumulating proofs that the Northern majority is implacable." No proffer of peace had emanated from the Republicans. In fact, propositions tendered by Southern statesmen had been "contumeliously rejected." Continuing on this point, the message concluded:

The common cry throughout the North is for coercion into submission, by force of arms, if need be, of every State, and of all the States of the South, which claim the right of separation, for cause, from a Government which they deem fatal to their safety. There can no longer be doubt of the wisdom of that policy which demands that the conflict shall come, and shall be settled now.[69]

Alexander Mouton was elected president of the convention, and the Committee of Fifteen was appointed to report on an ordinance of secession. On January 24 Joseph A. Rozier of Orleans Parish introduced an ordinance, as a substitute for the report of the Committee of Fifteen, calling for a convention of slaveholding states at Nashville on February 25, or soon thereafter, to propose amendments to the United States

[68] *Official Journal of the Proceedings of the Convention of the State of Louisiana,* 1861 (New Orleans, 1861), 13–14. Cited hereafter as *Journal of the Louisiana Convention,* 1861.
[69] *Ibid.*

Secession of Louisiana

Constitution "necessary and proper to secure the rights of the slaveholding States of the Union," and to settle all questions relating to slavery. In the event that such amendments and "such measures for the protection of Southern Slave States" were not made and accepted by the nonslaveholding states, this convention was to reassemble and to organize a separate confederacy of the slave states. Six delegates were to be chosen by this Louisiana convention for the proposed convention of all slaveholding states. This proposed ordinance was defeated, 106 to 24.[70]

Another co-operationist resolution, which was intended as a substitute for an ordinance of secession, was introduced by James O. Fuqua, senatorial delegate representing the parishes of East Baton Rouge, West Baton Rouge, and East Feliciana. It declared that Louisiana would not submit to the administration of Lincoln upon the principles of the Republican party and that any attempt to coerce any state that seceded would be regarded by Louisiana as an act of war upon all the slaveholding states and would absolve the state from all allegiance to the Federal Government. The resolution expressed Louisiana's desire to co-operate with her sister slaveholding states and provided for the acceptance of Alabama's invitation to meet in council at Montgomery. Fuqua's proposal received more support than Rozier's but was defeated 73 to 47.[71]

On January 25 Charles Bienvenu, who represented the district composed of the parishes of Plaquemines, St. Bernard, Jefferson, and a part of Orleans, introduced the following resolution which was defeated by a vote of 84 to 43:

Resolved, That whatever be the action of this Convention on the question whether or not this State ought to secede from the Union, it shall have no effect until the same shall have been ratified by the vote of the majority of the people at the ballot box, and, to this effect, an election shall be held at the various election

[70] *Ibid.*, 10–11, 15. [71] *Ibid.*, 11–12, 16.

precincts of the State, on the 25th day of February next, under the regulations and laws. . . .[72]

Former Governor John L. Manning, commissioner from South Carolina, and former Governor John A. Winston, commissioner from Alabama, addressed the convention on January 25. Manning said he came to present South Carolina's ordinance of secession and to ask for the co-operation of Louisiana in the formation of a Southern confederacy. It was necessary, he said, that each state should secede separately, with a view to a speedy confederation of all the slave states for the purpose of common defense. Winston told the delegates that the time had come to test the ability of the South to meet the emergency and urged them to act promptly. He predicted that in two years the South would be the greatest country upon which the sun had ever shone.[73]

On this same day, January 25, the convention received a communication from Senators Slidell and Judah P. Benjamin and Representatives John M. Landrum and Thomas G. Davidson, dated at Washington, January 15, favoring immediate secession. The message was read and twenty-five hundred copies were ordered to be printed.[74]

When an ordinance of secession was reported by the Committee of Fifteen, James G. Taliaferro, a delegate from Catahoula Parish, proved himself the most persistent and probably the most able opponent of secession in the convention. In a protest, which he asked leave to have spread on the journal, but which was refused, he gave the following reasons for his opposition to the secession of Louisiana: [75]

[72] *Ibid.*, 16. According to the resolution, the voters were to vote "Ratification" or "No Ratification."

[73] New Orleans *Daily Picayune*, January 26, 1861.

[74] *Ibid.; Journal of the Louisiana Convention*, 1861, p. 15.

[75] Jacob Barker, *The Rebellion: Its Consequences* (New Orleans, 1866), 94–96. Judge Taliaferro's protest is also found in *The War of the Rebellion: A Compilation of the Official Records of the Union and Confederate Armies*

Secession of Louisiana

1. The wrongs alleged might be redressed under the Constitution.

2. Secession did not provide a remedy; besides, "prospective evils depicted so gloomily may never come."

3. There was no certainty that the seceding states would ever be confederated again, or that the border states would secede.

4. "Because I believe peaceable secession is a right unknown to the Constitution of the United States."

5. The proper status of Louisiana was with the border states, "with which nature has connected her by the majestic river which flows through her limits," while an alliance in a weak government with the states east of her "is unnatural and antagonistic to her obvious interests and destiny."

6. By separate secession, Louisiana relinquished all its rights within the Government, surrendered its share in the public domain and all property belonging to the Nation, "and for this reason I oppose secession as being emphatically submission."

7. "Because secession will bring anarchy and war, as it will assuredly bring ruinous exactions upon property in the form of direct taxation, a withering blight upon the prosperity of the State, and a fatal prostration of all its great interests."

8. The act of dissolving the ties with the Federal Union was a revolutionary act which the convention, of itself, did not possess the legitimate power to perform. "Convened without authority of the people of the State, and refusing to submit its action to them for their sanction in the grave and vital act of changing their government, this convention violates the great and fundamental principle of American government—that the will of the people is supreme."

Mr. Roger Wallace Shugg was probably right in his con-

(Washington, 1880–1902), Ser. I, Vol. LIII, 614–15. Cited hereafter as *Official Records*.

clusions in his recent study of Judge Taliaferro's position. Mr. Shugg says:

In his unflinching fight against secession, however, Taliaferro reflected the attitude of his parish, Catahoula. Although it had voted for Breckinridge by a small plurality in November, 1860, it cast but a third of its votes for immediate secession two months later. Probably not more than a fourth of the voters in Catahoula were slaveholders, and nearly two-thirds of the plantations were less than fifty acres in size. Like most small farming parishes in Louisiana, Catahoula did not welcome secession.[76]

On January 26, by a vote of 113 to 17, the convention adopted the Ordinance of Secession, dissolving "the Union now subsisting between Louisiana and other States, under the name of The United States of America." [77] Upon the announcement of the vote, Mouton, president of the convention, declared the connection of Louisiana with the United States dissolved and pronounced Louisiana "a free, sovereign, and independent power." A beautiful Pelican flag was unfurled on the president's table.[78]

Some idea of the effect of the action of the convention upon the people of Louisiana may be had from the report of the *Picayune:*

When the news that the secession ordinance had been passed by the State Convention reached us by telegraph yesterday the effect, as might have been expected, was such as to suspend all thoughts of other matters, to concentrate the public mind on the one solemn event which changed the destinies of Louisiana.

The church bells proclaimed the fact in vibrating tones, whilst the deep voice of the cannon announced it even more loudly. From public edifices, hotels and private buildings, the Pelican

[76] Roger W. Shugg, "A Suppressed Co-operationist Protest Against Secession," in *Louisiana Historical Quarterly,* XIX (1936), 201.

[77] *Journal of the Louisiana Convention,* 1861, pp. 17–18, 231. The Louisiana Ordinance of Secession is also found in *Official Records,* Ser. IV, Vol. I, 80.

[78] *Journal of the Louisiana Convention,* 1861, p. 18; New Orleans *Daily Picayune,* January 27, 1861.

Secession of Louisiana

flag was hoisted and displayed its ample folds to the breeze. In the streets people met in groups, inquiring about the news and exchanging congratulations or comments upon the important step taken by the people of Louisiana.[79]

All was not joy, however. There must have been heavy hearts and clouded skies for some. The Shreveport *South-Western*, which had supported Bell and had never advocated secession, said on February 6:

As Louisiana is no longer a member of the federal government, we this day, as orderly citizens, lower the "stars and stripes" from our masthead! It is with heart-felt emotions, better imagined than portrayed, that we fold the saucy looking "star spangled banner" that we have always loved, and place the precious memento under our pillow.

[79] New Orleans *Daily Picayune*, January 27, 1861.

33

Chapter II

Political Adjustments and Military Preparations

LOUISIANA PLAYED A conspicuous role in the Confederacy. Her people contributed much to the cause of Southern independence, and they suffered keenly and terribly from the war and its aftermath. Her wealth, geographic position, military forces, and statesmen made Louisiana a leading Confederate state. Her position in the Confederacy was a vital and strategic one. The role of Louisiana in this significant era of American history can be understood and appreciated best if we are acquainted in the beginning with the people and the resources of this commonwealth.

Louisiana of 1860 was a rapidly growing community of 708,002 people. The population had more than doubled since 1840, and the increase for the last decade had been 36.74 per cent.[1] The state had attracted settlers by the abundance of rich, virgin soil adaptable to the cultivation of cotton and sugar cane and by the commercial advantages of New Orleans, a city of 168,675 inhabitants in 1860. The population movement had been a part of the westward migration common to the United States for that period. The birthplaces of the free American-born inhabitants of the state as revealed by the census of 1860 is a story of westward extension in itself. Mis-

[1] *Seventh United States Census,* 1850, Table V, p. 475; *Eighth United States Census,* 1860, *Population,* 194.

34

Adjustments and Preparations

sissippi, Alabama, and Georgia, in the order named, had contributed most (after Louisiana itself) to the free population of the state.[2]

Louisiana's population was rather heterogeneous. The foreign-born element numbered 81,029, which was slightly more than one fifth of the free residents of the state. The Irish with 28,207 and the 24,614 Germans led the list of foreign-born. This element was concentrated largely in New Orleans, where more than one third of the inhabitants were of foreign birth, chiefly Irish, German, and French. This does not include, of course, the many natives of French ancestry. Of the American-born residents, New York state was second to Louisiana in the number contributed to the population of the Crescent City. This indicates that rural Louisiana had attracted the farmer and planter element of the cotton states to the east, while New Orleans had been favored by the commercial classes of the North and the laboring classes of Europe.[3]

New Orleans had had a rapid, almost phenomenal, growth. From a town of 8,000 in 1803, it had become the busy city of 168,000 fifty-seven years later. Anyone familiar with the map of the United States will readily understand this growth. The city was the outlet for the export trade of a rapidly growing Mississippi Valley. The settlement of Kentucky, Tennessee, Ohio, Indiana, Illinois, Missouri, Arkansas, and Iowa, not to mention Louisiana and Mississippi, had contributed to the progress of the city near the mouth of the great river. Tobacco, cotton, pork, flour, corn, hay, oats, hides, whiskey, and many other products, most of which were destined for export, reached the city daily. One writer has expressed the idea in these words: "As to the variety of products reaching

[2] *Eighth United States Census,* 1860, *Population,* 195–96, 615.

[3] Statistics based on *ibid.* There were 4,088 residents of New Orleans in 1860 who had been born in New York state. Only 1,450 natives of New York were living elsewhere in Louisiana in 1860.

35

Louisiana in the Confederacy

New Orleans from the interior it would require all the letters of the alphabet to catalogue them." [4]

There were no other large cities in Louisiana in 1860. Shreveport, the metropolis of North Louisiana today with a population of almost 100,000, was a little town of 2,190 people in 1860. Baton Rouge, the capital with 5,428 residents, was much larger than Shreveport. Alexandria, in Central Louisiana, a city of about 30,000 people today, was a town of 1,461 inhabitants then.[5]

The slave population of Louisiana had grown from 69,064 in 1820 to 331,726 in 1860. The percentage of increase of slaves had been only slightly less than that of the white population. In 1860 almost half the population of the state—46.8 per cent—were slaves. The free Negroes numbered 18,647. More than half of these, 10,689, lived in New Orleans; but they were found in every section of the state, for only six of the forty-eight parishes were without free Negroes. Alexandria's 1,461 inhabitants, for instance, included 131 free Negroes, while Shreveport was the home of 46 "free persons of color." [6]

The free Negroes held an important place in the economic life of the state. Planters, overseers, and practicing physicians were found among their numbers. Many were slaveowners. The list of the large planters of ante-bellum Louisiana would not be complete without the names of several Negroes. Frederick Law Olmsted was impressed by the number of free Negroes in the section around Opelousas. Many of these, he learned, were wealthy and owned some of the best cotton and sugar plantations.[7]

[4] James E. Winston, "Notes on the Economic History of New Orleans, 1803–1836," in *Mississippi Valley Historical Review* (Cedar Rapids), XI (1925), 206. Professor Winston says that in the decade of 1830–1840 New Orleans made more progress than any other city in the United States.

[5] *Eighth United States Census, 1860, Population,* 195.

[6] *Ibid.,* 194–95.

[7] Frederick L. Olmsted, *A Journey in the Seaboard Slave States* (New

Adjustments and Preparations

According to a report of the state auditor, the total assessment of taxable property in Louisiana for the year 1859 was $400,450,757. The assessed taxable property of New Orleans was $106,646,838, more than one fourth of the total for the state. The ten wealthiest parishes, according to assessed property values, were, in order, Orleans, Concordia, St. Mary, Tensas, Iberville, Rapides, Carroll, Point Coupee, Jefferson, and St. Landry.[8]

New Orleans was noted for its strong banking facilities. According to a report of the United States secretary of the treasury, March 26, 1860, there were thirteen banks in Louisiana with a total capital of $24,496,866; deposits were $19,777,-812; and the specie in the vaults amounted to $12,115,431. Louisiana ranked first in capital stock, first in deposits, first in specie, and ninth in the number of banks among the slaveholding states.[9]

Reference has been made to the fact that there was a large element of French ancestry in the Louisiana population. As a matter of fact, most of these people were not merely of French ancestry—they were French—speaking the French language, retaining many French customs. The acts of the Legislature were printed in both French and English.

The French population was confined largely to South Louisiana, although there was then, as now, a French element in and near Natchitoches on Cane River. New Orleans and vicinity were particularly French. A European observer wrote of former Governor Roman's plantation: "It was curious to observe so far away from France so many traces of the life of the old seigneur." The same traveler said of New

---

York, 1861), 639; Alfred H. Stone, "Free Contract Labor in the Ante-Bellum South," in *The South in the Building of the Nation* (Richmond, 1909–1913), V, 135.

[8] New Orleans *Daily Picayune*, February 16, 1860.

[9] *Executive Documents Printed by order of the House of Representatives During the First Session of the Thirty-Sixth Congress, 1859–1860* (Washington, 1860) (Serial 49), 163–68, 278.

Louisiana in the Confederacy

Orleans: "There is an air thoroughly French about the people—cafes, restaurants, billiard-rooms abound, with oyster and lager-bier saloons interspersed; . . . the people in the streets are speaking French, particularly the Negroes, who are going out shopping with their masters and mistresses exceedingly well dressed, noisy, and not unhappy looking." [10]

The heterogeneous character of the American-born population of Louisiana—with the French predominating in South Louisiana and the Anglo-Saxon above the Red River —is explained in the history of the state. The first white settlers of the country were colonists from France. Colonization began with the founding of Natchitoches in 1713 and New Orleans in 1718. Other settlements were made, and the French language and customs were permanently planted in the region of the lower Mississippi. Spanish ways were introduced, and Spanish influence was felt when Louisiana was a part of Spain's empire from 1763 to 1800. Citizens of the United States who settled in Kentucky and Tennessee after the American Revolution found in New Orleans the port of export for the produce of their farms. Therefore, they—and hence the Federal authorities—were more than ordinarily interested in the political connections of the city. The repossession of Louisiana by France was a crisis in American history. But war in Europe, for once at least, came to our assistance, and Louisiana was severed permanently from European political control. The Stars and Stripes replaced the French tricolor in New Orleans in December, 1803.

And now, in 1861, the Stars and Stripes were lowered, and another flag was unfurled in New Orleans. This is no place to discuss the theories concerning secession—whether the states were out of the Union or whether a substantial number of their citizens were in rebellion against the authority and laws of the United States. The fact remains that the great

[10] William H. Russell, *My Diary North and South* (Boston, 1863), 230, 259. Russell made these observations in May, 1861.

Adjustments and Preparations

majority of the people of Louisiana, after January 26, 1861, considered their political ties with the United States broken; and their elected representatives acted accordingly.

A number of matters of vital importance engaged the attention of the members of the Louisiana convention after the adoption of the Ordinance of Secession. Because of the regular session of the Legislature in Baton Rouge, it was necessary for the convention to move to New Orleans, where a hall and other facilities were available. The transfer was made between January 26 and 29, when deliberations were resumed in New Orleans. On that day John Perkins, Jr., of the Committee on Confederation, reported an ordinance providing for the election by the convention of six delegates to the convention of seceding states which was to meet at Montgomery on February 4. The delegates were instructed to aid in the forming of a provisional government on the basis of the Constitution of the United States. This resolution was adopted, and the following delegates were elected: John Perkins, Jr., Alexander Declouet, Charles M. Conrad, Duncan F. Kenner, Edward Sparrow, and Henry Marshall.[11] The *Picayune* commended the convention on the choice of delegates to Montgomery, saying "the choice . . . is eminently judicious, and one that will give general satisfaction." The delegates were characterized as among the most eminent citizens of Louisiana, men of high character and deeply interested in the state's prosperity.[12]

On January 29 the Louisiana convention adopted an ordinance which provided (1) that all Federal officers in the civil service of the United States, and all laws of the United States relating to such officers, not incompatible with state laws, should be continued in force as officers and laws of the state, except the officers of the judiciary, postal, and land depart-

[11] *Journal of the Louisiana Convention,* 1861, pp. 19–24, 241; New Orleans *Daily Picayune,* January 30, 31, 1861.
[12] New Orleans *Daily Picayune,* January 31, 1861.

ments of the United States; (2) that the revenue, collection, and navigation laws of the United States should continue as laws of Louisiana, except that no duties were to be collected on imports from the states "forming the late Federal Union, known as the United States of America"; (3) that the president of the convention or the governor should require all Federal officers in the parish of Orleans to recognize the sole and exclusive authority of Louisiana and should administer to them the oath of office, and when any Federal officer should refuse to comply with the provisions of this ordinance, or to take the oath of office, the president of the convention, or the governor, should declare the office vacant and demand and take possession of all property, money, and effects held by such officer in his official capacity; (4) "That the State of Louisiana doth hereby guarantee and indemnify all Federal officers aforesaid, within this State, who comply with the Ordinances of this Convention, against all claims and demands of the United States arising out of such compliance." [13]

The convention appointed a committee to take an inventory of the public property in the hands of the officers of the "late Federal Government" within the parish of Orleans on February 1, 1861. The committee reported that there was $483,984.98 in gold and silver in the subtreasurer's vault at the Mint, "now in the custody of A. J. Guirot, an officer of the State of Louisiana." [14]

On February 4 a committee of three was appointed to design a flag for the state of Louisiana. John K. Elgee of Rapides Parish, who made the motion for the appointment of the committee, told the delegates that Louisiana had never adopted a flag and that it was necessary for ships sailing from New Orleans to have a flag to hoist. The committee reported on February 11, and the following "flag" ordinance was adopted:

[13] *Journal of the Louisiana Convention*, 1861, pp. 235–37.
[14] *Ibid.*, 34.

Adjustments and Preparations

We, the people of Louisiana, in Convention assembled, do ordain and establish, That the flag of the State of Louisiana shall consist and be composed of thirteen horizontal stripes, of the colors hereinafter described, and to be disposed in the following order, commencing from the upper line or edge of the flag, to wit: The first stripe blue; second, white; third, red; fourth, white; fifth, blue; sixth, white; seventh, red; eighth, white; ninth, blue; tenth, white; eleventh, red; twelfth, white; thirteenth, or bottom stripe, blue.

We, do further ordain and establish, That there shall be in the upper, or chief corner of the flag a square field, the color whereof shall be red, and the sides thereof equal to the width of seven stripes; and that in the center of said field there shall be a star, of due and proportional size, having five points or rays; and that the color of the said star shall be a pale yellow.

We do further ordain and establish, That the said flag, and no other, shall be the national flag of the State of Louisiana.[15]

On the morning of February 12 at eleven o'clock the members of the convention formed in double file, headed by President Mouton and Lieutenant Governor Henry M. Hyams, and marched to Lafayette Square, accompanied by military escort, to witness the unfurling of the new Louisiana flag. As the town clock struck eleven, the flag was run up from the staff at the City Hall and was greeted with a salute

[15] *Ibid.,* 47–48, 257; New Orleans *Daily Picayune,* February 12, 1861. Mr. Elgee made an eloquent speech in presenting the report of the committee on the flag. The stripes were retained, he said, because the memory of the "old thirteen" colonies "still lives." "We dedicate, therefore, our thirteen stripes to the memory of those whose unconquerable love of freedom has taught us this day how peacefully to vindicate our rights and protect our liberties." The colors blue, white, and red were dedicated to the French colonists; for the name of Louisiana and of New Orleans, and even the roll call each morning, "bade us remember that some tribute was due to the children and descendants of the founders of the colony." Spain, too, was remembered in the new flag, for her mild and paternal rule was even yet spoken of among the older inhabitants. "To the children of Spain we dedicate the colors of red and yellow, which we have woven into our plan. The star cannot fail to remind you that Louisiana has risen to take her place in the political firmament." New Orleans *Picayune,* February 12, 1861.

41

of twenty-one guns from the Washington Artillery. The *Picayune* said on this occasion:

After the firing of the salute, three hearty cheers were given in honor of the flag, when the members again marched in front of the military, which saluted them as they passed. The balconies of the private and public buildings, which surrounded the Square, were densely crowded with the fair ladies of our city, and as the breeze unfurled the heaven-born hues of Louisiana's flag against the sky, displaying the beauteous harmony of its combined colors, a thrill of joy and admiration filled the spectators.[16]

On February 7 the convention adopted an ordinance relating to citizenship. All white persons who were citizens of Louisiana on January 26 were declared to be citizens of the "independent" Louisiana. All those who were citizens of the United States, or of any one of the seceded states, and who had resided in Louisiana twelve months preceding January 26, 1861, would, upon taking an oath of allegiance to the state of Louisiana, become citizens thereof. However, the oath of allegiance would not be required, "after the formation of a Southern Confederacy, of persons coming into this State and being citizens of said Confederacy, and of any one of the States composing the same." [17]

The next business of the convention was the consideration of the status of United States courts and of cases pending when Louisiana withdrew from the Union. The laws of the United States relating to the organization and jurisdiction of circuit and district courts were adopted, and such courts were continued. All suits, actions, and proceedings pending in the courts when the Ordinance of Secession was passed were to continue "as if no interruption to the business of said courts had taken place." All suits pending in Louisiana heretofore instituted by the United States were to be carried on and

[16] *Journal of the Louisiana Convention*, 1861, p. 51; New Orleans *Daily Picayune*, February 12, 1861.

[17] *Journal of the Louisiana Convention*, 1861, pp. 249–51.

Adjustments and Preparations

prosecuted "in the name and for the benefit of the State of Louisiana." [18] A few days later the convention re-enacted and adopted the criminal laws of the United States, except laws defining and punishing treason and other offenses against the "late government of the United States." Prosecutions for violation of the former United States criminal code were to be carried on in the name and by the authority of the state of Louisiana.[19]

Meanwhile, the Legislature, in session in Baton Rouge, adopted on February 18 the following joint resolution on the right of secession:

Be it resolved. . . . That the right of a sovereign State to secede or withdraw from the Government of the Federal Union, and resume her original sovereignty when in her judgment such an act becomes necessary, is not prohibited by the Federal Constitution, but is reserved thereby to the several States, or people thereof, to be exercised, each for itself, without molestation.

That any attempt to coerce or force a sovereign State to remain within the Federal Union, come from what quarter and under whatever pretence it may, will be viewed by the people of Louisiana, as well on her own account as of her sister Southern States, as a hostile invasion, and resisted to the utmost extent.[20]

The convention adjourned on February 12, the birthday of Abraham Lincoln, and reassembled on March 4, the day when Lincoln, taking the oath of office as President of the United States, declared the ordinances of secession void and promised to use his power "to hold, occupy, and possess the property and places belonging to the government." The Louisiana convention, reassembling on this historic day, renewed its efforts to promote the movement which Lincoln condemned and promised to oppose.

On March 7 a resolution was adopted declaring all the

---

[18] *Ibid.*, 251–55.   [19] *Ibid.*, 259–61.
[20] Louisiana *Acts,* 1861, p. 10.

43

unappropriated public domain within the limits of Louisiana to be the property of the state. All laws, rules, and regulations of the "late Government of the United States" respecting the survey and sale of land, in force on January 26, 1861, and not inconsistent with the ordinances of the convention, would continue to be in full force in Louisiana. It was also provided that all registrars and receivers of land offices should continue in their offices, provided they took an oath of office and executed new bonds in favor of the state.[21] The question of public lands was evidently of considerable interest, for the Legislature adopted a somewhat elaborate land act on March 21. This act established a general land office, created the position of commissioner of public lands, and placed a minimum price of $1.25 an acre on public lands, except land subject to regular tidal overflow, and except lands remaining unsold for a number of years, which were made subject to the principle of graduation. The right of pre-emption up to 160 acres was allowed.[22]

The so-called permanent constitution of the Confederate States was adopted by the delegates at Montgomery on March 11 and referred to the seceded states for ratification. This document was laid before the Louisiana convention on March 19 and was taken up for consideration on the twenty-first. Several attempts were made to require the submission of the constitution to the people or to a specially elected convention for ratification or rejection. One proposed ordinance provided for the publication of the constitution in French and English for at least thirty days prior to the election. In case the constitution was rejected by a majority of the voters, the president of the convention was "to call together this Convention, at as early a day as practicable, with the view of determining upon the best course of action for the future welfare of the State." This proposal was defeated

[21] *Journal of the Louisiana Convention,* 1861, pp. 263–65.
[22] Louisiana *Acts,* 1861, pp. 205–12.

Adjustments and Preparations

74 to 26.[23] Ten of those voting for submission had voted against secession.

J. A. Rozier of Orleans Parish, who had voted against the Ordinance of Secession, favored the election of a new convention, fresh from the people, to adopt or reject the constitution. He condemned the "hasty action" of the convention in passing the Ordinance of Secession and charged that the policy of the secessionists had been "to trample on the rights of the people." He commended Arkansas, Tennessee, and Missouri for their hesitation in the present crisis. He did not wish to be forced to transfer his allegiance to South Carolina, Georgia, Alabama, and other confederated states, since the prosperity of New Orleans was tied to the western states. "We might pile ordinances miles in height," he declared, "but we could not divide the people of Louisiana from the people of the West." [24] Christian Roselius, who represented Jefferson Parish, was another opponent of the Confederate constitution who had voted against secession. He charged that the constitution of the Confederacy established an "unmitigated oligarchy," as the people played no part in forming this government, since the delegates to the Montgomery meeting had been appointed without the consent of the people. The Confederacy was but a league, a Hanseatic League, and the Montgomery convention "had dug the grave of American liberty." [25] But the opposition was ineffectual. The Constitution of the Confederate States was ratified by the Louisiana convention and declared binding upon the people of the state on March 21, 1861, by a vote of 101 to 7.[26]

Another act of the convention in making adjustments to

[23] *Journal of the Louisiana Convention,* 1861, pp. 69–70, 74.

[24] *Ibid.,* 74–75; New Orleans *Daily Picayune,* March 21, 1861.

[25] New Orleans *Daily Picayune,* March 21, 1861.

[26] *Journal of the Louisiana Convention,* 1861, pp. 75–76. Those voting against ratification were Charles Bienvenu, Isaiah Garret, George W. Lewis, Christian Roselius, Joseph A. Rozier, W. T. Stocker, and James G. Taliaferro, all of whom had voted against secession on January 26.

the new order was taken on March 25, the day before adjournment. By this ordinance it was declared that the state of Louisiana ceded to the Confederate States the "right to use, possess, and occupy all the forts, arsenals and lighthouses, the mint, customhouse and other public buildings in the State of Louisiana, late in the possession of the United States." [27] The convention adopted an ordinance providing for six congressional districts for the election of representatives to the Confederate Congress. The six districts were created and defined, and the first Monday in November was fixed as the day of election.[28]

The final act of the convention in making political adjustments was taken on March 26 by repealing and amending certain earlier ordinances in order to provide for Louisiana as a state within the Confederacy. All ordinances which provided for an independent Louisiana were either repealed or amended so as to deprive the state of an independent status. The word "national," for instance, was struck out of the ordinance pertaining to the flag.[29]

Both the convention and the state Legislature adjourned on March 26. In the two months following the adoption of the Ordinance of Secession much had been done in adjusting the affairs of Louisiana to the new political order. In addition, as a precaution against an armed conflict with the United States, the state had undertaken the task of military preparations. Attention must now be turned to this subject.

The bitter sectional feeling of the presidential campaign of 1860, the success of the Republicans, and the ever increasing talk of secession were bound to result in a certain belligerent attitude in both North and South. Southerners who talked of secession thought of the possibility of attempted "coercion" on the part of the Federal Government. Naturally, such thoughts soon found expression in preparations for defense against any attempt to prevent secession or to force them

[27] *Ibid.*, 281.   [28] *Ibid.*, 283–85.   [29] *Ibid.*, 289–91.

Adjustments and Preparations

back into the Union after the act of secession had taken place. Convinced as they were that they possessed the right to withdraw from the Union, they believed, when convinced of the necessity of withdrawing, that it was their duty to defend that right. Hence, they came to look upon the impending struggle as a defense of their homes and firesides.

There was a certain amount of military spirit and some military action in Louisiana before the convention adopted the Ordinance of Secession on January 26, 1861. Adjutant General Maurice Grivot, in his report to Governor Moore, December 4, 1860, stated that,

> . . . in anticipation of the present difficulties, there was evinced, prior to the Presidential election, both in the city of New Orleans and various parishes, a strong desire for the forming of volunteer corps, to protect their homes, their families, and their property, and scarcely a week has passed, but that requests, either verbal or written, have been made upon me for arms to equip the companies then organizing. I felt deep regret at being totally unable to comply with these demands. . . .
>
> Since the Presidential election, which has hurried matters to such a crisis, I have daily information of the organization of new companies in the city of New Orleans and in the parishes. The true spirit has been aroused, and Southern patriots are flocking to the standard of Southern rights. I am yet unable to comply with the urgent and daily demands for arms.[30]

On December 10 Governor Moore said to the members of the General Assembly, in special session: "In the temper of the Northern mind it is not possible to foresee the course or policy that Congress may determine upon, and it is the part of wisdom to prepare ourselves for any emergency that its legislation may produce." Louisiana was without arms to defend herself "should our sovereignty be assailed." It was

[30] Report of the Adjutant General, Louisiana *Legislature Documents*, 1861, pp. 9–11.

"our imperative duty," he said, to adopt immediate measures for "supplying ourselves with all materials for war." He recommended the creation of a military board to purchase and distribute arms to volunteer companies in the state and to prepare a plan for the reorganization of the militia. He recommended a liberal appropriation, "not less than half a million of dollars," to be expended under the authority of the board, in the purchase "of the best made arms, of the most improved patterns." [31]

As already indicated, the Legislature responded to the governor's recommendation by passing an act entitled "An Act to Promote the Formation of Military Companies, and to Provide for Arming and Equipping the Same." According to its provisions, a military board composed of the governor and four persons appointed by him was created. This board was authorized to purchase and distribute arms and munitions to volunteer companies, a portion of the arms being kept in New Orleans and a portion at the Seminary in Rapides Parish. The board was to report at the next session of the Legislature "some plan for the organization of the Militia or for the promotion of the formation of volunteer companies, as said Board may deem best." The sum of $500,000 was appropriated for the execution of the act.[32]

Governor Moore lost no time in strengthening the military position of Louisiana after it was evident that the state would join the secession movement. On January 10 he addressed the following communication to the commanding officer of the United States barracks and arsenal at Baton Rouge:

Sir: The safety of the State of Louisiana demands that I take possession of all Government property within her limits. You are, therefore, summoned hereby to deliver up the barracks, arsenal, and public property now under your command. With the

[31] Governor's message, *ibid.*, 7–8.
[32] Louisiana *Acts*, 1861, pp. 3–4.

Adjustments and Preparations

large force at my disposal this demand will be enforced. Any attempt at defense on your part will be a rash sacrifice of life. The highest consideration will be extended to yourself and command.[33]

Brevet Major Joseph A. Haskin, the commanding officer, sent the following message to Adjutant General Samuel Cooper at Washington:

BATON ROUGE, JANUARY 10, 1861

The barracks and arsenal at this place were surrendered this afternoon at 5 P.M., upon demand of the governor of the State, backed by a very superior force. Instructions asked where to proceed.[34]

The seizure of the arsenal at Baton Rouge added 47,372 pieces of small arms to the Confederate cause. Of this number, 29,222 were percussion muskets, 8,283 were flint muskets, and 2,287 were Hall rifles. It was reported that there was enough gunpowder in the Baton Rouge arsenal "to supply ten batteries of six guns each."[35] A portion of these military stores was sent immediately to the state arsenal at the State Seminary, where they were received by William Tecumseh Sherman. As superintendent, Sherman was required to receipt for and account for the arms received. "Thus I was made the receiver of stolen goods," he wrote, "and these goods the property of the United States. This grated on my feelings as an ex-army officer, and on counting the arms I noticed that they were packed in the old familiar boxes, with the 'U.S.' simply scratched off."[36]

Forts Jackson and St. Philip were seized by order of Gover-

[33] *Official Records*, Ser. I, Vol. I, 100.

[34] *Ibid.*, 489.

[35] Report of Major J. Gorgas, chief of ordnance, C.S.A., *ibid.*, Ser. IV, Vol. I, 292.

[36] Sherman, *Memoirs of General W. T. Sherman*, I, 182–83. Sherman resigned as superintendent of the Louisiana State Seminary of Learning in February, 1861, and went to his home in Ohio. In May he became a colonel in the Federal army. *Ibid.*, I, 192, 200.

nor Moore on the same day. In his message to the Legislature, January 22, he referred to the "aggressive purpose" of the Federal Government with reference to South Carolina and Florida and stated that, warned by these acts and the "uniform tenor of hostile language employed in Congress against free action in the South," he had decided to take possession of the military posts and munitions of war within the state, in order that the deliberations of the representatives of the people "shall be free and their action supported by the full possession of the whole territory of the State." He then reported the capture of the Baton Rouge barracks and arsenal, Fort Pike, on the Rigolets, and Forts Jackson and St. Philip, on the Mississippi. On February 18 the Legislature, by joint resolution, approved the "prompt, wise and energetic action" of Governor Moore in seizing the arsenal and forts.[37] The Louisiana convention, by a vote of 119 to 5, also adopted a resolution approving the executive's course in taking possession of the arsenal, forts, and munitions of war within the state.[38]

[37] *Official Records,* Ser. I, Vol. I, 493–96; Louisiana *Acts,* 1861, p. 10. The action of Governor Moore in ordering the seizure of Federal forts in Louisiana was the result of communications from Senators Benjamin and Slidell, January 10, warning the governor of Federal plans to garrison Southern ports. Benjamin and Slidell, at Washington, jointly wired Daniel W. Adams, of the Louisiana Military Board: "Secret attempts continue to be made to garrison Southern ports. We think there is special reason to fear surprise from Gulf squadron." On the same day Slidell wired Governor Moore: "The danger is not from Saint Louis, but from sea." See *Official Records,* Ser. I, Vol. I, 496, for both messages. As is well known, the Buchanan Administration had sent the *Star of the West,* on January 5, to reinforce Fort Sumter in the Charleston, South Carolina, harbor. The vessel was fired upon on January 9 by batteries manned by South Carolinians, and the *Star of the West* turned back to New York.

[38] *Journal of the Louisiana Convention,* 1861, p. 14. Those opposing the resolution were Cicero C. Meredith, David Pierson, Joseph A. Rozier, W. T. Stocker, and James G. Taliaferro. Fort Macomb was captured by a detachment of the First Regiment, Louisiana Infantry, on January 28. The Mint and Customhouse at New Orleans were seized on February 1. *Official Records,* Ser. I, Vol. I, 492, 498.

Adjustments and Preparations

Governor Moore reported to the Legislature that, in response to a request from Governor John J. Pettus, he had sent 5,000 flint lock muskets, 3,000 percussion muskets, 1,000 Hall rifles, 200,000 cartridges, 1,000 pounds of rifle powder, six 24-pounder guns and carriages, five hundred 24-pounder shot, and 1,000 pounds of cannon powder to the state of Mississippi. He had taken this action, he said, "not only from considerations of courtesy to a sister State, but in further execution of my duty to Louisiana regarding the approaches of Federal troops from above." [39]

There was considerable activity in Louisiana in January, 1861, in the formation of military companies and in the study and practice of military tactics. The *Picayune* of January 20 said: "Most of the fire companies [in New Orleans] are now drilling as military bodies, and will soon be equally prepared to fire at an enemy with their rifles, or to put out a fire with their pumps." The "Caddo Greys" made their debut on parade in Shreveport on January 8. A local paper complimented the organization for the "neat and becoming uniform" and added the wish "May they ever be ready to defend our firesides against abolitionists and intestine war." [40] A cavalry company was formed at Alexandria on January 14; and at a mass meeting of citizens of Morehouse Parish a company of "Minute Men" was raised, and officers were elected.[41] On January 22 a meeting of "Home Guards" took place in Shreveport. The "guards" were composed of men forty-five years of age and older. This particular meeting represented a part of Caddo Parish and resulted in the appointment of a committee to petition the governor "to furnish us with arms and ammunition to defend our firesides and the property of our fellow-citizens in case of danger." [42]

---

[39] *Official Records,* Ser. I, Vol. I, 495.
[40] Shreveport *South-Western,* January 9, 1861.
[41] New Orleans *Daily Picayune,* January 20, February 5, 1861.
[42] Shreveport *South-Western,* January 30, 1861.

Louisiana in the Confederacy

Governor Moore appointed Daniel W. Adams, Braxton Bragg, Isaac Garret, and Paul O. Hébert to serve with him on the Military Board, created by the Legislature in December. The Board issued a report on February 14 and made a number of recommendations for the state militia system. It recommended that the militia include all white male inhabitants between the ages of eighteen and fifty-five, divided into two classes, "active and sedentary," the active to be composed of those from eighteen to forty years old, subject to call for any duty, and the sedentary, those above forty, subject only to duty within their parishes. Each parish should be a separate militia district, the governor to appoint officers above the rank of captain, and company officers to be elected. The formation of volunteer companies in each parish was to be continued by issue of proper arms and by liberal appropriations from the military fund. The governor was to be commander-in-chief of the militia with full power to call out the militia and volunteers. The Board also recommended that its duties be transferred to the regular military staff of the state and reported certain of its actions as follows:

That unexpected circumstances have occurred requiring prompt action, in which they have taken responsibility not contemplated by the Legislature, perhaps, but justified, as they sincerely believe, by State necessity.

.   .   .   .   .:   .   .   .   .

In the practical execution of the trust, we have to report, that we have made a contract for the purchase of five thousand stand of the most approved small arms now in use in Europe, with ammunition, accoutrements, etc., which, with the arms since obtained, and some slight addition to the Artillery, and in matters of detail, will, in our opinion be all that is required for the present.[43]

[43] Special Report of the Military Board, February 14, 1861, Louisiana *Legislature Documents,* 1861.

Adjustments and Preparations

The Military Board reported that its regulations for the formation of military units had been published in the newspapers and that arms had been issued to the following companies: [44]

Name of company	Number of men on roll
Crescent Rifles	45
Louisiana Guards	100
Orleans Bacachas, No. 1	70
Atchafalaya Guards	46
Chasseurs St. Jacques	60
Orleans Bacachas, No. 2	56
Montgomery Guards	60
Orleans Cadets	40
Orleans Light Guards	42
Bienville Guards of Plaquemines Parish	60
New Home Guards	50
Co. No. 1 Orleans Guards	111
Co. No. 2 Orleans Guards	108
Co. No. 3 Orleans Guards	109
Co. No. 4 Orleans Guards	61
Terrebonne Guards	60
Grosse Tête Guards	45
Thibodaux Rifles	60
Shreveport Greys	00
Assumption Guards	40
Delta Rifles	60
Caddo Rifles	80
Clinton Guards	56
Pelican Rangers	38
Carter Minute Men	40
Madison Dragoons	30
Carroll Guards	38
Lake Providence Cadets	120

According to the report of the Military Board, the state of Louisiana, by February 14, 1861, had furnished arms to

[44] *Ibid.*

twenty-eight volunteer companies with a membership of 1,765.

Meanwhile, on February 5, the convention had adopted an ordinance providing for the establishment of a regular military force for the state, such force to consist of one regiment of artillery and one regiment of infantry and general and staff officers, with one major general; and all commissioned officers were to be appointed by the governor with the consent of the Senate. The pay and allowances and rules of war of the United States Army were adopted. The governor or the Legislature was empowered to disband this force "whenever the safety of the State no longer requires its services," or to transfer it to "such confederated government, as the State may join." Also, in order not to tie the hands of the state legislative body, the convention voted that the Legislature "may at any time alter, amend or abolish any of the provisions of this ordinance." [45]

By an act of the Legislature of March 7, the governor and the adjutant general were constituted a board to distribute arms to the volunteer corps of the state; and the Military Board, created by the act of December 12, 1860, was abolished.[46]

Meanwhile, the Provisional Congress of the Confederacy, which held its first session at Montgomery, Alabama, from February 4 to March 16, was confronted with the problem of military preparations. Acts providing for the creation of a Provisional Army of the Confederate States were adopted on February 28 and March 6. President Davis was authorized to receive into the service of the Confederacy such state forces as might be tendered and to receive from the states the arms and munitions acquired from the United States and all other arms and munitions which the states desired to turn over to the Confederate authorities. On March 9 the Confederate

[45] *Journal of the Louisiana Convention,* 1861, pp. 247–49.
[46] Louisiana *Acts,* 1861, p. 69.

Adjustments and Preparations

Secretary of War, Leroy P. Walker, appealed to Governor Moore for 1,700 Louisiana troops.[47]

The Louisiana convention, on March 13, requested the governor to communicate without delay to the President of the Confederate States the desire of the people of Louisiana to have the army of the state, or such portion as might be required, "transferred to the army of said Confederacy as soon as circumstances may permit." The governor was authorized by the Legislature on March 15 to transfer the regular military force of the state to the service of the Provisional Government of the Confederate States, and also to grant permission to the volunteer troops of Louisiana to volunteer for services in the Confederate army. At the same time, the governor was authorized to transfer to the Confederate Government "all the arms and munitions of war acquired from the late United States, or so much thereof as he may think proper, the said Provisional Government undertaking to settle for the same with the United States." [48]

The troops called for by the Confederate Government on March 9 (from all the seceded states) were used to garrison certain forts within the Confederacy. It soon became evident, however, that additional troops were needed to meet the menace of coercive measures of the United States Government. The refusal of the Lincoln Administration to receive the peace commissioners sent by the Confederate Government, "for the purpose of negotiating friendly relations between that Government [the United States] and the Confederate States of America," was the cause of a call on April 8 for additional troops for the Confederate forces. Louisiana was asked for 3,000 volunteers.[49] The Civil War was virtually be-

---

[47] *The Statutes at Large of the Provisional Government of the Confederate States of America* (Richmond, 1864), 43–44, 47–52; *Official Records*, Ser. IV, Vol. I, 135.

[48] Louisiana *Acts*, 1861, p. 113; *Journal of the Louisiana Convention*, 1861, p. 277.

[49] *Official Records*, Ser. IV, Vol. I, 211. Secretary Walker prefaced the re-

gun on April 12, when Confederate batteries at Charleston, South Carolina, fired on Fort Sumter, which was manned by United States soldiers under Major Robert Anderson. Lincoln's appeal for 75,000 volunteers on April 15 was followed the next day by a call of the Confederate Government for 32,-000 men. Governor Moore was requested "to hold in readiness for instant movement 5,000 volunteer troops, armed and equipped, or as nearly so as practicable." [50]

Moore responded to the calls for troops by proclamations appealing for volunteers for the Confederate service.[51] The appeals were answered promptly and generously from all parts of Louisiana. New Orleans was named as the rendezvous of the troops and, to take care of the soldiers who were arriving in the city, Camp Walker was established on the Metairie Course under the command of Brigadier General Edward L. Tracy. Later, because of the scarcity of water and the fear of disease, it was decided to move the camp to Tangipahoa, on the Jackson railroad, north of New Orleans.[52] Camp Moore, named in honor of the governor, was established there.

Military preparations involved, of course, immediate, heavy expenditures. The Confederate authorities, as we have seen, desired the states to arm and equip the troops. The Louisiana Legislature, on March 20, voted to appropriate $500,000 of the levee fund, for which there was an existing tax, for the purpose of state defense.[53] The parishes made liberal appro-

---

quest for troops with these words: "The discontinuance by the United States of negotiations with the commissioners representing this Government . . . leaves no doubt as to the policy we should pursue."

[50] *Ibid.*, 221–22.

[51] *Ibid.*, 747–48. Governor Moore's proclamations were made on April 17 for the 3,000 and on April 21 for the 5,000 additional troops. Problems in connection with the transfer of troops and arms from Louisiana to the Confederate authorities are discussed in Chapter VIII.

[52] *Ibid.*, 748.

[53] Louisiana *Acts*, 1861, p. 173.

priations for the support of the soldiers and their families. In April the Iberville Parish police jury appropriated $2,000 for the maintenance and equipment of the Iberville Grays and the sum of $852 "to go towards the payment of the arms used by the Company of the (Home Sentinels,) provided said arms, in case of the disbanding of the Company, shall be delivered to the President of the Police Jury, and by him kept and preserved for the Parish." In June the additional sum of $1,500 was voted for the Iberville Grays, and it was provided that $2,000 would be paid to any military company organized within the parish and accepted in the Confederate service.[54] This police jury also voted a pension of from $10 to $25 a month to the family (in needy circumstances) of every soldier who joined a company "leaving for the Seat of War from the Parish of Iberville." [55] Tensas Parish appropriated $16,000 for state use and paid $20 a month to each soldier besides pledging support to his family. East Feliciana voted an appropriation of $50,000 for military purposes. The East Baton Rouge Parish police jury appropriated $10,000 for the support of the families of those who volunteered, and Bienville Parish appropriated $30,000 for equipping volunteers and providing for the families of poor men in the military service. Many other parishes subscribed from $6,000 to $10,-000 for the same purposes.[56] Many individuals, particularly planters and to a lesser extent merchants, contributed generously to the expenses of equipping military companies. In some instances the benefactor was made captain of the or-

[54] Minutes of April 9, 25, June 3, 4, 1861, *Iberville Parish Police Jury Minutes, 1850–1862*, in *Transcription of Parish Records of Louisiana* (University, La., 1940).

[55] *Ibid.*, Minutes for June 3, September 2, 1861. On January 7, 1862, the Iberville Parish police jury adopted the following resolution: "Whereas the expenses of the Parish have been for the last six months very heavy and increasing daily. Therefore, Be it resolved, That from and after this date to the end of the war, no more pensions will be allowed (paupers excepted)."

[56] *Annual Cyclopaedia* (New York), I (1861), 431–32; New Orleans *Daily Picayune*, April 30, May 3, 8, 21, 22, 23, 1861.

ganization, while in others he was honored by having the company bear his name.[57]

Everywhere the scene was one of military preparation; and drills, parades, flag presentations, and departures for the war zones were the order of the day. The following description of New Orleans appeared in the *Picayune* of April 26:

Our city at this time presents the most warlike and military appearance that it has seen since the days of the war of 1814, or that of Mexico. . . .

The beat of the drum and heavy tramp of armed men is heard throughout the day and night. The wildest military enthusiasm and patriotism prevails. From the numerous armories, military rendezvous, arsenals, and recruiting offices on Camp, Chartres, Canal, Royal, St. Charles, Old Levee, St. Peter, and other streets, the flag of the Confederacy is flying. . . .

A visitor to New Orleans in May wrote: "The streets are full of Turcos, Zouaves, Chasseurs; walls are covered with placards of volunteer companies; . . . . In fact, New Orleans looks like a suburb of the camp at Chalons. Tailors are busy night and day making uniforms." [58]

Military spirit and preparations were by no means confined to New Orleans. A Baton Rouge paper said, "As the war news spreads the enthusiasm of the people of the interior begins to rise." News from Plaquemine was that "The talk here is war, and nothing but war." [59] The diary of a sugar planter of Assumption Parish reveals that on April 18 he was helping to get out handbills for a mass meeting at Napoleonville for the purpose of arousing a military spirit among the people.[60] In July it was reported that military companies were passing through Monroe almost daily.[61]

[57] Edwin A. Leland, "Organization and Administration of the Louisiana Army During the Civil War" (M.A. Thesis, Louisiana State University, 1938), 19–21.

[58] Russell, *My Diary North and South,* 231.

[59] New Orleans *Daily Picayune,* April 18, 19, 1861.

[60] Alexander F. Pugh Diary.

[61] New Orleans *Daily Picayune,* July 14, 1861.

Adjustments and Preparations

It has been estimated that Louisiana had at least 16,000 men under arms by June 1, 1861. Five thousand of these were in New Orleans, 4,000 at Camp Moore, 1,700 on seacoast and harbor defense, 1,000 in Arkansas, 2,100 at Pensacola, and 2,300 in Virginia or on the way.[62]

The departure of military units for the scene of conflict in Virginia or elsewhere was an occasion for an enthusiastic demonstration by the civilian population. Flags, fireworks, and oratory often joined hands to pay a farewell tribute to the boys in gray. A member of the Third Louisiana Regiment thus described the demonstration at its departure:

From Camp Walker the march of the regiment was one grand ovation, the balconies of the houses, banquets, and streets being crowded with countless thousands of men, women, and children, bidding the brave boys farewell. . . . The next evening the boats arrived at Baton Rouge. It having been telegraphed from New Orleans that the regiment would reach Baton Rouge early on the 21st, the population turned out *en masse* to give them a reception and take a last farewell of company K. Pelican Rifles.

After picturing the wonderful display of fireworks at Baton Rouge, the same observer adds: "Scenes similar to this occurred at Plaquemine, Lake Providence, wherever the regiment had friends and relatives, while the river banks at every plantation, hamlet, city and village poured forth their inhabitants to wave adieu to the men." [63]

Sometimes the occasion was one of solemnity, and the blessings of the church were bestowed upon the departing soldiers. The following description of a solemn occasion in New Orleans may be taken as typical:

The Sabbath of yesterday will long be remembered by our citizens as one of the most impressive, solemn and touching occasions which ever took place in our city.

[62] *Annual Cyclopaedia,* I (1861), 432.
[63] William H. Tunnard, *The History of the Third Regiment Louisiana Infantry* (Baton Rouge, 1866), 31–33.

Louisiana in the Confederacy

At Christ Church, a sermon was delivered by the Rev. Dr. Leacock to the members of the Washington Artillery, on the occasion of their departure, to-day, for the seat of the war. It was a strange and novel sight to see men-at-arms, with their accoutrements and sabres, kneeling at the throne of grace, and going through the forms of the Episcopal service, while the clang of steel echoing through the solemn vaulted aisles, gave a stern impression to the occasion.

The sermon of Dr. Leacock was most eloquent and appropriate, and when invoking the blessing of Divine Providence, and His protection over these gallant braves, and bidding them an affectionate farewell in departure for the field of battle, tears from the ladies flowed freely, for they had many a husband, brother and son among them.

At the Presbyterian church, Dr. Palmer also preached one of his eloquent and touching sermons to the Crescent Rifles, the galleries and aisles being crowded to hear the sermon.[64]

The parishes continued to make liberal appropriations for the military forces. For instance, in July, the police jury of Rapides Parish raised its appropriations for war purposes from $12,000 to $25,000 while Caldwell Parish appropriated $20,000 to arm, equip, and support the volunteers of that parish.[65] In August Iberville Parish appropriated the sum of $10,000 "or so much thereof as may be necessary" for the purchase of winter clothing, shoes, and blankets for volunteers who had enlisted in local companies. The money was to be raised by the sale of one- and two-year bonds bearing 8 per cent interest. A tax of seven cents on each one hundred dollars' value of taxable property was levied to redeem the bonds.[66] On August 9 the New Orleans Board of Aldermen

[64] New Orleans *Daily Picayune*, May 27, 1861.

[65] *Ibid.*, July 25, 28, 1861.

[66] *Iberville Parish Police Jury Minutes*, August 1, 1861. The president of the police jury and the treasurer of the parish were authorized to prepare the bonds "in such form and such sums as they may determine." On January 7, 1862, the police jury amended the earlier ordinance by authorizing the

appropriated $100,000 for the defense of the city and instructed the city treasurer to pay that amount to Major General David E. Twiggs, Confederate commander, "to be applied by him in such manner as he may deem proper for the construction of fortifications to defend the approaches of the city." [67]

At Shreveport the action of the New Orleans municipal authorities met with ridicule from at least one source. In an editorial entitled "The Defence of New Orleans," the *South-Western* said:

The council of this city, after doing little or nothing for its defence during the whole long summer, have at length appropriated the sum of $100,000 to fortify it. This is like throwing one bucket of water into the Mississippi river at a low stage of water to swell it. That sum will do about as much good towards successfully fortifying New Orleans as ten cents would do to protect Shreveport. If $10,000,000 had been appropriated something might have been done, if commenced in proper time.[68]

There was a wholesome rivalry between some of the parishes in furnishing troops for the defense of the country, and the newspapers praised individuals and communities for their patriotism. The *South-Western,* for instance, claimed that Caddo Parish was the "Banner parish of the State" when announcing the departure of the "Caddo Fencibles," the sixth company from Caddo, on August 14, 1861. The same paper on September 4 praised Rapides Parish for having sent six companies to the war and asserted that unless Caddo was more active, it would have to surrender the claim of being the banner parish. In Winn Parish, however, there seems to have

president to issue "the balance of said appropriations in bonds of twenty-five and fifty cents, without interest, payable on demand." Minutes of January 7, 1862.

[67] New Orleans *Daily Crescent,* August 10, 1861. For Major General Twiggs's report to Secretary of War Walker concerning this appropriation, see *Official Records,* Ser. I, Vol. LIII, 726–27.

[68] Shreveport *South-Western,* August 21, 1861.

been an element that was unwilling to support the military forces of the state. The *Southern Sentinel,* published at Winnfield, said in August:

There seems to be a very bad feeling existing between two classes of citizens in our parish. We are sorry to see such a condition of affairs, but it is so, and we cannot help it. The non-slaveholding population think that the slave-holders are not doing their duty, and therefore, should be made to do it.[69]

On September 28 Governor Moore, as commander-in-chief, issued an order setting forth rules and instructions concerning the organization of the militia. According to the instructions, a census of all persons from eighteen to forty-five years of age, subject to militia duty, was to be made. No volunteer companies, unless organized and commissioned by the governor, were to be recognized. No home guards, or companies organized for service only within the limits of a town, city, or parish, "will be acknowledged, except companies or corps the members whereof are subjects of a foreign prince or government, or composed exclusively of persons over forty-five years." It was made clear in the governor's order that any person refusing or neglecting to perform militia duty, or to attend drills, musters, or parades, would be marked as "suspicious" and be made subject to the fines imposed by an act of 1853.[70]

In another public notice Governor Moore recommended to banks and insurance companies that they close at two o'clock in the afternoon daily, and to merchants, builders,

[69] Quoted in *ibid.,* August 28, 1861. The Shreveport *South-Western* reported that a mass meeting was held in Winnfield on August 24, "for the purpose of devising means by which men of the parish who are able and not willing to support the volunteers, can be reached."

[70] New Orleans *Daily Crescent,* September 30, 1861; *Official Records,* Ser. IV, Vol. I, 753. The act of 1853 referred to imposed fines of from $5 to $200 upon officers (depending on the rank of the officer) and for a fine of $1 for noncommissioned officers and privates for failure to attend a review or for absence from parade. Louisiana *Acts,* 1853, pp. 355–56.

Adjustments and Preparations

manufacturers, and others that they close at three in order to afford their employees time to "obey the orders for the performance of a duty they owe to their country." [71] The executive's recommendation must have received a favorable response, for the New Orleans *Price-Current* of October 5, 1861, said:

The prompt and voluntary action of our citizens in organizing military companies, either specifically for the defense of the city or for the war, has occupied the attention of our mercantile classes to such an extent as to leave but a few hours for business pursuits. Our Banks and public offices now close their doors at 2 o'clock P.M. A large number of our merchants shut up at 3 P.M. The afternoons are devoted to drilling and every man in the community is preparing to meet and repulse the enemy should he dare attack us.

Officers, clerks, and employees of the Confederate States, of the state of Louisiana, and of telegraph offices, manufactories, dockyards, and foundries, "actually engaged on works for the state and Confederate Governments," were declared exempt by the governor from the operations of orders pertaining to the militia. [72]

According to Adjutant General Grivot's report of November 22 to the governor, there were 23,577 troops from Louisiana in the Confederate service. It was not possible to make a statement of the number enrolled in the militia, since many parishes had not made returns. Nine parishes had reported a total of 5,898. The First Division, made up of volunteer and regular militia forces, totaled 31,251 men. The grand total of Louisiana troops, so far reported, was 60,726. [73] Grivot was not entirely satisfied with the state's military system, and he recommended the adoption of a more stringent militia law. Officers, he said, should have full power to compel obedience

[71] New Orleans *Daily Crescent*, September 30, 1861.   [72] *Ibid.*
[73] *Official Records*, Ser. IV, Vol. I, 747–55; *Annual Cyclopaedia*, I (1861), 434.

to orders and attendance at drills and reviews, and during war the militia should be subject to "the strict and rigid rules and regulations of war." He also recommended that volunteer corps should be encouraged.[74]

When the Legislature convened, the recommendations of the adjutant general were presented for consideration. It was generally admitted that the militia system needed reform. On January 23, 1862, a measure was adopted entitled "An Act to Reorganize the Militia." The act stated that the militia of the state of Louisiana "Shall be composed of all the free white males capable of bearing arms residing in the State, and are eighteen years of age and not over forty-five." The following persons were declared exempt from militia service: members of the General Assembly, judges of the courts of record, secretary of state, treasurer and auditor of the state, the attorney general, district attorneys, the secretary and assistant secretary of the Senate, the clerk and assistant clerk of the House, clerks of courts of record, sheriffs, physicians in actual practice, ministers of the Gospel, mayors and recorders of cities, one apothecary in each store, the commissioner of the land office, registrars of the land offices of the state, keepers of public prisons, all persons engaged in the mail service, and all persons exempt under the laws of the Confederate States by virtue of their employment in the civil, military, or naval service of the Confederate Government. After thirty days from the passage of the act no additional volunteer companies should be formed without the consent of the governor, and no person should be received in any volunteer company without the consent of the major general of the militia.

According to the militia act, it was made the duty of tax assessors to enroll inhabitants of their parishes or districts subject to militia duty, and to return such a roll to the adjutant general. No detachment of the militia should be required to serve more than three months at one time, except

[74] *Official Records,* Ser. IV, Vol. I, 754.

Adjustments and Preparations

in case of urgent necessity, in which case the governor, as commander-in-chief, was authorized to detain the unit six months longer.[75]

The militia act provided for the election of a major general by the Legislature. John L. Lewis, who was elected to this office, entered upon his duties with laudable dispatch and determination. He issued instructions to military companies on February 15 and appealed to the people of Louisiana for their co-operation.[76] The governor was authorized by the militia law to appoint all other officers above the rank of captain, the consent of the Senate being required for the appointment of brigadier generals.[77]

The people of New Orleans received the news in December, 1861, that a Federal force had taken possession of Ship Island, Mississippi Sound. Naturally, such information created some excitement and furthered plans for local defense. Although the *Crescent*, in writing about the Federal forces at Ship Island, asked the question: "Why do they not come along?" and boasted that "Chalmette's glories will be repeated, with the difference only between defeating a brave and manly foe, and such a race of sneaking imbeciles as the Bull Runners of the North," it was critical of the Confederate naval authorities for not putting New Orleans in the strongest position for defense.[78] On February 20, 1862, the New Orleans council named sixty-four citizens as a "Committee on Public Safety." The purpose of this action was to provide for co-operation with the Confederate and state authorities in devising means for the defense of the city of New Orleans and its approaches.[79]

[75] Louisiana *Acts*, 1861–1862, pp. 61–72.

[76] New Orleans *Daily Crescent*, February 18, 1862.

[77] Louisiana *Acts*, 1861–1862, pp. 61–72.

[78] New Orleans *Daily Crescent*, January 10, 11, 1862. Ship Island is near Biloxi, Mississippi; it is fifty miles from Lake Pontchartrain and eighty miles from the mouth of the Mississippi.

[79] *Official Records*, Ser. III, Vol. II, 728–29; New Orleans *Daily Crescent*, February 25, 1862.

Louisiana in the Confederacy

New Orleans, while concerned with its own defense, was not unfaithful to the Confederate cause elsewhere. On March 3 the council appropriated $25,000 to purchase uniforms and equipment for all military organizations of the city needing assistance that might be mustered into the service of the state and be transferred to the command of General Beauregard, "to fight our battles in Columbus [Kentucky] or elsewhere." At the same time the mayor was authorized to issue municipal bonds to the amount of $1,000,000 in order to supply the Committee on Public Safety with funds to purchase arms, munitions of war, and provisions, or to provide any means for the successful defense of the city and its approaches.[80]

[80] *Official Records,* Ser. III, Vol. II, 730–31.

Chapter III

Problems of the New Order

THE ELECTION OF 1860 with the uncertainty concerning the future political status of the state, the severing of the old political ties, and the prospects of a war in defense of the right to sever those ties, with the consequent military preparations, combined to present to the people of Louisiana many serious problems. These problems were common for the entire state, and the economic policies adopted were the policies of the representatives of all the people until the Union forces gained control of New Orleans in April, 1862. After that date the history of Louisiana is the history of two sections—the southeast under Federal control, the rest of the state subject to the acts of the Confederate Government and of the state government acknowledging allegiance to the Confederacy.

The banks of Louisiana adopted a policy of sharp reduction of accommodations in the fall of 1860 when the election of Lincoln appeared probable. After the election this policy was continued, of course, with the result that there was considerable distress. The New Orleans *Price-Current* of November 3 said the money market showed "increasing tightness" because of the feeling of uneasiness that had pervaded the community for some time regarding the future course of political events. A month later it was reported that the stringency in the field of finance continued "to grow more and more severe from day to day," and in consequence every

67

Louisiana in the Confederacy

department of business was "laboring under great and un-usual depression." The banks were refusing all applications for new loans.[1] The Louisiana Board of Currency, charged with the duty of the supervision of the banks of the state, re-ported to the Legislature in January, 1861:

The Board has the satisfaction to state that amid the trials and embarrassments of the last few months, and the universal distrust engendered by the breaking up of the Federal Union, the banks of this State have maintained inviolate every engagement. Whilst other communities, compelled to resort to temporary palliatives, have sanctioned a suspension of specie payments, and even the banks of New York were forced into artificial combinations in order to avoid threatened insolvency, our own institutions never wavered for an instant. The steady maintenance of specie pay-ments by our banks was not without great sacrifices, but this is but another tribute to the wisdom of our banking system, and an illustration of the soundness of our commercial community, who were ready to submit to severe privations for the sake of preserving the integrity of our currency.[2]

On the day before adjournment the convention made an effort to strengthen the banking system of the state. An ordi-nance was adopted amending Article CXVIII of the constitu-tion by providing that two thirds of the capital stock be paid in specie before a bank should begin operation. No bank should issue notes exceeding in amount, at any one time, three fourths of the amount of capital paid in; and the cash liabilities of each bank should always be represented by at least one third in specie, and the balance in good paper, paya-

[1] New Orleans *Price-Current, Commercial Intelligencer and Merchant's Transcript,* December 1, 12, 1860. Cited hereafter as New Orleans *Price-Current.*

[2] Report of the Board of Currency, January, 1861, Louisiana *Legislature Documents,* 1861. The New Orleans *Price-Current* of December 15, 1860, quoted the *Boston Traveller* as follows: "The New Orleans banks are the strongest in the Union, and in fact the only ones it seems to us that conduct banking on safe and legitimate principles. The banks in the Northwestern States, and particularly in Illinois, are the weakest."

Problems of the New Order

ble in full at maturity, within ninety days. No bank was to issue from its counter any other than its own notes.[3]

The establishment of the Confederate Government and the appointment of commissioners to negotiate a peaceable arrangement with the authorities at Washington resulted in a decided improvement in the New Orleans money market. During March and for the first half of April the weekly bank reports showed increases in loans.[4] The beginning of hostilities at Fort Sumter on April 12, however, reversed this trend and brought a return of stringency and dullness to the exchanges. The New Orleans *Price-Current* of April 13 told its readers that "The dangerous aspect of political affairs, which culminated yesterday in actual hostilities at Charleston, has influenced the Money market in an adverse direction, and scarcely anything of importance has been done during the last few days"; and two weeks later, April 27, the paper declared, "In the present uncertain state of affairs it may be said that we no longer have a money market." On April 13 the New Orleans banks held $20,089,881 in deposits, $16,627,855 in specie, $14,143,746 in 90-day paper; and their circulation amounted to $8,684,486. On September 14 their condition was reported to be $14,710,698 in deposits, $14,173,258 in specie, $12,831,100 in 90-day paper, and the circulation $6,481,716.[5]

On September 16, 1861, Governor Moore recommended to

---

[3] *Journal of the Louisiana Convention*, 1861, p. 281. On March 16, 1861, the eleven New Orleans banks held $21,101,036 in deposits, $17,686,844 in specie, and $14,251,298 in 90-day paper. New Orleans *Price-Current*, March 20, 1861. See also Stephen A. Caldwell, *A Banking History of Louisiana* (Baton Rouge, 1935), 90.

[4] New Orleans *Price-Current*, March 13, 27, April 3, 10, 17, 24, 1861. The *Price-Current* of March 13 reported the money market better "under the impression that the prospect for peaceful solution of our political difficulties is assuming a more confident shape"; and on April 3 it said, "The money market continues to be abundantly supplied, and the tendency to increased ease for desirable paper and other investments, is quite apparent."

[5] *Ibid.*, April 17, September 21, 1861.

the banks of New Orleans that they suspend specie payments immediately. He admitted that under the laws of Louisiana banks could not suspend, nor could the Legislature legalize suspension. Nevertheless, he recommended such a course because of the issue of Confederate Treasury notes. Unless the creditors of the banks received the Treasury notes, he said, these notes could not be taken by them in payment, and would thus fail to answer the purpose of currency. The action of the banks in suspending could be referred to the people at such time as the Legislature might think proper; and the people, in convention assembled, "will decide whether the forfeiture of their charters by the Banks shall be exacted or relinquished." [6]

Governor Moore had been urged by Confederate authorities at Richmond to secure suspension by New Orleans banks. Christoper G. Memminger, Confederate secretary of the treasury, wrote Moore on September 11, saying: "I am directed by the President, with the concurrence of his cabinet, to request that you will unite with him in inducing the banks of New Orleans to suspend specie payments, and to place Treasury notes upon the same footing with their own notes." Memminger asserted that it was essential to the security of the government and necessary for self-defense that Treasury notes should circulate as currency. "This result had been obtained everywhere, except at New Orleans," he said, "and the urgency of the case has suggested the adoption of harsh measures to remove this exception. The Government of the Confederate States, however, has preferred adopting such measures as will effect the object with the least possible disturbance of private right and commercial integrity." [7] On the day he wrote to Governor Moore, Secretary Memminger addressed a letter to the presidents and directors of the New

[6] New Orleans *Daily Crescent,* September 16, 1861.

[7] *Reports of the Secretary of the Treasury of the Confederate States of America, 1861–1865* (Washington, 1878), 45 (Microfilm copy, University of Texas Archives).

Problems of the New Order

Orleans banks, calling attention to the fact that other banks in the Confederacy had suspended specie payments and urging the New Orleans banks to adopt "the only measure which can secure the credit of the Government, namely the temporary suspension of specie payments by the banks and the reception of Treasury notes as currency." [8]

On September 17 the *Crescent* commended the "wise and patriotic move" of the Louisiana State Bank, the Bank of Louisiana, and the Bank of America in suspending specie payments, and the next day announced the same action by the Crescent City Bank and the Citizens Bank of Louisiana. When announcing suspension by the banks, the *Price-Current* informed the public that that action was not due to "any inability on the part of the Banks to meet fully all their liabilities, but was mainly with the view of aiding the Government in introducing Treasury Notes into general circulation." [9] The Board of Currency reported on November 20, 1861, that all banks had suspended specie payments with the exception of the Southern Bank, which was still paying its liabilities in coin. [10]

The banks of Louisiana were protected against suits arising from their action in suspending specie payments. According to an act of the Legislature of January, 1862, no suit or proceeding should be instituted, and no protest made "during the existing war, and for the twelve months thereafter" for the nonpayment of bank notes in specie or for receiving and paying out other notes than their own at their counter, provided that the banks should continue to receive and pay out at par Confederate States Treasury notes. No

[8] *Ibid.*, 45–46.   [9] New Orleans *Price-Current,* September 21, 1861.
[10] New Orleans *Daily Crescent,* December 20, 1861. A New Orleans girl observed in her diary on September 22, 1861, that the people absolutely refused to give specie for paper and that it was impossible to get change. "A perfect mania has seized the community," she wrote, "and there is a dearth of silver money, and those who possess it will not part with it." Clara Solomon Diary (MS. in Louisiana State University Department of Archives).

bank was to sell any of its coin while this act was in effect. Finally, it was provided that nothing in this act was to be construed to prevent any bank from lending to the state or the Confederate States.[11]

In January, 1862, the Legislature enacted laws providing for the acceptance of Confederate States Treasury notes and bonds in payment of all sales of public land and in payment of all debts or claims due to the state or parish and city corporations. All fiscal agents were directed and authorized to receive such notes.[12] There was, however, some reluctance on the part of businessmen to receive the Confederate Treasury notes; and there was a good deal of speculation in connection with the currency. The New Orleans Committee on Public Safety adopted a resolution on March 5, 1862, condemning all persons who refused to take Confederate notes in payment of debts and other commercial transactions as "unworthy of the countenance and respect of patriotic citizens, and justly obnoxious to the indignation of the community." [13] Speculation, too, aroused the wrath of the authorities, and the Board of Provost Marshals (New Orleans and the surrounding territory were under martial law) published the following notice in the New Orleans papers in March and April, 1862:

All traffic in paper currency, tending to create distrust in the public mind, or otherwise to produce embarrassment, shall be held as acts of hostility against the Government, and will be dealt with summarily.

The traffic in Gold and Silver against the Notes of the Confederate States of America is hereby expressly prohibited.

[11] Louisiana *Acts*, 1861–1862, pp. 45–46. The Louisiana constitution of 1852 denied the Legislature the power to sanction, "directly or indirectly," the suspension of specie payments. The Legislature in 1853 provided for a hearing before a district court in case of the nonpayment of bank notes in specie. Unless the banks could show cause, the court should pronounce judgment of insolvency and provide for liquidation. *Journal of the Louisiana Convention*, 1852, p. 79; Louisiana *Acts*, 1853, p. 307.

[12] Louisiana *Acts*, 1861–1862, pp. 19, 82.

[13] New Orleans *Price-Current*, March 22, 1862.

Problems of the New Order

Delinquents will be visited by prompt and severe punishment.[14]

Not all the economic problems confronting the people of Louisiana in 1861 were caused by the state of war. The Federal blockade, the expense involved in military preparations, and the necessity of providing for many of the families of soldiers were serious problems indeed. But the situation was aggravated by a serious drought and overflow in 1860 in some sections of the state and by poor crops in 1861. On March 7, 1861, the Legislature, because of the "unprecedented drought and overflow which has visited many sections of the State of Louisiana during the year eighteen hundred and sixty," appropriated $30,000 to purchase corn or rice to be furnished the poor who were "actually in a state of suffering, or likely to be" from the effects of the drought and overflow. It was provided that no parish should receive more than $1,500.[15]

This economic distress was aggravated by the blockade. On May 27, 1861, the New Orleans *Picayune* announced that the U.S. man-of-war *Brooklyn* had arrived off Pass L'Outre bar at the mouth of the Mississippi at two o'clock the day before and had notified Major Johnson K. Duncan, in command at Fort Jackson, that the blockade would take effect from that moment. This event was of course not unexpected, and some Louisianians had made preparations for the interruption of trade. Food crops received greater emphasis in farm economy. A foreign observer reported in June that the planters along the Mississippi above New Orleans had planted an unusual quantity of Indian corn to have food for the Negroes without any distress from inland or sea blockade.[16] While such expedients might have aided the rural districts, they

[14] New Orleans *Daily Picayune*, April 7, 1862.

[15] Louisiana *Acts*, 1861, pp. 68–69.

[16] Russell, *My Diary North and South*, 264–65. See also the New Orleans *Price-Current*, March 21, April 3, 17, 1861, for reports of unusually large corn planting in the parishes of West Baton Rouge, Concordia, and Point Coupee.

could be of little or no value to New Orleans, where disruption of trade brought a business depression with a consequent increase in unemployment. A New Orleans resident wrote on July 20: "There is a great deal of suffering here at this time   many families are not able to pay their rent and [are] thrown out of employment."[17]   There is reason to believe that many men in New Orleans enlisted in the army as the only means of finding employment.[18]

The *Picayune* announced the receipt of North Texas flour, three hundred sacks from the mills near Bonham and a large consignment from Paris, Texas. According to that paper this was the first shipment of flour from this region to arrive in New Orleans, and the hope was expressed that the supply of breadstuffs would be drawn largely from Texas in the future. "The Lincoln blockade," it was said, "has not shut them out from an excellent market."[19]   But breadstuffs seem to have been among the few articles of food of which there was an ample supply in New Orleans by late September, 1861, as the following statement of the *Crescent* will show:

The supplies of many articles of consumption are running very low. There is scarcely a month's consumption of coffee in market. There is not a bag in first hands. In the meantime, substitutes have been proposed, among which is named the okra seed. As regards this, the thought of its becoming a substitute may as well be laid aside at once, for there are not twenty-five sacks of the seed available. The chief substitute will have to be rye. . . . The supplies of bacon, hams and pork are running low. Hams up to 25 cents per pound; lard 27 to 30 cents, the stock running very low. We shall have to fall back on Creole beef and mutton—return to first principles. Breadstuffs are in good supply and an abundance in the country.[20]

[17] Isaac Evans to E. P. Ellis, Ellis Collection (Louisiana State University Department of Archives).

[18] Roger W. Shugg, *Origins of Class Struggle in Louisiana* (University, La., 1939), 171–72.

[19] New Orleans *Daily Picayune*, July 13, 1861.

[20] New Orleans *Daily Crescent*, September 27, 1861.

Problems of the New Order

There were many evidences of speculation as early as October and November, 1861. The *Crescent* of November 6 reported "more talk about salt than anything else" and said: "Ten dollars per sack was asked yesterday. Speculation has been rife in the article for some time past." The Alexandria *Louisiana Democrat* was quoted as of October 30:

Some weeks ago the agents of certain jobbing houses in New Orleans visited this place and endeavored to buy up all the woolens, linseys and staple goods now on the shelves of our merchants. Strange as it may seem, they in part succeeded. Although the demand for such goods is, and will be, very great among our planters and the whole population, and though no doubt can possibly exist of the certain sale of all such articles, some of our merchants have, nevertheless, permitted these sharpers and Shylocks from New Orleans to denude their stores of the very things that our people will be suffering for before three months have expired. . . .

Last week another batch of these New Orleans runners arrived, and departed after having made large purchases. . . . About a month ago they sent up some military adventurers here, who were taken out of their handsome phaeton and given free lodging in jail. We propose to afford a more humble vehicle for these trading travelers—a slick pole with a dose of tar and the spare plumage of a Shanghai. The New Orleans papers will save some of their people some mortification by affording them an opportunity to read this warning.[21]

Prices in New Orleans were advancing rapidly in November. The *Crescent* reported a "steadily increasing scarcity of breadstuffs and other necessaries of life," and asserted: "Flour is advancing to famine figures. Each succeeding day is attended with an advance of 25 cents or more per barrel." Other articles—such as soap, candles, starch—were advancing in price "from day to day." [22] According to a New Orleans girl's diary, the price of a bar of soap advanced from twenty cents to

21 *Ibid.*, November 4, 1861.   22 *Ibid.*, November 9, 1861.

one dollar; coffee sold for one dollar per pound, and "Ma has notified us that we must soon say good bye to it." [23]

Already, the authorities of New Orleans had taken steps to protect the consumer by regulating the price of bread. On October 5 Mayor John T. Monroe announced a schedule of prices for the week commencing October 7, ranging from twenty cents for fifty-four ounces to five cents for fourteen ounces of first-quality bread.[24]

Business in general was seriously affected by the blockade and the war activity. A letter from Alexandria, Rapides Parish, dated November 21, 1861, read:

> Business in this place, as everywhere else, is almost entirely suspended, as regards commerce with other parts of the country, and the only lively feature of that sort I have noticed since my arrival is the spectacle of numerous ox teams from Texas, if an ox team, composed of a dozen or more animals hauling a single wagon load of wool, can be called a lively spectacle.[25]

The wagon commerce with Texas seems to have enjoyed expansion. It was reported from Alexandria in January, 1862, that wagons loaded with wool were arriving daily from all parts of Texas, with an average arrival and departure daily of twenty wagons, and that there were "over one hundred on the route from San Antonio alone, loaded with wool, coffee and hides, which will commence arriving in a few days." [26]

The New Orleans *Crescent* of February 19, 1862, appeared on a sheet half the usual size. In an editorial entitled "Our Half Sheet," the editor characterized the expedient as "mortifying to us" but explained that circumstances had rendered it unavoidable. Transportation difficulties were blamed for

[23] Clara Solomon Diary, November 2, 1861.

[24] New Orleans *Daily Crescent*, October 10, 1861.

[25] *Ibid.*, November 25, 1861. According to this writer, prices in Alexandria included ham at 45 cents and coffee at $1.50 per pound, while salt sold for $12 a sack.   [26] *Ibid.*, January 7, 1862.

the shortage of paper. A few days later the paper said: "It cannot be disguised that our bacon is running very low. From whence or how is the stock or supply to be replenished? Fifty dollars for a barrel of pork, one dollar for a bushel of corn, fourteen dollars per barrel for flour!" [27]

Scarcity of some articles in New Orleans, however, was not caused by a shortage of production within the state. Then, as in the twentieth century, the system of distribution was somewhat at fault. While New Orleans complained of food shortage and consequent high prices, North Louisiana complained of an oversupply of certain provisions. In March, 1862, the *Louisiana Baptist,* of Mt. Lebanon, Bienville Parish, stated:

We see by our city exchanges that the stock of corn and meat on hand is well nigh exhausted, and both articles are commanding high prices—corn worth over a dollar per bushel, and bacon twenty-five cents a pound.

We have an overstock of both of these articles in North Louisiana, and a great scarcity of money. Why, then, do not our planters send their corn and bacon to New Orleans, supply their wants, and bring back money, which is so much needed among us? [28]

Louisianians, in common with other Southerners, believed that cotton would be an important factor in the success of the foreign policy of the Confederacy. They had faith in the power of "King Cotton" and had visions of European interference in America in the interest of the Confederacy. William H. Russell, who was traveling among the Creoles along the Mississippi in June, 1861, said: "All these gentlemen to a man are resolute that England must get their cotton or perish. . . . Illimitable fields tilled by multitudinous negroes open on their sight and they behold the empires of Europe, with their manufactures, their industry, and their

[27] *Ibid.,* February 21, 1862.   [28] Quoted in *ibid.,* March 24, 1862.

wealth, prostrate at the base of their throne, crying out 'Cotton! More Cotton! That is all we ask.' " [29] The state's leading men were not less optimistic concerning the ability of cotton to bring foreign aid to the South.[30]

Southerners planned to hasten foreign intervention and at the same time cripple Northern industry by an embargo on cotton. England and France would be made to realize their dependence on the Confederacy and be stimulated to act at once to break the Federal blockade. Louisiana was not slow to co-operate in this Southern program. In fact, her leaders seemed to feel the responsibility resting upon the port of New Orleans in making a policy of cotton embargo a success.[31] In July, 1861, the cotton factors of New Orleans, numbering more than one hundred, advised cotton planters, through a public notice in the newspapers, not to ship any portion of their crops to New Orleans or to remove it from their plantations until the blockade was abandoned.[32] On September 23 ninety-five cotton factors of New Orleans addressed a petition to Governor Moore and Major General Twiggs, requesting them to take immediate steps to prevent the shipment of any cotton to New Orleans because cotton, "from the known inefficiency of the blockade, will find its way to foreign ports, and furnish the manufacturing interests of Europe and the United States with the product of which they are most in need." Governor Moore concurred in these views and responded by ordering that, after October 10, no cotton be brought to New Orleans or within that "section of the country between the fortifications above Carrollton and those below the city and extending back to the lake." Major General

[29] Russell, *My Diary North and South*, 259–60. See also *De Bow's Review* (New Orleans), XXX (January, 1861), 93.

[30] Frank L. Owsley, *King Cotton Diplomacy; Foreign Relations of the Confederate States of America* (Chicago, 1931), 22.

[31] *Ibid.*, 30.

[32] New Orleans *Daily Picayune*, July 23, 1861; New Orleans *Daily Crescent*, August 1, 1861.

Problems of the New Order

Twiggs announced that he would co-operate with the governor in the enforcement of the order.[33]

The cotton crop of Louisiana for 1861 was far below normal because of excessive rains in August and September in many portions of the state. Whereas excellent crop prospects were reported in June and July, long incessant rains in the succeeding months reduced the yield of cotton by about one half and in some places damaged the corn crop. News from Rapides Parish in mid-September was to the effect that the rainy season had lasted for forty days.[34]

The crop shortage and the embargo policy combined to reduce the cotton shipments to New Orleans to a minimum. The *Crescent* reported on September 25 that

The stock of cotton on hand yesterday was 10,639 bales, against 155,000 bales for the same time last year. The receipts this year since the first of September are 655 bales, against 121,000 for the same time last year. . . . The way cotton is coming to market at this time, it will take about twelve calendar months to load Com. Marcy's ship, the *Pettigrew*. The recommendations of the factors will be fully carried out by the planters.

On the following day the *Crescent* continued the discourse on the subject of cotton by saying: "In the absence of the king, the glory and prestige of Carondelet appears to have departed. No cotton coming to market, the brokers are taking it coolly and calmly." The *Crescent* reported on December 19 that the receipts of cotton for the week were 121 bales, "all in transitu for interior points." The total receipts at New Orleans, from September 1 to December 19, were 4,992 bales, as compared to 187,559 bales for the same period of 1860, a decrease of 182,567 bales. The shipments during the same period totaled 3,142 in 1861 as against 152,783 bales in 1860, a decrease of 149,641 bales.[35]

[33] *Official Records*, Ser. III, Vol. II, 725–27.
[34] New Orleans *Daily Crescent*, August 26, September 2, 16, 17, 1861.
[35] *Ibid.*, December 19, 1861.

Louisiana in the Confederacy

The limitation of cotton production by some form of state action was a mooted question in Louisiana as in the other cotton states in the years 1861–1865. But the idea received little support in the state, and the most its proponents were able to do was to secure the adoption of a resolution by the Louisiana House of Representatives on December 14, 1861, which instructed the Committee on Agriculture to inquire into the expediency and propriety of checking the cultivation of cotton in Louisiana during the blockade by a tax on cotton, and of encouraging the cultivation of articles of necessity by premiums on foods, wool, leather, material for clothing, iron, lead, and all munitions of war. Such an expedient, if adopted, was "to have effect, providing the blockade be in force on the 1st of April next." [36]

There was considerable feeling and controversy over the "Cotton Planters Relief Bill," which was adopted by the Legislature and vetoed by Governor Moore in January, 1862. The proposed act called for the issuing of $7,000,000 of paper money with cotton as security. Planters were to pledge their cotton to the state and receive treasury notes at the rate of five cents per pound. The notes were made payable one year after the raising of the blockade. The proponents of the measure advocated it as necessary to relieve the cotton planter from serious financial difficulties caused by inability to dispose of the cotton crop through regular channels. The opponents of the proposal charged that it was unnecessary, unwise, and unconstitutional. The *Crescent* was of the opinion that a better method of relief could be devised through the banks and issued the warning, "Whenever a State commences issuing her treasury notes, she always loses in character, credit and money. All experiences demonstrate this—and experience

[36] *Ibid.*, December 18, 1861. The Legislature took no action at this time or later restricting, directly or indirectly, the cultivation of cotton. The trade in cotton and the efforts to promote the manufacture of cotton cloth, 1863–1865, are discussed in Chapter VII.

is the only safe guide." [37] The *Price-Current* looked to the passage of the bill "with dismay" and declared, "It is the universal opinion among intelligent men, as far as we can learn, that the passing of such a bill . . . will, in the end, be productive of great and irreparable evils, not only to one, but to every department of industry throughout the State." [38]

Lewis Texada of Rapides Parish was one of the most ardent opponents of the measure. He opposed the bill not only as unnecessary and unconstitutional but as a positive evil in encouraging the North to believe that the South was already exhausted. Texada concluded his speech of January 17 in the Senate by saying:

Instead of leaving to the people to adopt their own method of obtaining supplies, and suspending the collection of taxes for the time, you publish to the world, to our enemies, that we are on the brink of ruin, that starvation is at our doors, and if not saved by the State we must perish.

. . . there would be more joy at Washington than the announcement of a battle won. The Abolition Cabinet of Abraham Lincoln will receive it as an omen of victory. Their organs will rally a people, now clamoring for peace to a continuance of the war. Louisiana, the richest State in the Confederacy, has to relieve the lords of the boasted interest which claimed to be king. Fight on, gallant Yankees, the proud Southron, who defies our enemies, and braves bayonet and bullet and bombshell, cannot reduce [sic] a curtailment of rations. Raised in luxury, he cowers when his supplies are exhausted.[39]

Governor Moore vetoed the bill because he considered it unconstitutional, and charged that it contravened the state constitution and violated the provisional constitution of the

---

[37] *Ibid.*, January 6, 1862. A copy of the bill was printed in the Shreveport *South-Western*, on January 1, 1862. It is also found in MS. Louisiana House Journal, 1861–1862 (Louisiana State University Department of Archives), 207.

[38] New Orleans *Price-Current*, December 28, 1861.

[39] New Orleans *Daily Crescent*, January 21, 1862.

Confederacy. "The cotton crop of Louisiana of 1861," he said, "cannot be pledged by the State, either for that or any other purpose. It is not her's to pledge." [40] The *Crescent*, in commenting on the veto, said: "Our Northern enemies will not have to exult over any supposed distress among our cotton planters, for it cannot be controverted that the cotton bill gave the strongest indications that the cotton planters were hopelessly involved." The editor charged that the proposed measure "was the perfect embodiment of an irredeemable and vicious currency, the entering wedge to an universal system of dependence in every branch of agriculture on legislative gratuities." [41]

Evidently there were violations of the governor's prohibition of cotton shipments to New Orleans. The civil and military authorities were compelled to adopt more severe measures to break up the trade. On February 10, 1862, Governor Moore, as commander-in-chief of the Louisiana militia, announced that any boat or railroad train that brought cotton to New Orleans without a special permit would be seized, together with the cotton, by the military authorities. Such cotton would be removed from the city "at the expense of the vessel or Railroad." On March 12 the governor announced that cotton must not be shipped from the interior of the state to any point on the Mississippi for storage or sale. Cotton shipped in violation of this order would be reshipped to some point in the interior at the expense of the owner. Naturally, such a measure was a precaution to prevent cotton from falling into the hands of the enemy.[42]

Military preparations and the blockade combined to give a stimulus to certain industries in the state. Manufactories were established, especially in New Orleans, for the production of many articles for which Louisianians were formerly de-

[40] *Ibid.*, January 25, 1862; MS. Louisiana House Journal, 1861–1862, pp. 204–11.   [41] New Orleans *Daily Crescent*, January 22, 1862.
[42] *Ibid.*, February 11, March 14, 1862.

pendent upon the North or Europe. A branch of the Trede-
gar Iron Works was located at New Orleans, and it was reported in June, 1861, that this establishment had made two
brass cannon, one for the police jury of St. Mary Parish and
the other for Tensas Parish. There was a plant on Canal near
Baronne for the making of cotton and woolen plantation
clothes, with 130 persons employed. By June 16, three thousand uniforms and three thousand knapsacks for state volunteers had been made there. Another business was a large
manufactory of machinery in New Orleans, which the
Picayune reported "is now manufacturing the Enfield rifle
with the sword bayonet." [43] One new concern of interest was
a shoe factory in New Orleans for the manufacture of plantation brogans. It was reported that the capital invested in this
plant was "upward of $40,000." Thirty-five men and boys
were employed there, and they turned out six hundred pairs
of shoes a day. *De Bow's Review* heralded the enterprise as
one "that appeals to the planting interest of the whole South"
and urged planters who came to the city to visit the factory
and examine the shoes made there. "Most of the machines,"
said the *Review*, "are of Yankee invention; and in their operation here, they will doubtless help to teach the Yankees that
their judgment in voting for president is far beneath their
ingenuity in contriving machines." [44]

A slaughter house was operated by the Confederate Government a few miles below Alexandria, where the meat was salted
and packed for the Confederate army. By Christmas, 1861,
more than two thousand barrels were ready for shipping. The
cattle were driven from Southwest Louisiana and Texas. Dur-

[43] See the item "New Orleans in the Revolution of 1861," in the New
Orleans *Daily Picayune*, June 16, 1861. The paper remarked that secession
and the military preparations to defend the South had done more "to draw
out our manufactured home resources and give a momentum to mechanics of
every branch than years of peace could have developed." See also New
Orleans *Daily Crescent*, September 16, 1861.

[44] *De Bow's Review*, XXX (March, 1861), 371–72.

ing the winter of 1861–1862 more than thirty thousand beeves were slaughtered and packed at this plant.[45]

A news item in the Shreveport *South-Western* of August 21, 1861, bore the title "Louisiana Flour" and announced the establishment of a flour mill in St. Mary Parish, "turning out three qualities of flour—superior, fine, and shorts; and bran enough to supply all the wants of the parish for the future." The editor added the comment, "We must have a flour mill in or near Shreveport." Three weeks later a flour mill was operating in Caddo Parish, and the editor of the *South-Western* was presented with a "sack of superior flour, ground from wheat raised in Caddo Parish." A broom factory was added to the industries of the state in September, 1861. It was located in St. Helena Parish and the corn was raised locally.[46]

Saltmaking was an industry which experienced considerable activity in Louisiana early in the war. Salt licks that had been the scenes of annual gatherings of country folk in the pioneer days when stores were scarce were again visited by hundreds of people in 1861 and for the remainder of the war. These salt works were located chiefly in Bossier, Bienville, and Winn parishes. It was estimated that saltmaking at Lake Bisteneau in December, 1861, was proceeding at the rate of 150 to 200 bushels per day.[47]

The question of the extension of railroad lines in Louisiana received much attention early in the war, although little actual

[45] New Orleans *Daily Crescent*, December 19, 1861; G. P. Whittington, "Rapides Parish, Louisiana—A History," in *Louisiana Historical Quarterly*, XVII (1934), 746.

[46] Shreveport *South-Western*, September 11, 25, 1861. The attention given to such enterprises by the newspapers is evidence of their novel character and of the realization that such industries were needed in the altered state of affairs. The Shreveport *South-Western* commented on the broom factory as follows: "This is the true and proper course to pursue instead of sending abroad for every necessary of life, either for household or plantation use."

[47] New Orleans *Daily Crescent*, December 9, 1861; Ella Lonn, *Salt as a Factor in the Confederacy* (New York, 1933), 22. Saltmaking is discussed more fully in Chapter VII.

construction was done because of the lack of materials, especially iron rails, and because of the occupation of Southeast Louisiana by Federal forces after April, 1862. The only railroads of importance in the state in 1860 were the New Orleans, Jackson and Great Northern, running from New Orleans to the west of Lake Pontchartrain and thence northward through Ponchatoula, Amite City, and Tangipahoa into Mississippi and points north (the Illinois Central line today); the New Orleans, Opelousas and Great Western, which extended from New Orleans to Brashear City (now Morgan City), a distance of eighty-eight miles; and the Vicksburg, Shreveport and Texas, which had been completed from the Mississippi opposite Vicksburg to Monroe on the Ouachita, a distance of about sixty miles.[48]

The Legislature attempted to promote railroad construction by chartering new companies and by granting rights of way and lands in the public domain. In March, 1861, two new companies—the New Orleans and Mobile, and the Delhi and Arkansas Branch—were chartered by the Legislature with grants of one-hundred-foot rights of way through lands owned by the state and with the right to use timber and other materials within one mile on either side of the tracks.[49] The greatest need for railroad construction in Louisiana, however, was for the completion of the rail, inland-water connections between New Orleans and Southeast Texas. This was especially desirable after the Federal blockade became effective in order to connect the Crescent City and the Lower Mississippi Valley with the resources of South Texas. On January 23, 1862, the Louisiana Legislature incorporated the New Orleans and Texas Railroad Company with the right to construct

[48] *Eighth United States Census*, 1860, *Mortality and Miscellaneous Statistics*, 329; *De Bow's Review*, XXX (April, 1861), 499–500.

[49] Louisiana *Acts*, 1861, pp. 143–46, 213–16. The Delhi and Arkansas Branch road was to extend from Delhi, in Carroll Parish (now in Richland) to the Arkansas line. As far as the writer knows, no work was done on either of these roads before the end of the war.

and operate a railroad from New Iberia to the Sabine River at Orange, Texas. The preamble to the act of incorporation said:

> Whereas, it is important not only for commercial purposes, travel, mail carriage, etc., in time of peace, but for military uses in the pending war, to build the Railroad from New Iberia to the Sabine River, so as to complete the channel of communication between New Orleans and Houston, Texas: Be it enacted. . . .

The company was to have a right of way through lands owned by the state to the extent of two hundred feet on each side of the road, with additional land for switches, depots, shops, and cattle pens. It was stipulated that construction be started within four months and the road be completed within five years thereafter.[50]

On March 22, 1862, the New Orleans City Council adopted resolutions declaring the New Orleans and Texas railroad a "military necessity of the first class" and requesting the Louisiana congressmen to "press the immediate consideration of the subject" upon the Confederate Government and to use their influence to obtain assistance from the government for the completion of the railroad. On April 19 the Confederate Congress authorized President Davis to aid the railroad to insure completion of the new line from New Iberia to Houston and appropriated the sum of $1,500,000 in Confederate bonds for that purpose.[51]

As mentioned before, most of the railroad construction in

[50] Louisiana *Acts*, 1861–1862, pp. 72–74; New Orleans *Daily Crescent*, February 3, 1862. New Iberia and Brashear City, the terminus of the New Orleans, Opelousas and Great Western road, were connected by Bayou Teche, which was navigable. Hence, the completion of the N. O. and T. line would join Texas and New Orleans by a short route, mostly rail. Actually, it was planned to connect New Iberia and Brashear City by rail. In May, 1861, it was reported that the roadbed between these points was almost completed. New Orleans *Price-Current*, May 29, 1861.

[51] *Official Records,* Ser. IV, Vol. I, 1013–14, 1073–74; *Public Laws of the Confederate States of America* (Richmond, 1862–1864) 1 Cong., 1 Sess., Chap. XXXVI.

Problems of the New Order

Louisiana for the period of the Confederacy was "on paper." There was a gap of some one hundred miles between Monroe and Shreveport, on the Vicksburg, Shreveport, and Texas railroad. Construction work on this line was abandoned in 1861 because of lack of materials. The fall of New Orleans in April, 1862, led to the abandonment of work on the New Orleans and Texas road between New Iberia and the Sabine River.[52]

Another great problem which engaged the attention of the authorities and the people of Louisiana was the question of direct relief to soldiers and to soldiers' families. Relief was rendered in many ways, such as direct financial assistance, food and clothing, especially food for distressed families and extra clothing and blankets for soldiers, and hospital and surgical supplies for the sick and wounded volunteers. One New Orleans physician, by newspaper advertisement in September, 1861, offered his professional services, free of charge, to the families of those who were absent from the city on military duty.[53]

Organizations and committees were formed to plan and to execute projects of relief. One of the first of these was "The Society of Ladies in Aid of the Confederate Army" which was organized for the purpose of making uniforms for the soldiers. The *Picayune* of June 10, 1861, said of the members of the society: "They have been toiling hard, and deserve every consideration which the sentiments of gratitude can express for them." The society met daily in the rooms of the Y.M.C.A., where some forty women were "daily and diligently occupied in making clothing for our devoted and gallant volunteers."[54] The women of Baton Rouge organized a "Campaign Sewing Society." Finding themselves in need of

[52] Maude Hearn O'Pry, *Chronicles of Shreveport* (Shreveport, 1928), 165–66; Charles W. Ramsdell, "The Confederate Government and the Railroads," in *American Historical Review* (New York), XXII (1916–1917), 802.

[53] New Orleans *Daily Crescent*, September 6, 1861.

[54] New Orleans *Daily Picayune*, June 11, 1861.

money to purchase the necessary supply of buttons, thread, needles, etc., these enterprising ladies held a "tombola," with articles of every description donated. Tickets, each drawing a prize from the collection of miscellaneous pieces, sold for $1.00 each. Eliza Ripley tells us that she purchased twenty tickets and drew nineteen lead pencils and a "frolicsome old goat." The "tombola" netted $6,000.[55]

In New Orleans a committee on "Aid to Volunteers' Families" was formed and accepted financial contributions from citizens. The committee, in acknowledging receipt of a contribution from German citizens, on July 12, 1861, reported that "Our position has brought us in contact with the families of our soldiers, and we have been forced to witness the distress of hundreds whose ordinary means of support have been cut off, and it has afforded us the highest pleasure to relieve them; to your generosity we are greatly indebted for the ability to do so." [56] The committee published a report on July 18 showing contributions totaling $7,469.30, and announced that this amount had been paid out "principally in sums of $10 per month to each family"; the report added that "the committee are unanimous in their opinion that a large amount of real distress exists amongst us caused by the departure of our patriotic working men to the seat of war." [57]

Various expedients were adopted to raise money for relief. A performance by artists of the German Theatre in New Orleans netted $400; a fair held by certain ladies in the De Soto schoolhouse (in New Orleans) brought $1,607.15; and a show given by Harry Macarthy, "the Arkansas comedian," for the benefit of the volunteer fund raised $176. A regular monthly subscription system was established among the German population of New Orleans to aid families of soldiers.[58]

[55] Eliza M. Ripley, *From Flag to Flag* (New York, 1889), 14–16.

[56] New Orleans *Daily Picayune*, July 12, 1861.

[57] *Ibid.,* July 18, 1861.

[58] *Ibid.,* July 12, 13, 17, 1861; New Orleans *Daily Crescent*, August 7, 10, 1861. The New Orleans *Daily Picayune*, July 13, said it had been informed

Problems of the New Order

A free market for the relief of indigent families of absent soldiers was established in New Orleans and opened for the first time on August 16, 1861. The City Council appropriated the new building of the city waterworks, at the head of Canal Street, as a depot for the reception of contributions of vegetables and provisions. A volunteer relief committee of the City Council made a public appeal for aid in the way of provisions of all sorts. This committee sat daily at the City Hall to register the names of distressed families of absent volunteers. Applicants for relief at the free market had to have a ticket issued by this committee in order to obtain assistance.[59]

On the day the free market was opened, relief was given to 723 families, which were estimated by the *Crescent* at 2,129 persons. Meats, breadstuffs, and vegetables were given to the applicants.[60] The committee on relief reported to the City Council on October 1 that the market had been open every Tuesday and Friday and that an average of 1,350 families had been served on each day. Provisions valued at $8,966.58 and cash to the amount of $3,626.33 had been donated. The expenditures for supplies had totaled $2,722.53, leaving a cash balance of $903.80.[61] Some idea of the magnitude of the market may be obtained from a newspaper account in the early part of December, 1861. The reporter said:

Yesterday was the heaviest day yet at this institution, as 1,883 families came forward for supplies, yet so briskly did the committee go on with their work, that at the hour of closing not a single person remained unattended to. The following list of provisions was given out: 2,000 loaves of bread; 160 bushels of corn meal; 10 bbls. rice; 11 bbls. molasses; 9 beeves; 26 kits mackerel; 2 boxes codfish; 85 sacks sweet potatoes; 13 sacks

by the citizens' committee that of the sum already received by them, more than one half had been contributed by German citizens.

[59] New Orleans *Daily Crescent*, August 5, 15, 1861; New Orleans *Price-Current*, October 5, 1861.

[60] New Orleans *Daily Crescent*, August 15, 1861.

[61] *Ibid.*, October 12, 1861.

turnips; 500 cabbages; 400 bunches greens; 300 bunches leeks; 200 bunches turnips and 640 pumpkins.[62]

There were many difficulties connected with the work of administering relief. Doubtless people of that generation were not essentially different from people of our day. That all was not pleasant is evidenced by the following notice of the relief committee, of August 19, 1861, addressed "To all Good Citizens."

As this Committee has received, with deep regret, positive proof that impositions have been practiced upon the public generosity, by persons obtaining relief who were not entitled to the same, they hereby appeal to all good citizens, who may come to the knowledge of any such cases of fraud, to inform members of the Committee in person, or leave such information, with as little delay as possible, at their office, Secretary's Room of Board of Assistant Aldermen.[63]

The committee reported on November 20 that "we are disposed to think that many take advantage of the liberality of our citizens." It was stated that many families were desiring the services of nurses, servants, etc.; but that, although liberal wages were offered, families found it impossible to obtain help. "Whether this is owing to the fact of the full supplies given by the Free Market," the report said, "and inducing persons to vacate their places in consequence thereof, is a problem to be solved." [64]

Money for the free market was raised in various ways. Perhaps the most common method was the presentation of a play or a musicale by local talent with the proceeds going to the market fund. A group of New Orleans citizens formed a "Free Gift Lottery Association" to raise funds for the free market. The management of this association announced on

[62] *Ibid.*, December 7, 1861. A description of the work of the free market is given by Marion Southwood, *"Beauty and Booty," The Watchword of New Orleans* (New York, 1867), 77–82.

[63] New Orleans *Daily Crescent*, September 11, 1861.

[64] *Ibid.*, November 21, 1861.

Problems of the New Order

December 24, 1861, that the drawing of the lottery had been postponed "in consequence of having received so many generous contributions, amounting thus far to $40,000 in value," the classification of which required so much additional time and labor. The association reported in February, 1862, that the lottery made a clear profit of $59,789.50.[65] Contributions to the free market were not limited to the city of New Orleans. Henry Laurance, the agent of the market, traveled by horse and buggy in the winter of 1861–1862 through the parishes of St. Mary, St. Martin, Lafayette, Vermilion, St. Landry, Rapides, Avoyelles, and West Feliciana. On his return to New Orleans he reported generous contributions of provisions from the parishes.[66]

The business of the free market continued to expand. Cash donations for the month of March, 1862, amounted to $12,631.50; and donations in kind were valued at $4,118.05. The number of families served during this month ranged from 1,862 on March 7, to 1,921 on March 25.[67] In May the market passed under the control of Major General Benjamin F. Butler of the United States Army.

While the distressed families of soldiers were being ministered to, the soldiers themselves were not neglected. The people of Louisiana were called upon to supply the needs of the men in the ranks, and they responded generously. At a public meeting in New Orleans in July, 1861, a committee of twenty-four was appointed to solicit contributions for the relief of the sick and wounded soldiers. A subcommittee, by means of newspaper notices, appealed to the public for aid, saying, "It behooves those who enjoy the safety and comforts

[65] *Ibid.*, December 24, 1861, February 3, 1862.

[66] *Ibid.*, January 11, 1862. Julia Le Grand said: "Free market kept up by contribution. Planters all over country send in to support it." Kate M. Rowland and Mrs. Morris L. Croxall (eds.), *The Journal of Julia Le Grand* (Richmond, 1911), 37.

[67] Report of the committee, in New Orleans *Daily Picayune*, March 30, 1862.

of home to testify in a material form, their appreciation of the perils and sufferings of our brave volunteers." The people were asked to contribute blankets, bedclothes, and articles of nourishment, particularly sugar, coffee, tea, rice, tapioca, arrowroot, cordials, pure liquors, and wines.[68] In August, 1861, Governor Moore made an appeal for blankets for sick soldiers to be sent to his agent in New Orleans. The appeal was directed especially to the planters.[69] It met with a hearty response. In some places the women were very active in answering the appeal. The good work of the women of Lafourche Parish seems to have been typical of the loyalty and devotion of the women of Louisiana. A letter from Thibodaux in September, 1861, said:

> The Ladies Volunteer Aid Association of Lafourche just do things the right way. Having read the call of Gov. Moore on the good people of Louisiana to contribute blankets for the sick and wounded soldiers of the Confederacy in Virginia, they went immediately to work and in one week collected one hundred and five pairs of blankets, had them baled so as to bear shipment to any part of the Confederacy, and shipped to A. B. James, Esq., agent of Gov. Moore. . . . The Ladies of Lafourche are now busily engaged in making uniforms, knitting socks and neck comforts for the Lafourche Creoles. . . . May they reap for their reward the independence of their Sunny South, peace, plenty and a happy future.[70]

A contemporary tells us that during the winter of 1861–1862 teams went from house to house in Baton Rouge collecting blankets and bedding for the soldiers in camp. Later, when New Orleans was occupied by Federal troops, and the people of Baton Rouge feared that they might be cut off from communications with Louisiana soldiers in service, "Carpets were ripped from the floors of many houses, cut into suitable blanket-size," and sent via Camp Moore to the Confederate army in Virginia and Tennessee. Our informant tells us that

[68] New Orleans *Daily Crescent*, September 6, 1861.
[69] *Ibid.*, August 22, 1861.   [70] *Ibid.*, September 16, 1861.

she and a negro servant "drew the tacks from every carpet at Arlington; brussels, tapestry, and ingrain, old and new, all were made into blankets and promptly sent to the front." [71]

In January, 1862, the Louisiana Legislature gave official recognition and aid to the work of hospitalization of soldiers. An act was adopted which incorporated an organization known as the "Association for the relief of the sick and wounded soldiers of Louisiana," with New Orleans as a domicile. It was granted full power to appoint agents, employees, and nurses; to establish hospitals in any of the Confederate States for the relief and comfort of the sick and wounded soldiers of Louisiana; and to "maintain and supply said Hospitals to the extent of the means which may be at their command by voluntary contributions and appropriations by the Legislature of the State." The Legislature appropriated $150,000 to assist the association in carrying out its program of hospitalization. [72]

At least one other form of relief was extended to the soldier in this first year of the conflict. In December, 1861, the Legislature voted that "no suit or other judicial proceedings shall hereafter be instituted, or had against any person or persons of the State who may be at the time in the military or naval service of the State, or the Confederate States." All suits begun prior to the adoption of the act were to be suspended, except for the purpose of taking testimony. The act was amended in January, 1862, with the statement that "it shall not be construed so as to interfere with the collection of taxes, or with the revenue laws of the State or of the Confederate States." [73]

The Legislature came to the relief of the general debtor class by a form of moratorium in a measure entitled "An Act to Regulate Forced and Judicial Sales of Property." This "Stay Law," as it was called, seems to have aroused consider-

[71] Ripley, *From Flag to Flag*, 17–18.
[72] Louisiana *Acts*, 1861–1862, pp. 36, 38.   [73] *Ibid.*, 12, 34.

able feeling; and vigorous opposition to the principle of "stay laws" was expressed by the press while the bill was before the Legislature. The Thibodaux *Union,* of January 6, 1862, declared: "This piece of legislation appears to be extremely unpopular in this parish. A petition bearing the signatures of a very large number of the most influential merchants, planters and mechanics residing in Lafourche, has been addressed to the Governor, praying that in the event the bill, known as the 'Stay Law' pass the Senate, his Excellency should veto the same." [74] The Baton Rouge *Gazette* opposed the "Stay Law" bill and on January 7, 1862, asserted that "Stay Laws are wrong in principle." The Franklin *Planters' Banner* also expressed disapproval of the bill in an editorial of January 11.[75]

In spite of such opposition, however, the bill was enacted and approved by Governor Moore, January 17, 1862. According to the act appraisers of property in forced sales were required to adopt as a standard of appraisement the value of such property on April 1, 1861. If the price offered by the highest bidder did not equal the amount of the appraisement, "then the property shall not be adjudged, and the sale shall be postponed for twelve months" after the signing of a peace treaty between the United States and the Confederacy. In the meantime, the property was to be returned to the defendant in the case. The act, however, was not to apply to fiduciaries or defaulters of trust funds, nor to the collection of taxes, "nor to the interest due minors or [*sic*] money loaned, nor to moneys due charitable institutions for rents or subscriptions." Claims due the state of Louisiana, having the force and effect of a judgment in the contract, were also exempt from operations of the law.[76]

On January 23, 1862, the Louisiana Legislature made an-

[74] Quoted in the New Orleans *Daily Crescent,* January 8, 1862.

[75] The Baton Rouge *Gazette* and the Franklin *Planters' Banner* are quoted in the New Orleans *Daily Crescent* of January 10 and 13, 1862, respectively.

[76] Louisiana *Acts,* 1861–1862, p. 40.

other acknowledgment of the abnormal times by adopting the first of a series of acts permitting postponement of the payment of state taxes. The act suspended the payment of all state taxes, except "licenses on trades, professions or occupations," until February 1, 1863.[77]

A few days prior to the passage of the above act the Legislature took action to increase the war chest of the state by providing for the issuance and sale of state bonds. The governor was authorized and required, "in consequence of the war, and to repel invasion," to issue the coupon bonds of the state for $1,000,000, in certain denominations, payable in five equal installments of $200,000 each, at eight to twelve years inclusive, bearing interest at the rate of 6 per cent per annum. The governor was required to advertise for the sale of the bonds and to place the proceeds to the credit of the military funds "for the purpose of purchasing arms and munitions of war, and equipments, for the volunteers and militia of the State."[78] Governor Moore announced the sale of bonds for the week beginning February 24. "I take occasion to observe," he said, "that a loan for so patriotic a purpose should be participated in by citizens generally, who may thus contribute to the protection of our homes and firesides." He reported to the Legislature in 1864 that all but $74,000 of this bond issue was sold.[79]

On January 23 the Legislature voted another bond issue to meet the needs of the general treasury. It was stated in the preamble that Louisiana had expended large sums of money for military purposes and had assumed the payment of the Confederate war tax, and that "during the existing state of affairs the collection of taxes cannot, with sufficient cer

[77] *Ibid.*, 79.   [78] *Ibid.*, 29.

[79] New Orleans *Daily Crescent*, February 24, 1862; *Official Journals of the House and Senate of Seventh Legislature*, Session of 1864 (Shreveport, 1864), 6 (hereafter cited as Louisiana *House Journal* and Louisiana *Senate Journal*, with date). The governor's message is found also in Shreveport *Semi-Weekly News*, February 2, 1864.

tainty, be relied upon to meet the accumulated wants of the Treasury." The governor was empowered and directed to borrow "on behalf of the State, from time to time, as the wants of the Treasury may require, a sum not exceeding seven millions of dollars, either by the issue of bonds, or of treasury notes of the State, or of both, provided, that the amount of Treasury notes shall not exceed the sum of two million dollars." The bonds were to bear interest not exceeding 8 per cent and to be payable in from three to ten years, at the discretion of the governor. The treasury notes were to be noninterest bearing, were to be receivable in the payment of state taxes and all other public dues, and "shall be redeemable twelve months after a definite treaty of peace between the Confederate States and the United States." The act also provided for the payment of interest and principal by the assessment of a "War tax" of not less than ten cents nor more than twenty cents per annum on the one hundred dollars of assessed valuation on all movable and immovable property that was assessed in the state.[80] In accordance with this act bonds to the amount of $5,000,000 were issued. Governor Moore reported in January, 1864, that $226,000 of these bonds remained unsold.[81]

The actions of the Legislature in January, 1862, were evidences of serious economic problems which were to confront the people of Louisiana for the next four years. The inability of the people to pay taxes necessitated a suspension of collection, while the increased need of revenue forced the state to the only other means of financing itself, the issue of bonds and treasury notes.

[80] Louisiana *Acts,* 1861–1862, pp. 84–86.

[81] Louisiana *House Journal,* 1864, p. 6; also found in Shreveport *Semi-Weekly News,* February 2, 1864.

Chapter IV

Federal Occupation of New Orleans

A FEDERAL ATTACK ON New Orleans was expected by many Louisianians as early as April, 1861. Louisiana authorities were apprehensive of the danger and desired to strengthen the city's defenses. Governor Moore wrote to L. P. Walker, Confederate secretary of war, on April 10:

The news from Washington creates considerable anxiety here. The ships sent from New York are believed to be destined for this place [New Orleans]. The forts can be passed. We are disorganized, and have no general officer to command and direct. I doubt the policy of draining this place of troops to be sent to Pensacola. They are needed here, especially if this place be selected to collect revenues. What can we do with a fleet opposite the customhouse? [1]

Moore wired Judah P. Benjamin, the attorney general of the Confederacy, on April 11, that there were great fears of a Federal attack in New Orleans and that the sending away of troops had created dissatisfaction. Benjamin replied that the Federal fleet was not destined for New Orleans and the "fears of our people are without cause." Benjamin had written from Montgomery to a friend in New Orleans on April 9 that "it is confidently believed here" that the defenses of New Orleans were sufficient to repel attack.[2]

[1] *Official Records*, Ser. I, Vol. LIII, 669. "The ships sent from New York" were evidently those dispatched under secret orders by President Lincoln to the relief of Fort Pickens at Pensacola. Their destination was, of course, generally unknown. [2] *Ibid.*, 668–69.

97

Louisiana in the Confederacy

The views of Moore and Benjamin are typical. The one believed the defenses of New Orleans inadequate; the other seems to have shared the opinions of those at Montgomery who considered them "sufficient." The Confederate authorities, that is, the civil authorities, do not seem to have ever fully realized the danger to which New Orleans was exposed. On the other hand, Governor Moore was not alone in his views of the dangers confronting the city. The *Picayune* of July 28 urged the necessity of the immediate construction of gunboats for the defense of the lake shores and "the avenues to the Mississippi" leading to New Orleans. Major General Twiggs, commanding, at New Orleans, Department No. 1, wrote to Secretary Walker on August 9 concerning rumors of a Federal descent on New Orleans and made this prophetic statement: "I am told that they are building and equipping a powerful fleet of iron-clad gun-boats, with which they expect to pass our shore batteries. This might be successfully accomplished in a dark night by the rapidity with which they can move." [3] In September former Governor Roman wrote to President Davis that "the prevailing opinion here [New Orleans] is that the more exposed points of our sea-coast are soon to be attacked" and added that it "is generally admitted that we are not now prepared to offer . . . an efficient resistance." Another resident of New Orleans wrote to Benjamin on September 30 that "the city is not in a condition to defend itself against such an expedition, and will not be unless we are largely re-enforced from the army of Virginia, and unless a greater unity and energy are infused into the direction of our military force here." [4]

When Major General Mansfield Lovell assumed command of New Orleans and vicinity in October, 1861, he set to work

[3] *Ibid.*, 722.

[4] Roman to Davis, *ibid.*, 739; Alexander Walker to Benjamin, *ibid.*, 746–47. It is shown in a subsequent chapter that an almost universal cause of complaint in Louisiana was the age and infirmities of General Twiggs. General Lovell succeeded Twiggs in October, 1861.

to improve the defenses of the city. He found himself considerably handicapped, however, by the failure of the Confederate authorities to meet his requests for big guns and an adequate naval force. Obstructions were sunk in Pearl River and in the numerous bayous surrounding New Orleans. Intrenchments of more than eight miles were constructed around the city to repel attack by land. More than sixty guns were mounted on the intrenchments. A powder mill and a cartridge manufactory were established in New Orleans.[5]

The main defense of New Orleans consisted chiefly in Forts Jackson and St. Philip, located on opposite sides of the Mississippi, seventy-five miles below the city. Lovell placed larger guns on these forts and strengthened the garrisons. A raft of cypress trees held together by $2\frac{1}{2}$-inch chain cables was placed across the river near the forts.[6] In all this work General Lovell was aided materially by the municipal authorities of New Orleans. The raft was constructed with funds furnished by the City Council. A "Committee on Public Safety" was appointed in New Orleans, and a million dollar bond issue was voted to strengthen the defenses of the city.

The measures for the protection of New Orleans seem to have given the citizens a sense of security and satisfaction, and they seem not to have realized the danger to which the city was exposed. A contemporary related that, although there was a certain amount of uneasiness in New Orleans "that could not be disguised" and a great fear of Federal spies, confidence in the ability of the city to defend itself against Federal attack was "expressed on all sides."[7] Major General Lovell wrote to Secretary of War Benjamin on Jan

---

[5] *Ibid.,* Ser. I, Vol. VI, 559–64. The above paragraph is based upon the testimony of General Lovell before the Court of Inquiry.

[6] *Ibid.,* 560, 564–65; John R. Spears, *David G. Farragut* (Philadelphia, 1905), 183–86.

[7] Madame Loreta Janeta Velazquez, *The Woman in Battle* (Richmond, 1876), 176.

Louisiana in the Confederacy

uary 3, 1862: "The enemy is in force at Ship Island, but I am fully prepared for him. I have recalled the two regiments from Columbus, as we are short of armed men, but I have no fears about results." Lovell stated in this communication, however, that "the Navy Department here does not produce results at all commensurate with the amount of money expended," and complained that the naval authorities "are not doing justice to the Government." [8]

Newspapers, too, shared the general optimism concerning the safety of New Orleans. In an editorial entitled "Defenses of the City and River," the *Crescent* said:

. . . we do not believe that any vessel of the enemy built, or to be built, can pass our forts at Charleston, Savannah, Mobile or New Orleans. We hold that these great fortifications are impregnable to any force the enemy can bring against them; and as long as they remain intact it will be impossible for the foe to make important permanent conquests. Still, plenty of gun-boats, of the most approved description, should have been constructed long ago. . . .

. . . .

We do not apprehend much danger of an attack from the sea. We think we can successfully beat the enemy off if he approaches from the seaward. The only real danger we apprehend comes from the Upper Mississippi.[9]

Extremely high water and the accumulation of drift destroyed the cypress-log raft early in March. A new obstruction was made of parts of the old raft attached to schooners anchored and fastened together by chains. This obstruction was broken and scattered by high water and windstorms. This left Forts Jackson and St. Philip, manned by a force of fifteen hundred men, as the almost sole defense of New Orleans from an attack from the mouth of the Mississippi.

[8] *Official Records,* Ser. I, Vol. LIII, 765–66.

[9] New Orleans *Daily Crescent,* February 14, 1862. The last sentence refers to the capture of Fort Henry on the Tennessee River by General Grant on February 6 and the Federal movements down the Mississippi.

Federal Occupation of New Orleans

Major General Lovell had about three thousand troops in New Orleans. A small Confederate naval force patrolled the river above the forts.[10]

While preparations against a military attack were being made, defense against the enemy at home was not neglected. In the early months of the war rumors of Federal sympathizers and spies had inspired protests and warnings from some, and it was urged that a closer check on strangers should be made.[11] The Confederate disasters at Fort Henry and Fort Donelson in February, 1862, and the growing apprehension of an attack on New Orleans led the state and Confederate authorities there to resort to drastic means to protect the city from subversive acts. On March 12 Governor Moore and Major General Lovell appealed to President Davis to declare martial law in New Orleans. The next day Davis authorized such a proclamation for the parishes of Orleans, Jefferson, St. Bernard, and Plaquemines. On March 15 Lovell declared these parishes under martial law. According to the proclamation, all adult white males, except unnaturalized foreigners, were required to take an oath of allegiance to the Confederacy. All persons unfriendly to "our cause" were notified to leave the district embraced by martial law "without delay." A system of registry and passports was established. Good citizens were requested to report to the provost marshals "all who are suspected of hostility to the Government." "A number of persons who have no ostensible business, nor any interest in the city or State, have recently arrived in New Orleans," Lovell declared. "They must satisfy the provost-marshals of their good intentions and objects here, or leave immediately." [12]

---

[10] *Official Records*, Ser. I, Vol. VI, 562; Clement A. Evans (ed.), *Confederate Military History* (Atlanta, 1899), X, 35–39. On February 25, 1862, Lovell requested Governor Moore to send him 10,000 militiamen. *Official Records*, Ser. I, Vol. VI, 561.

[11] New Orleans *Daily Crescent*, October 8, 15, 22, 1861.

[12] *Official Records*, Ser. I, Vol. VI, 856–58; Vol. LIII, 793; New Orleans *Price-Current*, March 22, 1862.

Louisiana in the Confederacy

By General Orders No. 11, issued on March 18, Lovell directed that every white male over sixteen years old, residing temporarily or otherwise in the parishes of Orleans and Jefferson, Confederate citizen or alien, should appear before a provost marshal to have his name registered and to furnish such information as was required. Aliens would be sworn to "the effect that they will abide by the laws of this State and of the Confederate States . . . and that they will, under no circumstances, convey to our enemies any information relative to the military or political affairs of the country." Persons who came to Louisiana or to New Orleans after May 21, 1861, from any of the states at war with the Confederate States were subject to arrest and imprisonment, unless they procured a permit to remain in the city or the parish of Orleans or Jefferson, signed by the commanding general or by the provost marshal of the district in which they resided.[13]

The authorities at Washington appreciated, of course, the importance of obtaining possession of the Mississippi River. Control of the river by Federal forces would divide the Confederacy and check the flow of supplies from the Southwest to the heart of the South. Thus, the capture of New Orleans was an essential step in getting possession of the Mississippi.

Gustavus V. Fox, assistant secretary of the Navy in the Lincoln Government, conceived a plan of capturing New Orleans with an armed fleet that should run by Forts Jackson and St. Philip. Commander David Porter recommended, however, that the forts be reduced by a mortar flotilla before passage by the fleet. David G. Farragut, who was given command of the expedition, held Fox's view that the forts could be passed, but was willing to make an attack, although he had doubts of the ability of the mortar boats.[14]

[13] *Official Records*, Ser. I, Vol. VI, 860–61; New Orleans *Price-Current*, March 22, 1862.

[14] James F. Rhodes, *History of the Civil War, 1861–1865* (New York, 1917), 118–19; Walter G. Shotwell, *The Civil War in America* (London, 1923), I, 236–40.

Federal Occupation of New Orleans

The Federal fleet which appeared in the Mississippi River in April, 1862, consisted of twenty-four ships—eighteen in Farragut's squadron and six mortar steamers under Porter— and nineteen mortar boats. The fleet was accompanied by a large force of Federal troops under command of Major General Benjamin F. Butler. The mortar boats began to bombard Fort Jackson on April 18; and, after forty-eight hours of terrific firing, Farragut decided to execute the plan of running by the forts. After arrangements had been carefully completed, early on the morning of April 24, in complete darkness and under a smoke screen, thirteen of the Federal boats passed by the forts and proceeded toward New Orleans. On April 27 about 250 men of the garrison of Fort Jackson spiked their guns and surrendered to the land forces under Major General Butler. On the next day the forts surrendered, and the lower Mississippi River was lost to the Confederacy.[15]

An eyewitness describes the scene in New Orleans on April 25:

The wildest excitement prevailed when it was understood that New Orleans was about to fall into the hands of the Federals, and great wrath and indignation were excited by what was believed to be the inefficiency of the defense. . . .

Late in the morning of the 25th of April, 1862, the Federal fleet could be seen coming up the river, but it must have dampened the enthusiasm of the Yankee sailors somewhat to find steamboats, cotton, and all kinds of combustible property blazing for miles along the levee. It was a terribly magnificent spectacle . . . and it impressed me more strongly with an idea of the horrors of warfare than all the fighting and slaughter I had ever seen done.[16]

[15] Rhodes, *History of the Civil War*, 120–23; Shotwell, *The Civil War in America*, I, 241–48; *Official Records*, Ser. I, Vol. VI, 505. For the reports of Farragut and Porter, see *Official Records of the Union and Confederate Navies in the War of the Rebellion* (Washington, 1895–1927), Ser. I, Vol. XVIII, 155–59, 356–59. Cited hereafter as *Official Records, Navy*.

[16] Velazquez, *The Woman in Battle*, 236. Clara Solomon wrote in her

Great, indeed, must have been the destruction wrought by the excited citizens of the city. Hogsheads of sugar were emptied in the streets and barrels of molasses were poured out, so that "molasses was running in the gutters, like water." [17]

When Farragut's fleet anchored at New Orleans, Captain Theodorus Bailey and Lieutenant George H. Perkins were detailed to visit the mayor and demand the surrender of the city. These officers were conducted to the City Hall, where they presented the demand of surrender to Mayor Monroe, coupled with the demand that the flag of the United States be raised over the Customhouse, the Mint, the Post Office, and the City Hall. Mayor Monroe replied that he was not the military commander of the city and, therefore, had no authority to surrender it. Major General Lovell was sent for. He stated that he would not surrender the city, but explained that he had marched all his soldiers out of New Orleans. This meant, of course, that the Federal forces could occupy the city without further resistance. New Orleans was lost to the Confederacy.[18]

It seems strange, at first glance, that the largest city of the Confederacy surrendered without firing a shot. But a closer examination of the facts surrounding the capitulation leaves no doubt of the wisdom of that action. In relating the story of the fall of New Orleans Major General Lovell said, in part:

I will here state that every Confederate soldier in New Orleans, with the exception of one company, had been ordered to Corinth,

diary: "Standing at a corner we saw one of our finest boats, of our own accord committed to the flames. Oh! *never* shall I forget the 25th of April, 1862. Such expressions of woe as were on the faces of everyone, and such sadness as reigned in every heart." Clara Solomon Diary, entry for May 4, 1862. [17] Southwood, "*Beauty and Booty*," 21.

[18] The events connected with the surrender of New Orleans are discussed at length in Southwood, "*Beauty and Booty*," 23–37, and James Parton, *General Butler in New Orleans* (New York, 1864), 269–78. The correspondence between Mayor Monroe and Farragut is in *Official Records, Navy*, Ser. I, Vol. XVIII, 229–36.

to join General Beauregard in March, and the city was only garrisoned by about 3,000 ninety-day troops, called out by the governor at my request, of whom about 1,200 had muskets and the remainder shot-guns of an indifferent description.[19]

According to Lovell, he ordered the removal of government property and the evacuation of New Orleans by the troops because he recognized "the perfect absurdity of confronting more than 100 guns afloat of the largest caliber, well manned and served, looking down upon the city, with less than 3,000 militia, mostly armed with indifferent shot-guns." Resistance, he said, "would have been a wanton and criminal waste of the blood of women and children, without the most remote possibility of any good result." [20]

The primary cause of the fall of New Orleans was the failure of the Confederate naval and coast defenses to protect the approaches to the city. Several factors contributed to this failure. Brigadier General Johnson K. Duncan, Confederate commander of the coast defenses, attributed the success of the Federals in passing Forts Jackson and St. Philip to the damaging of the defenses by heavy rains and windstorms and to the failure of naval officers to co-operate. The disaster, he charged, was "but the sheer result of that lack of cheerful and hearty co-operation from the defenses afloat . . . and to the criminal negligence of not lighting up the river at night when the danger was imminent and the movements of the enemy absolutely known almost to the hour of the final attack." [21] Major General Lovell gave the following reasons for the failure of the defenses of New Orleans:

1. The want of a sufficient number of guns of heavy caliber, which every exertion was made to procure without success.

2. The unprecedented high water, which swept away the obstructions upon which I mainly relied, in connection with the forts, to prevent the passage of a steam fleet up the river.

---

[19] Major General Lovell to General S. Cooper, May 22, 1862, *Official Records*, Ser. I, Vol. VI, 513.   [20] *Ibid.*, 515.   [21] *Ibid.*, 521–34.

3. The failure, through inefficiency and want of energy of those who had charge of the iron-clad steamers *Louisiana* and *Mississippi* to have them completed in the time specified so as to supply the place of obstructions; and, finally, the declension of the officers in charge of the *Louisiana* to allow her, though not entirely ready, to be placed as a battery in the position indicated by General Duncan and myself.[22]

Whatever be the facts concerning the naval defense of New Orleans, there is no doubt that after the defense by water failed there was nothing left to do but to surrender. The city was not in a position to withstand a siege. The river was high, and the boats of the enemy, standing several feet above the level of the city, were in a position to sweep the streets. There is evidence that lack of provisions was also an important element in determining the surrender.[23]

On April 26, while negotiations for surrender were pending between Farragut and the authorities of New Orleans, some of Farragut's men raised the United States flag over the Mint.[24] It was this flag that William B. Mumford, a citizen of New Orleans, pulled down on April 27, two days before the city surrendered to United States Flag-Officer Farragut. A few weeks later Mumford was convicted of treason against the United States "in tearing down a United States flag from a public building of the United States" and sentenced to be executed. Major General Benjamin F. Butler, who took for-

[22] *Ibid.*, 517.

[23] Sarah A. Dorsey, *Recollections of Henry Watkins Allen* (New York, 1866), 92, 103. Governor Moore wrote to President Davis from New Orleans, April 17: "A danger as formidable as the fleet of the enemy now threatens us. There will be, and indeed now is, a scarcity of provisions in this city which, unless speedily remedied, will incapacitate us for any protracted defense." On the same day Provost Marshal H. M. Spofford wrote the President that New Orleans had been cut off from its main source of supply of wheat and flour, and "in consequence we are now upon the verge of a bread famine, the stock of wheat and flour in the hands of dealers here being totally exhausted." For both letters see *Official Records*, Ser. I, Vol. LIII, 801–02.

[24] Evans (ed.), *Confederate Military History*, X, 51; Spears, *David G. Far-*

mal possession of New Orleans on May 1, approved the verdict and ordered the execution.[25]

This execution was the first of many acts that made the name of Butler hated throughout the South. To the people of the South, Mumford was a hero and a martyr and Butler a plain murderer. Governor Moore wrote to President Davis on June 12 concerning the Mumford case and suggested as retaliation "for this brutal murder" the execution of one James W. Connelly, a Federal lieutenant, captured after he had burned bridges and other property in a raid along the Opelousas railroad.[26] On December 23, 1862, President Davis issued a proclamation setting forth the facts of the case of Mumford and added:

Now, therefore, I, Jefferson Davis, President of the Confederate States of America, and in their name, do pronounce and declare the said Benjamin F. Butler to be a felon, deserving of capital punishment. I do order that he be no longer considered or treated simply as a public enemy of the Confederate States of America, but as an outlaw and common enemy of mankind, and that in the event of his capture the officer in command of the capturing force do cause him to be immediately executed by hanging; and I do further order that no commissioned officer of the United States taken captive shall be released on parole before exchange until the said Butler shall have met with due punishment for his crimes.[27]

Naturally, Butler is not without his defenders. A member of the United States military forces stated:

I heard Butler swear by all that was sacred, that if he caught Mumford, and did not hang him, might he be hanged himself. He caught him, and he kept his oath. There never was a wiser act. It quieted New Orleans like a charm. The mob, who had assembled at the gallows fully expecting to hear a pardon read

---

[25] *Official Records,* Ser. I, Vol. XV, 465, 469; Shotwell, *The Civil War in America,* I, 249, 253–54.   [26] *Official Records,* Ser. II, Vol. III, 899.
[27] *Ibid.,* Ser. I, Vol. XV, 906–08.

at the last moment, and prepared to create a riot if he were pardoned, slunk home like whipped curs.[28]

Butler himself claimed that it was not merely a question of the fate of Mumford, but a question of whether a mob of thugs and gamblers should rule New Orleans or whether the city was to be ruled by the commanding general of the United States forces. He told a Philadelphia audience that he was inclined to spare Mumford, but the threat of the associates of Mumford made it impossible for him to grant clemency. It was a question of the authority of the United States or mob rule.[29]

One of Butler's first acts after occupying New Orleans was to take possession of the New Orleans and Opelousas railroad and use it to bring provisions into the city. He sent a regiment out to Brashear City, eighty-eight miles away, and to Berwick Bay, which resulted in the capture of field guns, ammunition, powder, and other ordnance stores.[30]

Perhaps no single act of the Civil War received as much unfavorable comment as Butler's famous "Woman Order" of May 15, 1862. Because his officers and soldiers had received an unfriendly welcome and were sometimes the objects of hostile attitudes, called "repeated insults" by Butler, on the part of New Orleans women, the Federal commander in General Orders No. 28 ordered "that hereafter when any female shall by word, gesture or movement insult or show contempt for any officer or soldier of the United States she shall be regarded and held liable to be treated as a woman of the town plying her avocation." [31] The order was interpreted by state and Confederate authorities as a permission to the Federal troops to offer insults to the women of New Orleans. Mayor Monroe immediately protested and characterized the order

[28] Wickham Hoffman, *Camp Court and Siege* (New York, 1877), 22.
[29] *Annual Cyclopaedia*, II (1862), 649.
[30] Butler to Stanton, *Official Records*, Ser. I, Vol. VI, 506.
[31] *Ibid.*, Ser. I, Vol. XV, 426.

as "extraordinary and astounding" and "a reproach to the
civilization, not to say the Christianity, of the age, in whose
name I make this protest." [32]   Butler replied to the mayor's
protest in these words:

No lady will take any notice of a strange gentleman, and *a
fortiori* of stranger simply, in such a form as to attract attention.
Common women do. Therefore, whatever woman, lady, or mistress, gentle or simple, who by gesture, look, or word insults,
shows contempt for (thus attracting to herself the notice of) my
officers and soldiers, will be deemed to act as becomes her vocation as a common woman, and will be liable to be treated accordingly. This was most fully explained to you at my office.
I shall not abate, as I have not abated, a single word of that
order. It was well considered. If obeyed, will protect the true
and modest woman from all possible insult. The others will take
care of themselves. . . .[33]

After an exchange of notes and after several interviews concerning the "Woman Order," Butler suspended the mayor
from office and ordered Monroe, his secretary, and the chief
of police committed to Fort Jackson.[34]

James Parton, General Butler's biographer, contends that
the threat that any woman insulting or showing contempt for
any officer or soldier of the United States "shall be regarded
and held liable to be treated as a woman of the town plying
her avocation" meant that such a woman would, under the
laws of New Orleans, "be arrested, detained over night in the
calaboose, brought before the magistrate in the morning, and
fined five dollars." [35]   Butler himself later asserted that the
way gentlemen treat a common woman, plying her vocation
in the streets, is to ignore her. She is arrested when she becomes a nuisance.[36]

[32] *Ibid.*, Ser. I, Vol. LIII, 526; Shotwell, *The Civil War in America*, I, 255.
[33] *Official Records*, Ser. I, Vol. LIII, 527.
[34] Parton, *General Butler in New Orleans*, 331–37; Shotwell, *The Civil War
in America*, I, 255.   [35] Parton, *General Butler in New Orleans*, 327.
[36] *Ibid.*, 342–43. See also *Private and Official Correspondence of Gen. Ben-*

Louisiana in the Confederacy

After all, the meaning of the famous order hinges on one's interpretation of the words "she shall be regarded . . . and held liable to be treated." In this connection one is reminded of the ambiguity in the United States Constitution which was the source of trouble in the Hayes-Tilden election in 1876. By whom, let us ask, "shall she be regarded and held liable to be treated as a woman of the town plying her avocation"? By Major General Benjamin F. Butler? By the police officers of New Orleans? By the Federal soldiers, gentlemen and otherwise?

Parton quotes the following conversation between Butler and a member of his staff which occurred before the publication of the order:

After all, general, is it not possible that some of the troops may misunderstand the order? It would be a great scandal if only one man should act upon it in the wrong way.

Let us, then [replied Butler], have one case of aggression on our side. I shall know how to deal with that case, so that it will never be repeated. So far, all the aggression has been against us. . . . I do not fear the troops; but if aggression must be, let it not be all against us.[37]

The famous order was published by Butler on May 15. Governor Moore on May 24, at Opelousas, where the executive officers had been moved after the Federal occupation of New Orleans (leaving Baton Rouge open to a naval attack), issued a stirring appeal addressed "To the People of Louisiana." After quoting in full the General Orders No. 28 (Butler's "Woman Order"), the governor said:

The annals of warfare between civilized nations afford no similar instances of infamy to this order. It is thus proclaimed to the world that the exhibition of any disgust or repulsiveness by the women of New Orleans to the hated invaders of their home and

---

jamin F. Butler During the Period of the Civil War (Norwood, Mass., 1917), I, 581–83; II, 35–36.   [37] Parton, *General Butler in New Orleans*, 327–28.

Federal Occupation of New Orleans

the slayers of their fathers, brothers, and husbands shall constitute justification to a brutal soldiery for the indulgence of their lust. The commanding general, from his headquarters, announces to his insolent followers that they are at liberty to treat as women of the town the wives, the mothers, the daughters of our citizens, if by word, gesture, or movement any contempt is indicated for their persons or insult offered to their presence. Of the nature of the movement and the meaning of the look these vagabond refuse of the Northern States are to be the judges.

What else than contempt and abhorrence can the women of New Orleans feel or exhibit for these officers and soldiers of the United States? The spontaneous impulse of their hearts must appear involuntary upon their countenances and thus constitute the crime for which the general of those soldiers adjudges the punishment of rape and brutalized passion.

.   .   .   .

Louisianians! will you suffer such foul conduct of your oppressors to pass unpunished? Will you permit such indignities to remain unavenged? A mind so debased as to be capable of conceiving the alternative presented in this order must be fruitful of inventions wherewith to pollute humanity. Shameless enough to allow their publication in the city, by the countenance of such atrocities they will be multiplied in the country. Its inhabitants must arm and strike, or the insolent victors will offer this outrage to your wives, your sisters, and your daughters. . . . Organize, then, quickly and efficiently. If your enemy attempt to proceed into the interior let his pathway be marked by his blood. It is your homes that you have to defend. It is the jewel of your hearts—the chastity of your women—you have to guard. Let that thought animate your breasts, nerve your arms, quicken your energies, and inspire your resolution. Strike home to the heart of your foe the blow that rids your country of his presence. If need be let his blood moisten your own grave. It will rise up before your children as a perpetual memento of a race whom it will teach to hate now and evermore.[38]

[38] *Official Records*, Ser. I, Vol. XV, 743–44; *De Bow's Review*, XXXIII (July, 1866), 61–62.

Louisiana in the Confederacy

Major General Butler reported to the Federal authorities at Washington that New Orleans was "very turbulent and unruly, completely under the control of the mob." He was not pleased, naturally, when he was met with cheers for Davis and Beauregard; and severe punishment was visited upon those who committed such "insults." Butler wrote to Secretary Stanton on May 8 that "the last man that was heard to call for cheers for the rebel chief has been sentenced by the provost judge to three months' hard labor at Fort Jackson, which sentence is being executed." [39]

Butler laid a heavy hand on the city of New Orleans. His was not a mild rule. His administration, by any modern standard, and by comparison with that of his successor, must be considered harsh. He was not content with having deprived the Confederacy of the great city of New Orleans but wished to stamp out every vestige of Southern sentiment within the area under his control. The slightest manifestation of sympathy for the cause of the Confederacy was considered as rebellion and treason that must be punished. His activities in this direction were nothing less than petty tyranny. Incidents that would have been ignored by a Grant or a Lee were magnified and utilized by Butler to humiliate a conquered people. He seems to have enjoyed such occasions as opportunities to exercise his authority. Indeed, he seems to have been more interested in ruling a great city than in furthering military conquests in Louisiana. John Rose Ficklen said of Butler's rule in New Orleans: "In fact, his political administration, in its unbending severity and its total disregard of the feelings of those whom the chance of war had placed in his power, reflects methods of military occupation which had been obsolete for several centuries." [40]

Upon assuming command in New Orleans, Butler issued a

[39] *Official Records*, Ser. I, Vol. VI, 506.
[40] John R. Ficklen, *History of Reconstruction in Louisiana (Through 1868)* (Baltimore, 1910), 33.

proclamation, May 1, placing the city under martial law and forbidding the publication of news of movement of troops within the department. No Confederate bonds were to circulate. All assemblages of persons in the streets, day or night, were forbidden. All persons in arms against the United States were required to surrender themselves and their arms to the Federal authorities; and all "ensigns, flags, devices, tending to uphold any authority whatever," except the flags of the United States and those of foreign consulates, were ordered suppressed.[41]

It was agreed between Major General Butler and the municipal authorities of New Orleans that the mayor and council would continue to administer the government of the city, with the exception of taking cognizance of political offenses or interfering with Federal military authority. There was much friction from the beginning, and within three weeks, as has been related, Mayor Monroe was suspended from office and imprisoned. Parton said, "Order No. 28 [the "Woman Order"] was the spark which blew up the city government." [42]

On May 20, by order of Butler, Brigadier General George F. Shepley of Maine, military commandant of New Orleans, took over the government of the city "in the absence of the late mayor" and "until such time as the citizens of New Orleans shall elect a loyal citizen of New Orleans and of the United States as mayor of the city." [43] General Shepley immediately announced that Captain Jonas H. French, provost marshal, would exercise the functions of chief of police. Captain French was entrusted with the duty of organizing the city police force and "will continue in office those found to be trustworthy, honest, and loyal." At the same time, the city recorders were suspended from office; and Major Joseph M. Bell, provost judge, was appointed to "hear and determine all complaints for the violation of the peace and good order

[41] Parton, *General Butler in New Orleans*, 292–95.   [42] *Ibid.*, 330.
[43] *Ibid.*, 336; New Orleans *Daily Picayune*, May 21, 1862.

113

of the city, of its ordinances or of the laws of the United States." [44]

On June 10 Butler announced that all officers of the law who exercised any office or held any trust which called for the doing of any legal act would be required to take an oath of allegiance to the United States. Naturally, all officers who retained their allegiance to the Confederacy resigned. On June 27 Brigadier General Shepley announced that the legislative power vested in the common council of the city was suspended and the seats of the aldermen and assistant aldermen had been vacated, one class of them by the expiration of their term of office, and the remainder by their neglect to take the oath of allegiance to the United States. [45] Shepley announced that he would be assisted in governing the city by a "bureau of finance" and a "bureau of streets and landings," each consisting of three persons appointed by himself. [46]

Practically every phase of the life of the people of New Orleans was affected by Butler's desire to be "thorough." Churches, newspapers, banks, schools, and other agencies and institutions were reminded of the presence and the power of the Federal authority. When Confederate authorities at Richmond set a day to be observed throughout the South as a day of fasting and prayer and the churches of New Orleans were planning to join in this observance, Butler published General Orders No. 27 on May 13, commanding that no such religious exercises be held in the churches of the city. [47] One of Brigadier General Shepley's first orders, dated May 28, concerned religious services in New Orleans. It read:

Hereafter in the churches in the city of New Orleans, prayers will not be offered up for the destruction of the Union or consti-

[44] Parton, *General Butler in New Orleans*, 336. Shepley's correspondence as military commandant is found in the Letter Books, 1860–1862, Mayor's Office, New Orleans (MSS. in New Orleans City Hall Archives).

[45] Parton, *General Butler in New Orleans*, 450, 452. [46] *Ibid.*, 453.

[47] New Orleans *Daily Picayune*, May 17, 1862; Southwood, *"Beauty and Booty,"* 70.

tution of the United States, for the success of rebel armies, for the Confederate States, so called, or any officers of the same, civil or military, in their official capacity.

While protection will be afforded to all churches, religious houses, and establishments, and religious "services are to be held as in times of profound peace," this protection will not be allowed to be perverted to the upholding of treason or advocacy of it in any form.

Where thus perverted, it will be withdrawn.[48]

Parton, commenting on the above proclamation of Brigadier General Shepley, said: "This order was complied with only in the letter. Thenceforward, in reaching that part of the service where prayers were accustomed to be offered for Jefferson Davis, the minister would say: 'Let us now spend a few moments in silent prayer,' "[49] As a matter of fact, this practice precipitated a crisis between Butler and three Episcopal ministers of New Orleans. The ministers Dr. W. T. Leacock, The Reverend William Fulton, and The Reverend Mr. Goodrich—refused to take the oath of allegiance to the United States. They were ordered by Shepley to read the service adopted by the Protestant Episcopal church in the United States, including the prayer for the President of the United States. They refused and, when examined by Butler, explained that they could not comply because their bishop, Major General Leonidas Polk, had prescribed a different form of service. They were put under arrest and banished from the city.[50]

The newspapers of New Orleans found the sailing rough when Butler came to the town. They were placed under a strict censorship and forced to be colorless. Statements of war news had to be submitted to an officer appointed by Butler, and no editorial comments were allowed on movements of the armies.[51] Practically no news was published concern-

[48] Parton, *General Butler in New Orleans*, 337–38.   [49] *Ibid.*, 338.
[50] *Correspondence of Gen. Benjamin F. Butler*, II, 407–08.
[51] Southwood, *"Beauty and Booty,"* 55–56.

ing the activities of Governor Moore and other state officials or agencies. In fact, the newspapers of New Orleans cease to be of value, after May, 1862, in the study of that part of the state of Louisiana that remained under Confederate control. Marion Southwood quotes a New Orleans newspaper as follows:

There are a great many things occurring in and around the city, accounts of which would be of interest to our readers, but, the fact is, we find it so difficult to discriminate between that which is and that which is not contraband intelligence, that we are under the necessity of disappointing them. It is not a matter of choice, but one of necessity, as our limits are somewhat circumscribed.[52]

Some editors were not so discreet, and several failed to discriminate between "that which is and that which is not contraband intelligence." Between May 13 and November 14, Butler suppressed five New Orleans newspapers—the *Crescent, Bee, Commercial Bulletin, Picayune,* and *Daily Advocate,* and he seized the office of the *Delta* and operated the paper under direction of the United States authorities. Suppression was not permanent in every case, however. The *Bee,* for instance, was suppressed on May 16 for "having published an elaborate, though covert argument in favor of the cotton burning mob," but was allowed to resume publication on May 29, after assuring Butler it had not intended and did not intend to advocate destruction of cotton or of other crops.[53] The publication of the *Picayune* was ordered discontinued on July 31 for "having published an editorial article in today's issue directly in violation of the proclamation of the commanding general of May 1, reflecting upon the officers and tending to influence the public mind against the Government of the United States." The publication was discontinued until the publishers and editors should "exhibit

[52] *Ibid.,* 56–57.   [53] New Orleans *Daily Picayune,* May 17, 29, 1862.

their loyalty" by taking the oath of allegiance.[54] At least one editor was sent to prison. John C. Dinnies, associate editor of the *Commercial Bulletin,* was ordered by Butler on August 1 to be sent to Fort Jackson for "having written and published a seditious article," and the publication of the *Bulletin* was suspended.[55]

New Orleans banks were made to feel the regulating hand of Major General Butler. With the approach of Federal forces the banks sent their specie out of the city to keep it from falling into the hands of the enemy. When Butler announced a guarantee of protection of property, a committee of the bankers of the city approached him and received his promise that such specie might be returned to New Orleans with a guarantee of protection through the lines and in the city "so long as it is used in good faith to make good the obligations of the banks to their creditors by bills and deposits." The Confederate Government, however, refused to allow the specie to be returned to New Orleans, and Secretary Memminger wrote: "They may proceed to conduct their business in the Confederate States upon this deposit, just as though it were in their own vaults." [56]

On May 16 Butler ordered that neither the city of New Orleans nor any bank should issue or exchange any Confederate notes, bills, or bonds. All circulation of Confederate notes and bills was to cease on May 27. Most of the banks, in order to avoid loss, immediately notified their depositors to withdraw Confederate notes before May 27. The notifications were in the form of newspaper advertisements. Butler decided to make the banks take the loss and issued General Orders No. 30 on May 19, commanding the banks to pay out no more Confederate notes to their depositors or creditors,

54 *Official Records,* Ser. I, Vol. XV, 533.
55 *Ibid.;* Ser. II, Vol. IV, 322.
56 Parton, *General Butler in New Orleans,* 415–16.

and ordering that all deposits be paid in the bills of the bank, United States Treasury notes, gold, or silver.[57]

The banks found it difficult to operate. The loss of their specie, the accumulation of Confederate notes, the special taxes levied upon them by Butler, and the general business stagnation all combined to weaken them. By the end of February, 1863, seven of the New Orleans banks had closed their doors.[58]

It will be recalled that when the Federal forces took New Orleans approximately two thousand families were being fed by the free market, an institution which was opened in August, 1861, and supported by voluntary contributions in money and provisions, not only of citizens of New Orleans, but of residents of South and Central Louisiana. The city's supply of food seems to have dwindled in the weeks immediately preceding its capture by the Union army. The cattle trade with Texas and the steamboat traffic from the Red River country gradually ceased as the danger of the surrender of New Orleans increased. It must not be forgotten, also, that excited citizens destroyed much food when Federal boats appeared in the Mississippi opposite the city in April.

Major General Butler therefore found himself in possession of a city of 168,000 people threatened with a food shortage and with at least nineteen hundred families dependent upon charity for their existence. In all fairness to Butler, it must be said that he realized the gravity of the situation and devoted himself energetically to the task of procuring food for the inhabitants. The third day after his arrival he issued an order on the subject of provisions and said, in part:

The Commanding General of this Department has been informed that there is now at Mobile a stock of flour purchased by

---

[57] New Orleans *Daily Picayune*, May 17, 18, 21, 1862. For a detailed account of the relation between Butler and the New Orleans banks, see Parton, *General Butler in New Orleans*, 413–31.

[58] Caldwell, *A Banking History of Louisiana*, 96.

the city of New Orleans for the subsistence of its citizens. The suffering condition of the poor of this city, for the want of this flour, appeals to the humanity of those having authority on either side.

For the purpose of the safe transmission of this flour to this city, the Commanding General orders and directs that a safe conduct be afforded to a steamboat, to be laden with the same, to this place. This safe conduct shall extend to the entire protection of the boat in coming, reasonable delay for discharge, and return to Mobile.[59]

On May 3 Butler "authorized and required" the directors of the Opelousas railroad to run cars over the road for the purpose of bringing to New Orleans "provisions, marketing, and supplies of food which may be offered, in order to supply the wants of the city." [60]

Butler charged that the New Orleans City Council was failing to provide for the cleaning of the streets. He decided, therefore, to attack the problem of relief of the poor in the light of the need for improved sanitation. On June 4 he addressed a communication to Brigadier General Shepley, military commandant, and to the City Council, commanding that the city should employ upon "the streets, squares, and unoccupied lands in the city" some two thousand men with proper implements for at least thirty working days "in putting those places in such condition as, with blessing of Providence, shall

[59] "General Orders No. 19," *Correspondence of Gen. Benjamin F. Butler,* I, 112.

[60] "General Orders No. 20," *ibid.* Butler wrote to United States Secretary of War Stanton, May 8, 1862: "My action in regard to provisions was made absolutely necessary by the starvation which was falling upon the 'just and the unjust.'" It appears from Butler's correspondence with Stanton that the provisions were obtained. *Ibid.,* 452–55. But George S. Denison wrote from New Orleans to his brother Jimmy, July 6, 1862: "There was a scarcity of food three or four weeks ago which is becoming greater every day. Thousands of people in this city today are hungry and cannot obtain sufficient food. Well dressed men and women apply to the soldiers for bread for themselves and children." George S. Denison Papers (microfilm copy, University of Texas Archives).

insure the health as well of the citizens as of the troops." Each laborer was to be paid out of the city revenue fifty cents per day for ten hours and an equivalent sum issued by Federal authorities in food.[61]

There seems to be no doubt of the success of Butler's street-cleaning project. Even such a severe critic as Marion Southwood credits him with cleaning up New Orleans. This Southern contemporary said of Butler:

Persons are not wholly bad, there are always some good qualities intermixed. So with Butler. He had an eye to cleansing the city; he was the best scavenger we have ever had among us. . . . It was quite a grotesque sight to see a battalion of stalwart men, with brooms and spades, rallying forth on a hot summer morning to scrape and sweep the streets, and, without doubt, the city has been much more healthy since. The broom brigade would have served as a reserve corps in case of an emergency, it was so extensive.[62]

Whatever might have been the faults of Benjamin Butler, he was not a man of one idea. On the contrary, he was entirely too resourceful with his ideas for the comfort of his enemies. In June, as we have seen, he combined the matter of poor relief with the need for a cleaner and more sanitary city. In August he added to these the plan of punishing leaders of the secession movement. By General Orders No. 55, an assessment was laid on all citizens of New Orleans who had subscribed to the funds raised for the defense of the city and on all cotton brokers who had had a part in publishing the proclamation in October, 1861, advising planters not to send or bring their cotton to New Orleans. Each person or firm was assessed one fourth of the amount subscribed to the fund "to aid treason against the United States." For example, the Citizens' Bank of Louisiana had subscribed $306,400 for the defense of New Orleans. It was assessed $76,600 by Butler.

[61] Parton, *General Butler in New Orleans,* 307.
[62] Southwood, *"Beauty and Booty,"* 182.

Federal Occupation of New Orleans

The total assessment against the subscribers to the defense fund was $312,716.25. Ninety-six cotton brokers were assessed a total of $29,200, from $100 to $500 per firm. Butler stated the purpose of the assessment in these words: "The money raised by this assessment to be a fund for the purpose of providing employment and food for the deserving poor people of New Orleans." [63]

Two days after announcing the assessments to provide employment and food for the poor, Butler authorized the city surveyor and street commissioner to employ at least one thousand men, including those already employed, to work on the streets, wharves, and canals. After stating specifically that the laborers would be paid out of the employment and relief fund raised by the assessment order, the announcement said:

> While this force was paid by taxation of the property of the City, the Commanding General felt authorized to employ it only in [the] most economical manner, but it now being employed at the expense of their rebellious neighbors, the Commanding General proposes that they shall be paid the sum that was paid them by the same party for work on the fortifications, to wit: One Dollar and a half for each day's labor. The rations, heretofore a gift to the laborers by the United States, will now be discontinued. [64]

One advantage accruing to New Orleans by the Federal occupation was the resumption of trade with Northern ports. President Lincoln, by proclamation on May 12, 1862, lifted the blockade on the port of New Orleans "except as to persons, things, and information contraband of war." Several

[63] *Official Records*, Ser. I, Vol. XV, 538–42; Shotwell, *The Civil War in America*, I, 252–53.

[64] New Orleans *Daily Picayune*, August 8, 1862. See also "Special Order No. 244" in *Correspondence of Gen. Benjamin F. Butler*, II, 158. Aid continued to be given, however, to families in destitute circumstances. The United States Relief Commission in New Orleans reported that relief—pork, beef, and bread, chiefly—had been given to 9,892 families for the week ending October 18, 1862. Of this number, 1,031 were families of Confederate soldiers. New Orleans *Daily Picayune*, October 22, 1862.

ships left New Orleans in May and June, carrying turpentine, tar, and sugar to the North.[65] Naturally, a city of 168,000 people, so largely cut off from the rest of the Confederacy, became more and more dependent upon imports by sea. Flour was one of the chief items of trade. It must have been imported in large quantities in the summer of 1862, for the price dropped from $16 a barrel on July 22 to $6 on September 12.[66] The *Picayune* of August 5 announced the arrival of three steamers from the North bringing 14,946 barrels and 333 sacks of flour.

Butler endeavored to open up trade with that portion of Louisiana within the Confederate lines, especially in cotton and sugar. On July 21 he wrote to Reverdy Johnson, special agent and investigator sent to Louisiana by Lincoln, that "no merchandise, whether cotton or sugar, will in any event be seized or confiscated by the United States authorities here." He promised safe conduct, open market, and prompt shipment for merchandise sent to New Orleans, and added that "the owner, were he Slidell himself, should have the pay for his cotton, if sent here under this assurance." [67]

The possession of New Orleans and vicinity by forces of the United States created new and embarrassing problems for the state authorities. Since Baton Rouge was untenable, the

[65] For Lincoln's proclamation, see *Official Records*, Ser. III, Vol. II, 31. The New York *Times*, June 13, 1862, said that the *Flying Dragon* had left New Orleans on May 22 and arrived at Boston on June 12 with a cargo of turpentine and tar. Butler was informed by a letter of July 2 from a New York business house that a cargo of sugar shipped from New Orleans in the *General Butler* had arrived at Boston. *Correspondence of Gen. Benjamin F. Butler*, II, 34. Most of these early shipments from New Orleans were made by General Butler personally and by his brother, Colonel A. J. Butler. See *ibid.*, I, 533–34.

[66] New Orleans *Daily Picayune*, July 24, September 13, 1862.

[67] *Ibid.*, July 22, 1862. Reverdy Johnson was a distinguished Maryland lawyer who served in the United States Senate from 1845 to 1849, resigning to become attorney general under President Taylor. He was one of the defense attorneys in the case of Dred Scott *v.* Sanford. He was a United States senator-elect when he came to New Orleans in 1862.

offices of the state were moved to Opelousas. Normal relations between the area around New Orleans and the rest of the state were broken. This was a matter of no little importance, for New Orleans was then, as now, the financial and commercial center of Louisiana. The city then, as now, contained more than one fifth (23 per cent in 1860) of the state's population. It was, of course, the chief marketing point, not only of Louisiana, but of the Southwest.

The Federal authorities were not unwilling to permit trade, under proper regulations, between New Orleans and that part of the state still under Confederate control. Especially was this true in the matter of obtaining the staple products of Louisiana for Northern consumption. Louisiana cotton was still highly valued though it might be polluted by slave labor and tainted with rebellion. Louisiana sugar and molasses were just as sweet and appetizing as they had ever been. Northern gold had no objection to being exchanged for Confederate cotton and sugar. In fact, as the war progressed, it became a matter of doubt whether Federal advances into Louisiana were military campaigns or cotton expeditions.[68]

Governor Moore, a cotton planter of Central Louisiana, viewed the situation with suspicion and alarm and hastened to put his official disapproval on trade with the enemies of the Confederacy. On June 18, from his new gubernatorial office at Opelousas, in the heart of the Evangeline country, he issued a stirring address "To the People of Louisiana." He opened his message in the following words:

The occupation by the enemy of a portion of the territory of our State imposes upon us new and unaccustomed responsibilities. It creates an anomalous condition of affairs, and establishes between the citizens of New Orleans and all other of our towns in the actual occupation of the enemy and those of the

[68] See George H. Gordon, *A War Diary of Events in the War of the Great Rebellion, 1863–1865* (Boston, 1882), 312–26; H. L. Landers, "Wet Sand and Cotton—Banks' Red River Campaign," in *Louisiana Historical Quarterly,* XIX (1936), 150–95.

country parishes relations very different from those which regulate their ordinary intercourse. . . .

New Orleans is the commercial depot of the State. . . . The channels of trade constantly flow between it and the country . . . thus binding our urban and rural populations together by the strong bands of mutual dependence and reciprocal benefit.

A state of public war, resulting in the armed occupancy of New Orleans by the enemy, changes these relations. There cannot be a war for arms and a peace for trade between two people at the same time. The armed occupants of that city are our enemies. To each loyal citizen of Louisiana and of the Confederacy every citizen of the country hostile to us is an enemy. We cannot barter our produce for theirs. We cannot exchange our corn, cattle, sugar, or cotton for their gold.[69]

The governor then set forth regulations controlling the relations between that part of Louisiana occupied by Federal forces and the rest of the state. (1) Communication with New Orleans, except under a flag of truce, would not be permitted. (2) Use of the enemy's passports must cease because they always contained, the governor said, the following conditions for egress from New Orleans: "This pass is given upon the parole of honor of the holder that he will in no way give information, countenance, aid or support to the so-called Confederate Government or States." (3) Conscripts or militiamen, having in their possession such passports and seeking to shun duty under the pretext of a parole, were to be treated as public enemies. No such papers would be held as sufficient excuse for inaction by any citizen. (4) Trading with the enemy was prohibited under all circumstances. (5) The utmost vigilance should be used by officers and citizens in the detection of spies and salaried informers, and their apprehension should be promptly effected. (6) Confederate notes must be received and used as the currency of the country. (7) River steamboats should in no case be permitted to be captured, but

[69] *Official Records*, Ser. I, Vol. XV, 504–10. The entire message is found here.

should be burned when they could not be saved. (8) Provisions might be conveyed to New Orleans only in charge of officers and under precautionary regulations governing communication between belligerents.

New Orleans, indeed, was in an anomalous position. Considered by Federal authorities as a conquered city whose inhabitants were Confederates to be watched and subjected to military rule, it found itself cut off from the Confederacy and considered as enemy territory by the governor of the state of Louisiana. Perhaps it would not be an exaggeration to say that for nearly three years thousands of residents of New Orleans were men without a country. The editor of the *Picayune*, in July, 1862, aptly described the position of the city in an editorial entitled "New Orleans in a Stress." In addition to complaining of "twenty-five cents for a loaf of very indifferent bread, and very scarce at that," the editor declared:

We are pressed on both sides; indeed, on all sides. Whilst the United States authorities hold us as captives under martial law, the Confederates and Gov. Moore forbid all intercourse with the country. The people with whom the one authority allows us to have commercial intercourse are willing to trade, but the people under the other authority are not permitted to send us the only articles which we might exchange for what the former brings and is ready to sell.

We are thus subjected to the hardships of a sort of double siege. Both parties virtually treat us as enemies. Martial law, with all its rigors, presses us in all directions. To a people so long accustomed to the most unrestricted commerce and freedom, these are very hard conditions. God grant some early conclusion of this most anomalous and uncomfortable state of affairs in our once great and prosperous city.[70]

Butler, therefore, enjoyed only a limited success in his attempt to establish trade between New Orleans and the Confederate lines. He wrote to Secretary Salmon P. Chase on

[70] New Orleans *Daily Picayune*, July 2, 1862.

Louisiana in the Confederacy

October 22, 1862: "As you are aware, from the time that I came here I have endeavored in every possible way to open trade in cotton through the rebel lines. . . . Owing to the peculiar action of the Confederate authorities, I have not been able as yet much to succeed." [71]

The Federal occupation of Baton Rouge was a natural consequence of the capture of New Orleans, for the Louisiana capital, about one hundred and thirty miles up the Mississippi from New Orleans, had been dependent on the coast and river defenses of the Crescent City. Soon after the fall of New Orleans the Federal gunboats moved up the river, and on May 8 Captain James S. Palmer of the *Iroquois* landed a small force at Baton Rouge and took possession of the arsenal and other public property.[72] Later Butler dispatched Brigadier General Thomas Williams with a force of forty-five hundred to occupy the town. Williams and his men arrived at Baton Rouge on May 28.[73] The Louisiana capital was taken by the Federal forces without a struggle.

Great, indeed, was the excitement in Baton Rouge at the approach of the Federals. Perhaps the one single thought of the citizens was the destruction of property to prevent the "Yankees" from getting it. Cotton, especially, was the object of destruction. Wagon loads of "King Cotton" were taken to vacant squares, piled high, and burned. Barges were loaded and taken out in the Mississippi, to go up in smoke. Liquors, too, were destroyed, so that the Federals might be disappointed; and it was reported that gutters and pavements were filled with a variety of strong drinks.[74]

[71] *Correspondence of Gen. Benjamin F. Butler,* II, 394–96. Butler was accused of using his military command to engage in mercantile speculation. See Secretary Salmon P. Chase to Butler, *ibid.,* I, 632; II, 422–23. See also *Diary and Correspondence of Salmon P. Chase,* in *Annual Report of the American Historical Association, 1902* (Washington, 1903), Vol. II, Pt. IV; and James F. Rhodes, *History of the United States* (New York, 1920), V, 303–13.

[72] *Official Records, Navy,* Ser. I, Vol. XVIII, 473–76.

[73] Evans (ed.), *Confederate Military History,* X, 63–64.

[74] Sarah Morgan Dawson, *A Confederate Girl's Diary* (Boston, 1913), 16–18.

Federal Occupation of New Orleans

In this brief campaign, which resulted in the fall of Baton Rouge, Louisianians were initiated into the tactics of wanton destruction that were to characterize their foes all too often and to make Louisiana suffer as perhaps no other state suffered for the period of the war. Brigadier General Williams reported on May 29:

I regret to say I believe there is just ground against the Wisconsin and Michigan regiments for the charge of pillaging and marauding preferred against them by the inhabitants of Kenner Station. . . . These regiments, officers and men, with rare exceptions, appear to be wholly destitute of the moral sense, and I believe that they believe, in the face of all remonstrances, exhortations, and disgust, expressed in no measured terms, that they regard [sic] pillaging not only right in itself but a soldierly accomplishment.[75]

A Federal colonel reported that in an expedition around Baton Rouge in June his men destroyed outhouses, fences, "ornamental" trees, an "extensive and valuable sugar mill," and "left nothing but the blackened chimneys as monuments to the folly and villainy of its guerilla owner."[76]

On August 5 the Confederate forces, numbering about three thousand, under Brigadier General John C. Breckinridge, attacked Baton Rouge. Breckinridge had expected the co-operation of the ram *Arkansas,* but the machinery of this boat became disabled about five miles from the city, and the Confederates were without its services. The battle was fiercely fought with heavy casualties on both sides. The Federal commander, Williams, was killed, and Colonel Henry Watkins Allen of the Fourth Louisiana (Confederate), while leading his men across an open field, was severely wounded. Both sides claimed the victory. The Federals retained possession of Baton Rouge but evacuated the city two weeks later.[77] Butler, who ordered the evacuation, feared an attack

[75] *Official Records,* Ser. I, Vol. XV, 22–23.   [76] *Ibid.,* 19–21.
[77] For official reports concerning the engagement at Baton Rouge, see *ibid.,*

on New Orleans and therefore desired a concentration of the Union forces.[78]

Baton Rouge suffered sorely from the operations of May–August, 1862. During the battle on August 5 most of the inhabitants fled to the country. A contemporary reported "about five hundred tired, exhausted, broken-down, sick, frightened, terrified human beings" at her home four miles from town.[79] A Federal colonel wrote from Baton Rouge to Major General Butler on August 13: "This place has been nearly completely sacked by the soldiery. Scarcely a single house has escaped, all the citizens having fled. . . . Even officers' tents are filled with furniture from deserted houses." [80]

When Butler ordered the Federal forces to evacuate Baton Rouge, he directed Colonel Halbert E. Paine to destroy the town because the "shelter of Baton Rouge to them is a necessity in the long winter campaign, to say nothing of its advantages as a summer residence." On August 19, however, Butler wrote Colonel Paine:

Upon your representation . . . of the state of the public charitable and penal institutions at Baton Rouge, wherein the orphan, the insane, and the helpless are confined and housed, so that the innocent and helpless must be so greatly the sufferers, I am inclined to countermand my order for burning the town.

.   .   .   .

With New Orleans it would be different, which must be held at all hazards or destroyed. It is the key to the river and the arsenal and banking-house of the rebellion.[81]

The Federals evacuated Baton Rouge on August 21. This assured the Confederate forces, for a while at least, of control

---

39–108. Allen was shot in both legs, the bones in his right leg being shattered. Because of his wounds, he resigned his command in January, 1863. In August of that year President Davis made him a brigadier general. *Ibid.*, Ser. I, Vol. XXII, Pt. II, 974; see also Luther E. Chandler, "The Career of Henry Watkins Allen" (Ph.D. Dissertation, Louisiana State University, 1940), 136–38.
[78] *Official Records,* Ser. I, Vol. XV, 552. [79] Ripley, *From Flag to Flag,* 36.
[80] *Official Records,* Ser. I, Vol. LIII, 533–34; *Correspondence of Gen. Benjamin F. Butler,* II, 187. [81] *Official Records,* Ser. I, Vol. XV, 552–53.

of the Mississippi from Baton Rouge to Vicksburg, including the mouth of the Red River. The Confederate Major General Earl Van Dorn had already realized the importance of the occupation of Port Hudson, forty miles below the mouth of the Red River and eighteen miles north of Baton Rouge, and had begun to strengthen that place. Port Hudson was favorably situated for defense of the Mississippi because hills touched the river and commanded it.[82]

When the Federals withdrew from Baton Rouge, they took with them the state library and Powers's statue of Washington, as well as other property. The library was taken to New Orleans and stored there, and the statue was sent to the mayor of New York "to be held in trust for the people of the State of Louisiana," so Butler wrote the mayor, "until such time as they shall return to their senses." [83] Butler wrote to Mrs. Butler: "I have brought off the State library and the Statue of Washington by order, besides pretty much all the plunder of the town *without order*. I have put a stop to that, however. We are fast coming, however, to the point where devastation is a *necessity*." [84]

In addition to the country along the Mississippi River, that part of Louisiana north of Lake Pontchartrain and the region directly west of New Orleans experienced expeditions and raids by the Union army in the year 1862. The lake district, however, was generally neglected by the Federals in favor of the rich sugar district west of the Mississippi. The section between New Orleans and Franklin on Bayou Teche was especially susceptible to attack, as the region is a vast network of rivers, bayous, and lakes, through which vessels of considerable size can pass. Also, as previously mentioned, the tracks of the New Orleans, Opelousas and Great Western railroad ran from the west bank of the Mississippi at New Orleans to

[82] Evans (ed.), *Confederate Military History*, X, 72; Richard Taylor, *Destruction and Reconstruction* (New York, 1879), 116.
[83] *Correspondence of Gen. Benjamin F. Butler*, II, 233, 235–36.
[84] *Ibid.*, II, 233.

Berwick Bay, a distance of eighty-eight miles. From Berwick Bay to New Iberia, fifty miles to the northwest, along the beautiful Teche, extended a prosperous country of sugar planters. Major General Richard Taylor has given us an inimitable picture of this country, with its stately mansions, verdant prairies, and roaming herds on the west bank, and fields of luxuriant cane running back from the east side of the famous Teche; and he concludes his description with these words: "In all my wanderings, and they have been many and wide, I can not recall so fair, so bountiful, and so happy a land." [85] Because of the ease of communications and the natural wealth of the country, Butler constantly harassed the district between the Mississippi and the Teche. Light-draft steamers, equipped with light guns, were used to navigate the many bayous and lakes.

On July 30, 1862, Major General Taylor, who had already participated in operations in Virginia, was ordered by the Confederate authorities to assume command of the District of West Louisiana. Taylor was a Louisianian, whose estate was in St. Charles Parish, west of the Mississippi, between New Orleans and Baton Rouge. He was the son of General Zachary Taylor, hero of the war with Mexico and twelfth president of the United States. Taylor had served in the Louisiana senate, where he was chairman of the Committee on Federal Relations, and he reported to the senate the bill calling a convention in January, 1861. He was a member of the secession convention and was made chairman of the Military and Defense Committee.[86]

Major General Taylor visited Governor Moore at Opelousas, where he remained for two days in consultation with the state's chief executive. From there he went to Alexandria, about eighty miles north of Opelousas, and busied himself

[85] Taylor, *Destruction and Reconstruction*, 105. This section and the country for about fifty miles north of New Iberia, to Opelousas, is the Evangeline country, immortalized by Henry Wadsworth Longfellow.

[86] *Ibid.*, 12, 111.

with the task of organizing his department. He then made a tour of inspection of the country between Alexandria and Berwick Bay. He gives us the following description of the situation in the autumn of 1862:

Melancholy indeed was the condition of the "District of Louisiana," to the command of which I was assigned.

Confederate authority had virtually ceased with the fall of New Orleans in the previous April. Fortifications at Barataria, Berwick's Bay, and other Gulf coast points had been abandoned, the garrisons withdrawn, works dismantled, and guns thrown into the water. The Confederate Government had no soldiers, no arms or munitions, and no money, within the limits of the district. Governor Moore was willing to aid me to the extent of his ability, but, deprived by the loss of New Orleans and the lower river parishes of half the population and three fourths of the resources of his State, he could do little.

. . . Without hope of aid from abroad, I addressed myself to the heavy task of arousing public sentiment, apathetic if not hostile from disaster and neglect, and the creation of some means of defense. Such was the military destitution that a regiment of cavalry could have ridden over the State, while innumerable rivers and bayous, navigable a large part of the year, would admit Federal gunboats to the heart of every parish.[87]

The early military operations of the Federals in the country between the Teche and the Mississippi had been in the nature of skirmishes and marauding expeditions. A more formidable attack was under way in late October, 1862, when Brigadier General Godfrey Weitzel landed at Donaldsonville with four thousand men and advanced down the Lafourche. According to Major General Butler, the purpose of this expedition was to disperse the forces assembled in Western Louisiana under Richard Taylor. Taylor's district had been strengthened by the arrival of Brigadier General Alfred Mouton, son of former Governor Mouton of Louisiana, the Eight-

[87] *Ibid.*, 102–03.

eenth Louisiana Regiment, and the Crescent Regiment of New Orleans, both veterans of Shiloh.[88]

Weitzel was marching his forces down both sides of Bayou Lafourche toward Thibodaux. The Confederate forces, numbering about one thousand, attempted to check his advance; and on October 27 an engagement occurred at Labadieville, eight miles from Thibodaux. The Federal forces probably numbered less than two thousand, for the column on the right bank of the bayou had advanced more rapidly than the other detachment. The Confederate troops were defeated, and the Confederate Colonel G. P. McPheeters was killed.[89]

The year 1862 closed with the armies of Mouton and Weitzel skirmishing along Bayou Teche. Mouton took a stand on high ground midway between Berwick Bay and Franklin. He had about thirteen hundred men. The Confederate gunboat *J. A. Cotton* was patrolling the Teche. Weitzel, who was following Mouton, advanced up the Teche, accompanied by gunboats, in January, 1863. Confederate pickets were driven back and the *Cotton* was subjected to heavy firing. Mouton, who thought his forces too weak to check Weitzel, caused the *Cotton* to be turned across the bayou and burned to arrest the advance of the Federal boats. On January 14 Weitzel, evidently despairing of overtaking Mouton's little army, ordered his own to move back to Berwick Bay.[90]

Every available source indicates that South Louisiana was in a destitute condition by the autumn of 1862. Both inhabitants and soldiers were suffering from extreme hardships. Sarah Morgan Dawson attended a dress parade near Baton

[88] Evans (ed.), *Confederate Military History*, X, 75–77; Taylor, *Destruction and Reconstruction*, 113. For Butler's statement of the purpose of the expedition, see his letter to Major General H. W. Halleck, October 24, 1862, in *Official Records*, Ser. I, Vol. XV, 158–60.

[89] Evans (ed.), *Confederate Military History*, X, 78–79; Taylor, *Destruction and Reconstruction*, 113; *Official Records*, Ser. I, Vol. XV, 167–76.

[90] Taylor, *Destruction and Reconstruction*, 120–21; *Official Records*, Ser. I, Vol. LIII, 462–63.

Rouge on September 24, 1862, and wrote: "Men that had fought at Shiloh and Baton Rouge were barefooted. Rags was their only uniform, for very few possessed a complete suit, and those few wore all varieties of colors and cuts." [91] Major General Taylor wrote to Brigadier General Paul O. Hébert, October 19, and reported "a total want of everything necessary for troops in the field, with the fewest imaginable facilities for creating that which was needed in the several departments." Brigadier General Henry Hunter Sibley, who had just arrived at Opelousas, reported on December 25 that "this part of the State of Louisiana, by far the richest in the Confederacy, is in a lamentably defenseless condition. . . . In short, this country is absolutely destitute, I fear, both of men and material." [92]

Louisianians west of the Mississippi in the fateful year of 1862 suffered in common with their fellow citizens around New Orleans and Baton Rouge from plundering and pillaging by the enemy. Major General Taylor reported that the capture of a Federal post on Bayou des Allemands, between New Orleans and Thibodaux, yielded "books, pictures, household furniture, finger rings, ear rings, breastpins and other articles of feminine adornment and wear." Taylor complained to Butler of such plundering and threatened to treat the marauders as robbers rather than as prisoners of war. The conduct complained of was stopped. [93]

About the time Taylor was complaining to Butler concerning the propensity of Federal troops to plunder, Lieutenant F. A. Roe of the United States Navy protested to Commodore Henry W. Morris concerning the action of the Federal troops at Donaldsonville on September 10 in pillaging an occupied residence in a "brutal manner"—carrying off wines, silver

[91] Reprinted by permission of the publishers, Houghton Mifflin Company, from Dawson, *A Confederate Girl's Diary*, 234.

[92] *Official Records*, Ser. I, Vol. XV, 838, 910–11.

[93] Taylor, *Destruction and Reconstruction*, 111–12; *Official Records*, Ser. I, Vol. XV, 565.

plate, and clothing belonging to ladies. He asked to be relieved of the duty of protecting (by boats) "drunken, undisciplined, and licentious troops in the wanton pillage of a private mansion," since he did not care to further "prostitute the dignity of my profession, as I conceive I have done today." General Butler endorsed Roe's protest as an "improper, bombastic, and ridiculous rhodomontade of a sub-lieutenant of the Navy." [94]

The Confederate attack on Baton Rouge on August 5 seems to have caused an uneasiness within the Federal ranks in New Orleans, and it resulted in another general order affecting the life of the inhabitants of the city. On August 11 Godfrey Weitzel, assistant military commandant, issued the following order:

It being a fact that numbers of the inhabitants of Baton Rouge, who have been allowed by the United States authorities to retain their private arms, were found dead and wounded on the battlefield, it is hereby ordered, to prevent any repetition of such breach of trust, that all arms, of whatever description, now in this city, be turned in as follows: . . . .[95]

It was explained by a subsequent announcement that shipment of arms to any portion of the United States "that is loyal," or to Havana or Europe, would be allowed. Butler published a notice offering rewards for information leading to the discovery of weapons concealed unlawfully, ranging from ten dollars for a serviceable gun to three dollars for a "dirk, dagger, bowie knife, or sword cane." It was also promised by Butler that "every slave giving information that shall discover the concealed arms of his or her master, shall be held to be emancipated." [96]

[94] *Official Records,* Ser. I, Vol. XV, 568–69.
[95] New Orleans *Daily Picayune,* August 12, 1862.
[96] *Ibid.,* August 14, 19, 1862. Parton says that New Orleans was practically disarmed and estimates the number of arms surrendered at six thousand. Parton, *General Butler in New Orleans,* 466.

Federal Occupation of New Orleans

The Congress of the United States in July, 1862, passed an act authorizing the seizure of property of rebels after sixty days' notice. Butler had already taken steps in that direction when, in June, he had ordered the property of Major General David E. Twiggs sequestered; he had also appropriated freely private residences, including the home of General Twiggs, for the accommodation of his staff. On August 11, without the formality of a notice, he ordered all the property of John Slidell confiscated.[97] By a general order of September 18, all transfers of property of any kind, except necessary food, medicine, and clothing, by any citizen who had not returned to his allegiance to the United States, were forbidden. The person transferring, either by sale, gift, pledge, payment, lease or loan, and the person receiving were made liable to punishment by fine, or imprisonment, or both.[98]

Butler's next act was to issue a general order on September 24 to put the confiscation law into effect. According to the order, all persons, eighteen years of age or older, who had ever been citizens of the United States and who had not renewed their allegiance to the United States, were required to furnish the nearest provost marshal with a descriptive list of all their property, and to register their place of residence and occupation, receiving at the time "a certificate from the marshal of registration as claiming to be an enemy of the United States." It was stated, however, that "Every person who shall, in good faith, renew his or her allegiance to the United States previous to the first day of October next, and shall remain truly loyal will be recommended to the president for pardon of his or her previous offenses."[99]

Parton says that Butler's order requiring registration of property "led to a run on the oath offices." By October 21,

97 *Official Records*, Ser. I, Vol. XV, 500; Ficklen, *Reconstruction in Louisiana,* 38; New Orleans *Daily Picayune*, August 12, 1862. The sixty days' notice was not required in the case of officers of the Confederacy.

98 *Official Records*, Ser. I, Vol. XV, 572–73.

99 *Ibid.*, 575–76; Caskey, *Secession and Restoration of Louisiana*, 61.

according to a report of Provost Marshal General French, 67,-920 persons in New Orleans and its suburbs had taken the oath of allegiance. Of this number, 27,929 had taken the oath subsequent to September 24, the date of Butler's proclamation.[100]

On December 4, 1862, Major General Nathaniel P. Banks sailed from New York with reinforcements and arrived at New Orleans on Sunday evening, December 14. According to Banks, no one in New Orleans had anticipated his arrival, and a Federal officer testifies that "No one was more surprised than Butler. He had supposed that Banks's expedition was directed against Texas." On December 17 General Banks relieved Butler and assumed command of the Department of the Gulf.[101]

Banks immediately instituted a policy in New Orleans which was as conspicuous for its mildness as that of Butler had been for its harshness. A contemporary Southern woman wrote: "General Banks has, so far, by equitable rule commanded the respect of his enemies. . . . Every rich man is not his especial foe, to be robbed for his benefit." This was in December, 1862. A few weeks later the same writer observed, "There is a difference even among some devils, it seems, as some of Banks' people do try to be kind to us, while Butler's were just the reverse." [102]

One of the first conciliatory acts of Major General Banks

[100] Parton, *General Butler in New Orleans*, 474; New Orleans *Daily Picayune*, October 22, 1862. Ficklen wrote that "somewhat less than 4,000 registered themselves as enemies, and many of these left the city." Ficklen also says, "A large amount of property belonging to persons who were absent in the Confederate army and who were thus unable to take or refuse the oath was promptly seized and sold." On the other hand, according to the same authority, the evidence seems to show that the property of *registered* enemies was not confiscated. Ficklen, *History of Reconstruction in Louisiana*, 39, and footnote.

[101] *Official Records*, Ser. I, Vol. XV, 611, 613; Frank M. Flinn, *Campaigning With Banks in Louisiana* (Boston, 1889), 54.

[102] Rowland and Croxall (eds.), *The Journal of Julia Le Grand*, 55–56, 77.

was to rescind "provisionally" Butler's order which had closed the Episcopal churches of New Orleans because the rectors had persisted in omitting from the services the prayer for the President of the United States. In his General Orders No. 118, relating to the closed churches, Banks made this interesting comment: "Where the head of the state is also head of the church an omission like that referred to would be in contravention of political authority; but the Government does not here assume that power, and the case presented does not seem to require a continued intervention of military authority." Banks made it clear, however, that clergymen were subject to the ordinary restrictions imposed upon other men; they were to make no appeal to the passions or prejudices of the people nor to excite hostility to the United States Government. The order came as a Christmas gift to the Episcopalians, as it was issued on December 24 and permitted the churches to be opened on and after Christmas Day.[108] In an editorial entitled "Free Breathing," the New Orleans *Picayune*, of December 28, 1862, said:

The course of Major General Banks and his subordinates is eliciting the approbation of our citizens. It is conceded to be honorable and liberal. People begin to breathe more freely. A marked contrast is felt. The houses and other property of many of our citizens have been restored to them. The military authorities, when they require premises for any purpose, hire them, instead of taking them by force under the plea of military necessity—the tyrant's plea—while some scores of our citizens, in durance vile, are to be released upon giving their parole of honor to do nothing against the Government of the United States. The order re-establishing the freedom of the Episcopal Churches in the city gives much satisfaction, not only to the members and friends of that denomination, but to the community in general.

A Union chaplain who was in and around New Orleans in 1863 explains the policy of Banks by saying ". . . since But-

[108] *Official Records*, Ser. I, Vol. XV, 624.

ler had stroked the cat from tail to head, and found her full of yawl and scratch, it was determined to stroke her from head to tail, and see if she would not hide her claws, and commence to purr." [104]

[104] George H. Hepworth, *The Whip, Hoe, and Sword* (Boston, 1864), 27–28.

Chapter V

War and War Measures, 1863-1864

THE FEDERAL OCCUPATION of New Orleans and vicinity was a matter of vital importance to the people of Central and North Louisiana. The city was a social and financial center and contained almost one fourth of the state's population. When Confederate authority was superseded by Federal rule there, the Confederate state was cut off from an important source of revenue; and the ordinary channels of trade were interrupted. The loss of New Orleans was, indeed, a staggering blow to the pride and the purse of Louisianians.

But that was not all. New Orleans in Federal hands and in communication with the North by sea was a constant menace to the safety of the interior of the state. Port Hudson, near Baton Rouge, offered the only resistance to a Federal fleet seeking to enter the Red River from New Orleans. That river was navigable as far as Alexandria, some one hundred miles northwest of Baton Rouge and near the geographic center of the state. During high water, the Red River was navigable to Shreveport in the northwest corner of Louisiana. Besides the Red, the Ouachita, the Teche, the Atchafalaya, and other streams offered routes for gunboats to penetrate the interior of the state.

North Louisianians were not unaware of the dangers. In fact, they seem to have been keenly alive to the situation. As early as May, 1862, soon after the fall of New Orleans, "committees of safety" were appointed in many North Louisiana parishes. The Caddo Parish committee provided for a special messenger between Shreveport and Natchitoches for the purpose of keeping the people of the parish informed of the happenings south of Shreveport. The committee of safety of Natchitoches Parish appointed a subcommittee to establish couriers to correspond with committees in other parishes "touching matters of mutual interest in the present exigency of affairs." Courier service was established with Alexandria and from there to the mouth of the Red River.[1]

On November 22, 1862, representatives of the parishes of Bienville, Bossier, Caddo, De Soto, and Winn, and of Harrison County, Texas, met in Shreveport to consider measures for the protection of the Red River Valley. The delegates concluded that the Red River ought to be obstructed, and committees were appointed to confer with the military authorities. Subscriptions of the parishes for the defensive works were set as follows: Bossier, $20,000; Caddo, $25,000; De Soto, $20,000; Winn, $4,500; Harrison County, $10,000. An executive committee was appointed. The members of this committee were R. C. Cummings of Bossier, D. J. Elder of Caddo, Samuel Clark of De Soto, J. D. Strother of Winn, Thomas Hunter of Natchitoches, and W. T. Scott of Harrison County.[2] This executive committee issued an appeal to the people from Natchitoches on December 3, asserting that they needed slaves for work on the river defenses and assuring slaveowners that slaves would be cared for and properly supervised and not overworked. Twenty-five dollars a month would be paid for each slave. The Negroes were to bring their own clothing and bedding and such tools "as may be within the power of the owner to lend to the work."[3]

When the Legislature convened at Opelousas in December, 1862, one of its first acts was to empower the executive committee of the Shreveport convention of November 22, which

[1] Shreveport *Semi-Weekly News*, May 16, 1862.
[2] *Ibid.*, December 2, 9, 1862.   [3] *Ibid.*, December 9, 1862.

was charged "with the execution of such works, on the banks and in the channel of said river, as they may deem adequate to the defense of the same," to (1) use such force and expend such sums of money as might be placed at their disposal; (2) select the points on the Red River and determine the character of the works to be erected; (3) expropriate timber on or near the Red River and seize any other property or material necessary, with adequate compensation to owners.[4]

By this same act of December 29, the Legislature authorized police juries to appropriate money and levy a tax, in aid of the river defense program. Police juries were also authorized to order out a force of able-bodied slaves between the ages of eighteen and forty-five, and to requisition each owner for his pro rata share. They were also empowered to demand subsistence, working tools and implements, boats, wagons, carts, oxen, mules, and horses from owners; and "the persons furnishing them shall be entitled to demand and receive reasonable compensation therefor, as well as the hire of their slaves."

Richard Taylor, who assumed command of the District of West Louisiana in July, 1862, tells us of the efforts of the Confederate authorities to improve the river defenses of Central Louisiana:

To protect Red River against anything that might chance to run the batteries of Vicksburg and Port Hudson, two thirty-twos were placed in position on the south bank, thirty odd miles below Alexandria [Fort De Russy], where the high ground of Avoyelles Prairie touches the river; and for the same purpose two guns were mounted at Harrisonburg [Fort Beauregard] on the west bank of the Washita. An abrupt hill approached the river at this point, and commanded it.[5]

It was necessary to protect the Atchafalaya, for through it access could be had to the Red and the Ouachita (Washita).

4 Louisiana *Acts*, 1862–1863, pp. 5–6.
5 Taylor, *Destruction and Reconstruction*, 119.

Louisiana in the Confederacy

A large mound on the west bank of the Atchafalaya, called "Butte a la Rose," was selected for the site of Fort Burton; and two twenty-fours were mounted there.[6]

On January 3, 1863, Governor Moore approved a measure of the Legislature entitled "An Act To raise an Army for the defence of the State of Louisiana." According to its terms, the governor was authorized to raise by enlistment any number of men not exceeding twenty thousand for the defense of the state, to serve for twelve months, unless discharged earlier. Each private and noncommissioned officer enlisting in the state service for twelve months was to receive a bounty of $50 to be paid at the time of enlistment and eighty acres of land at the close of the war; in the event of death, the soldier's heirs were to receive the land.[7] The act declared that the governor "shall proceed immediately . . . to raise an army for the defence of the State, which shall be known as the army of the State of Louisiana, and shall not be compelled to operations [sic] out of the State." [8]

On January 3, 1863, the Legislature adopted a new militia law. This act differed in several respects from the militia act of January 23, 1862, which was repealed. The act of 1862 had enrolled in the militia all free white males, with certain exemptions, between the ages of eighteen and forty-five. The new law placed the age limits at seventeen and fifty and added to the list of state exempts engineers of railroads in actual service, and a track master for every fifteen miles of road, professors and students "now members of the Louisiana State Seminary and Military Academy of Alexandria," and one justice of the peace in each parish. It was specifically stated that "no exemptions from service in the armies of the Confederate States shall entitle any person to claim exemption from military service in this State." The governor was au-

[6] *Ibid.*

[7] As mentioned previously (p. 42), the state, by an act of the convention, March 7, 1861, took over the Federal lands within its borders.

[8] Louisiana *Acts,* 1862–1863, pp. 18–20.

142

thorized to call out the militia for a time not to exceed six months, "or for as much longer as may be necessary." Section 25 provided that any person subject to military duty under this act, failing to report within ten days after public notice given by the enrolling officer, would be held as a deserter, tried by court-martial, and punished according to the articles of war of the Confederate States of America.[9]

There was some criticism of the militia law. The act was condemned by many citizens on two scores mainly. It was charged that it was too sweeping in its application and failed to exempt many who were needed in essential civil capacities, and that the penalty for failure to report for service was too severe. One newspaper devoted two editorials to condemning the act. Its chief complaint was that the law did not exempt editors and printers from military service.[10] The Franklin *Banner* condemned the law in the following language:

The Opelousas law makes a clean sweep of the balance of the men in this State, and leave[s] but little behind besides the slave population and defenceless women and children. Thousands of plantations will be without protection, if the law should be enforced. Who will make bread for the army and the people the coming year? Who will enforce order? Who will attend to the families of absent soldiers? These even now are too much neglected. The hard treatment Louisiana has received at the hands of the general government is more than emulated by the

[9] *Ibid.*, 36–40. When the Louisiana militia law of January 23, 1862, was adopted, the Confederate Government was depending on voluntary enlistments. On April 16, 1862, the Confederate Congress adopted the first conscription act, placing the age limits at eighteen and thirty-five. On September 27, 1862, the Confederate conscription law was amended to include men between the ages of thirty-five and forty-five. The new Louisiana militia law of January 3, 1863, extended the age limits to seventeen and fifty, doubtless, in order to include men below and above those embraced in the Confederate law. For the Confederate conscription acts of April 16 and September 27, 1862, see *Public Laws of the Confederate States*, 1 Cong., 1 Sess., Chapter XXVII, and 2 Sess., Chapter XV.

[10] Shreveport *Semi-Weekly News*, January 20, 27, 1863.

State government. The Legislature and Governor now propose to crucify the State.[11]

The Shreveport *Semi-Weekly News* told its readers on January 30: "Our contemporary of the Natchitoches *Union* insinuates that some of the folks in his town, since the passage of the Militia Law, have a sudden anxiety for Texas air."

On February 14, 1863, Adjutant General Charles Le D. Elgee, from headquarters of the Louisiana army, at Alexandria, issued instructions concerning the volunteer and militia service. Persons liable to militia duty had the privilege of volunteering until March 1. The privilege would not be granted after the militia was called out on that date. Volunteers were to receive the cash bounty and $16 a month, besides the eighty acres of land at the end of the war. "Militiamen will receive neither bounty nor land," said the announcement, "and but $11 a month, and in the event of their not reporting within ten days after notice of call by the enrolling officer, which call shall be made on the 1st of March, they shall be considered deserters and liable upon conviction to the death penalty." [12]

The Legislature met in extra session in May, 1863, at Shreveport, which had been made the seat of government. In June the militia act of January 3, 1863, was repealed and a new militia law was adopted. According to the new law, any one failing to respond without delay to a call of the militia would, upon conviction by court-martial, be sentenced to a fine of from $50 to $5,000, or imprisonment of from ten to ninety days, "or to such other less punishment as the court martial may decree, and after execution of the sentence . . . he shall be retained in service." The following classes of persons were added to the list of those exempt from militia duty: mayors and treasurers of towns; "persons who reside in parishes occupied by the enemy, and who have fled from

[11] Quoted by the Shreveport *Semi-Weekly News*, February 13, 1863.
[12] *Official Records*, Ser. IV, Vol. II, 398–99.

their homes"; the editor of each newspaper and compositors necessary to carry on business; every head of a family consisting of ten white persons or children depending upon his personal exertions for support; overseers on plantations owned by persons in the army or by widows or minors; presidents of incorporated railroad companies and employees needed to run the trains; millers owning steam and water mills "and now grinding corn for the public"; and all tanners "who shall make affidavit, that they had at the time of the passage of this act, not less than five hundred hides in tan." [13]

While Louisiana and Confederate authorities were making plans for the defense of the interior of the state, the Federals were planning an attack. Directly after Banks was assigned to the command of the Department of the Gulf, in November, 1862, he was instructed by Major General Henry W. Halleck to open the Mississippi River, with two objects in view. The first object was to capture Vicksburg and destroy the railroads at Jackson and Marion, Mississippi, cutting off all connection by rail between North Mississippi and Mobile and Atlanta. The second object was to ascend the Red River with a naval and military force and open an outlet "for the sugar and cotton of Northern Louisiana." It was suggested to Banks that the Red River would form the best base for operations in Texas. [14]

Banks arrived at New Orleans on December 14. Two days later, without transshipping troops or stores, he dispatched Brigadier General Cuvier Grover with ten thousand men to take possession of Baton Rouge, which Banks called "the first rebel position on the Lower Mississippi." General Grover and his forces arrived at Baton Rouge at daybreak, December 17, and immediately occupied the town. The Confederate forces, which Grover estimated at five hundred, withdrew upon the arrival of the Federal expedition. [15]

[13] Louisiana *Acts*, Extra Sess., 1863, pp. 37–41.
[14] *Official Records*, Ser. I, Vol. XV, 590.   [15] *Ibid.*, 191, 613.

Louisiana in the Confederacy

There was considerable excitement in Louisiana early in 1863 because of naval operations on the Mississippi and Red rivers. Major General U. S. Grant appeared on the west bank of the Mississippi near Vicksburg with a large army, a fleet of gunboats under Rear Admiral David Porter co-operating. The work of digging a canal through the peninsula opposite Vicksburg, which had been begun the previous summer, was continued. The Federals, of course, were making a desperate effort to deprive the Confederates of control of the Mississippi between Vicksburg and Port Hudson. Between these two places was the mouth of the Red River. The Confederates, therefore, as long as they controlled this section of the Mississippi, enjoyed a traffic of tremendous importance to their cause. Rear Admiral Porter decided to send some vessels by the batteries at Vicksburg in order to interfere with the Confederate trade below. The gunboat *Queen of the West* ran the batteries on February 2. Proceeding down the Mississippi below the mouth of the Red, two Confederate steamers, one of which carried provisions for the army, were captured; and a third steamer, also carrying provisions, was taken at the mouth of the Red River.[16]

The *Queen of the West* returned to a point near Vicksburg on February 5. The Federals managed to float a barge loaded with coal past the Vicksburg batteries on the seventh. The *Queen of the West*, accompanied by the *De Soto*, a small boat captured from the Confederates, returned to the mouth of the Red and started up that river. At Fort De Russy, however, the Confederates disabled and captured the *Queen*, though most of the crew escaped to the *De Soto*, which beat a retreat.[17]

The people of Alexandria, the first town of importance on the Red River, were greatly excited at news of the approach

[16] Alfred Thayer Mahan, *The Gulf and Inland Waters* (New York, 1883), 124–26; Spears, *David G. Farragut*, 280.

[17] Mahan, *The Gulf and Inland Waters*, 126–27; Taylor, *Destruction and Reconstruction*, 122–23.

of the Federal boats. It was not their last excitement. The *Queen* was towed to Alexandria for repairs. In the meantime, the Confederate boat *Webb* had been sent in pursuit of the crew of the *Queen*. The *Webb* entered the Mississippi but retreated when it sighted the *Indianola,* a Federal heavy ironclad which had passed the Vicksburg batteries on the night of May 12.[18] When the *Webb* returned to Fort De Russy with the news of the *Indianola,* the authorities planned an expedition to destroy the Federal ironclad. The *Webb* and the *Queen of the West* were manned by volunteers from Fort De Russy, and Major Joseph L. Brent, of General Taylor's staff, was placed in command of the expedition. On the night of February 24 the Confederate boats overtook and attacked the *Indianola* in the Mississippi, about sixty miles below Vicksburg. The *Indianola* surrendered after a stiff fight and was sunk in shallow water on the east bank of the Mississippi. The Confederates were again undisputed masters of the Red River and of the Mississippi between Vicksburg and Port Hudson.[19]

There was considerable military activity in South and Southeast Louisiana in the early part of 1863. In March the Federals occupied the town of Ponchatoula, only to be driven out by the Confederate forces a week later. This one week, however, was sufficient time for the town to be systematically pillaged and plundered. A Federal officer wrote:

All kinds of papers, books, daguerreotypes, articles of household furniture and female wearing apparel, are scattered here and there on the ground. Doors and windows are wide open, most of the people having fled to hiding places in the woods, wherever they can find shelter.[20]

[18] Taylor, *Destruction and Reconstruction,* 123–24; Mahan, *The Gulf and Inland Waters,* 126–28.

[19] Taylor, *Destruction and Reconstruction,* 124–25; Mahan, *The Gulf and Inland Waters,* 128–31.

[20] Edward Bacon, *Among the Cotton Thieves* (Detroit, 1867), 65, 71. Lieutenant Colonel Horace H. Miller, C.S.A., reported to Lieutenant General

Louisiana in the Confederacy

Early in April Major General Banks left New Orleans on the first of his expeditions that carried him into the heart of Louisiana. He advanced to Brashear City and from there moved upon Bayou Teche. His forces attacked Fort Bisland on April 13, and the Confederate defenders evacuated the fort the following day. The Federals were retarded in their advance by the troops under Major General Richard Taylor, who was ably assisted by Colonel Thomas Green and his Texas cavalry and by the gunboat *Diana* under the command of Captain Raphael Semmes. The troops under Banks, however, succeeded in advancing; and the gunboats *Diana* and *Queen of the West* were destroyed. Opelousas was taken on April 20; Major General Taylor retreated northward toward Alexandria and Natchitoches; and Brigadier General Mouton was ordered to the country west of Opelousas.[21]

Banks's army remained at Opelousas a fortnight and then marched to Alexandria, about eighty miles to the north. That town was taken by the Federals on May 7. Rear Admiral Porter had arrived with several gunboats a few hours ahead of Banks and his army, as the Confederates had abandoned Fort De Russy on the Red River south of Alexandria.[22]

Banks did not tarry long in Alexandria. He wrote to Halleck on May 8 that he would be glad to follow the enemy to Shreveport and "complete his entire destruction"; but it "would occupy too much time, which can be more advantageously used in another enterprise nearer at hand and more decisive in its results." Porter's boats could not pass the

John C. Pemberton that the Federals had burned the depot filled with their commissary stores and had set fire to many other buildings at Ponchatoula and destroyed much private property. See *Official Records*, Ser. I, Vol. XV, 288.

[21] *Official Records*, Ser. I, Vol. XV, 704–05; Taylor, *Destruction and Reconstruction*, 129–35.

[22] *Official Records*, Ser. I, Vol. XV, 313; Taylor, *Destruction and Reconstruction*, 136.

148

falls at Alexandria, and Banks was probably unwilling to risk a campaign in Northwest Louisiana without naval support. Meanwhile, Grant was urging Banks to join him at Vicksburg. He decided, therefore, to abandon the Red River campaign. His forces were moved southward from Alexandria on May 14. Brigadier General Weitzel, whose troops had followed the Confederates sixty miles above Alexandria, withdrew from that section and joined Banks's retreating army.[23]

Banks considered his expedition to Alexandria a success. He wrote to Halleck from Port Hudson in June, stating that he had marched to Alexandria for the double purpose of dispersing the Confederate army concentrating at Alexandria under Kirby Smith and "destroying the materials upon which an army could be organized or supported in that country." He claimed success in both objects, since the enemy had been driven "into the pine woods" seventy miles above Alexandria, foundries and shops had been destroyed, and horses and carts had been seized, making it "impossible to organize and supply a large force from that country." [24]

The campaign, however, was not an unqualified success. Although the Confederate authorities had made Alexandria a concentration point for supplies and war materials, had built there a packing plant and foundry, and had established above the falls a shipyard where steamboats were converted into gunboats, Porter's boats could not pass the falls; and the

---

[23] *Official Records*, Ser. I, Vol. XV, 313, 316–18. Banks wrote Halleck from Alexandria on May 12 that it was not within his power to join Grant at Vicksburg. On the following day, however, he wrote Halleck: "Contrary to my dispatches of yesterday, thorough reconnaissances . . . satisfy me that it is possible for my command to join General Grant at Vicksburg. I shall make every sacrifice and hazard everything to accomplish this object with the least possible delay. . . ." *Ibid.* On the same day Banks wrote Farragut and Grant to the same effect, saying to Grant: "I can add about 12,000 to your column." *Ibid.*, 731.

[24] *Ibid.*, Ser. I, Vol. XXVI, Pt. I, 535.

Louisiana in the Confederacy

Confederates had moved guns, machinery, and supplies to Grand Ecore and Shreveport before the arrival of Banks.[25] But if measured in terms of disaster to the residents of Central Louisiana, the expedition was a success. Cultivation of crops was most seriously interfered with. Teams were taken, and cattle were turned into cultivated fields. Fences and houses were destroyed. Plantations were abandoned; and slaves became demoralized, about four thousand following the Federal army on its withdrawal, taking with them property of their owners.[26]

Many planters abandoned their homes and sought refuge in Texas, taking with them their slaves and other property such as furniture, etc. Lieutenant Colonel Arthur J. L. Fremantle, traveling in East Texas, observed on May 7 several planters, with their families and Negroes, moving to Texas, "after having abandoned their plantations in Louisiana on the approach of Banks." One of them, he observed, "had as many as sixty slaves with him of all ages and sizes." Two days later Fremantle recorded seeing more planters moving toward Texas, with families, slaves, furniture, and "everything that they could save from the ruin that had befallen them on the approach of the Federal troops." On May 10, between Shreveport and Monroe, our chronicler said: "The road today was alive with negroes, who are being 'run' into Texas out of Banks' way. We must have met hundreds of

[25] Whittington, "Rapides Parish, Louisiana—A History," in *loc. cit.,* XVIII (1935), 5–8.

[26] *Ibid.* A letter written from near Alexandria on May 31, 1863, said: "The country in many places below is *ruined*—fences were torn down and burnt—houses and provender destroyed, cattle turned into the fields, and the negroes on many plantations driven off in a body—This is no fiction—For instance—Mrs. Jobez Tanner's and Ralph Smith's all left save some 4 or 5 old ones on both places—the Helm's all left but 9—and only 3 hands among them, and then recollect that every mule, horse and wagon was taken at the same time. Below those places on the road to Simsport [*sic*] the destruction of property and crops was greater if possible." John H. Ransdell to Governor Thomas O. Moore, Thomas O. Moore Papers (Louisiana State University Department of Archives).

them, and many families of planters, who were much to be pitied, especially the ladies." [27]

The expedition was highly successful in the matter of obtaining equipment and supplies. Banks wrote to Major General Halleck from Opelousas on May 4:

In the progress of this army I have deemed it expedient, in order to prevent the reorganization of the rebel army and to deprive the rebel Government of all possible means of support, to take possession of mules, horses, cattle, and the staple products of the country—cotton, sugar, and tobacco. I have given the people to understand that those who are well-disposed and entitled to the favor of the Government will receive compensation for this property. . . . In round numbers, I may say that 20,000 beeves, mules, and horses have been forwarded to Brashear City, with 5,000 bales of cotton and many hogsheads of sugar [28]

When the army was encamped near Opelousas, the wagon trains were employed in gathering cotton to be shipped to New Orleans. A member of the expedition wrote: "Cotton is king for the army is doing nothing else but gathering cotton." [29]

Mention has been made of the destitute condition of South Louisiana in 1862. Military activities aggravated the evils in 1863. Louisianians realized the truth of Sherman's famous words long before that notable spoke them. A Federal chaplain has left us the following picture of the country near Brashear City when Banks's army was operating there in 1863.

Our boys droves to the rear every pony and mule, every ox and cow and sheep. They did not leave, on an average, two chickens to a plantation. Wherever they encamped, the fences served as beds and firewood. A more forlorn and destitute set of people never were seen. . . . Another thing which struck me

[27] Lieutenant Colonel Arthur J. L. Fremantle, *Three Months in the Southern States* (New York, 1864), 82–87.

[28] *Official Records*, Ser. I, Vol. XV, 309–10.

[29] Flinn, *Campaigning With Banks in Louisiana*, 62, 65.

with some surprise was the general scarcity of food. The richest planters could give us nothing better than cornbread and the coarsest Texas beef. They had no coffee, and said that they had had none for more than a year. . . . There is but little doubt that the breadstuffs of the Confederacy are very low.[30]

When the forces of Major General Banks left Alexandria, a portion moved down the river in boats; and the remainder marched by land to Simmesport, crossing the Atchafalaya River there, and then marched to the Mississippi, crossed to Bayou Sara on May 23, and moved directly to Port Hudson on May 24. By this time Banks had decided that he could not reinforce Grant at Vicksburg. He feared that the transfer of any considerable number of his troops and artillery to Vicksburg would leave his trains and fugitive Negroes to the chances of capture by the Confederates. He feared also that, unless Vicksburg fell immediately, either the Confederate garrison at Port Hudson, which he estimated at from 16,000 to 18,000, or Taylor's army, reinforced from Texas, would threaten New Orleans and South Louisiana. He suggested that Grant assist him with from 10,000 to 20,000 men and expressed the opinion that "the movement against Port Hudson can delay us but a few days." [31] Instead of sending help to Grant at Vicksburg, Banks concentrated his forces near Port Hudson and began the investment of that place on May 25. He had been joined by Major General Christopher C. Augur and 3,500 men from Baton Rouge. According to Banks's official report, his total forces, including Augur's command, numbered less than 13,000.[32]

When Banks's command withdrew from the Red River

[30] Hepworth, *The Whip, Hoe, and Sword,* 272–74.

[31] *Official Records,* Ser. I, Vol. XV, 732; Ser. I, Vol. XXVI, Pt. I, 12. Banks's estimate of the number of Confederates at Port Hudson was far too large. According to a report of Major General Franklin Gardner, C.S.A., May 19, 1863, there were 8,007 Confederate troops at and in the vicinity of Port Hudson. See *ibid.,* Ser. I, Vol. XXVI, Pt. II, 10.

[32] *Ibid.,* Ser. I, Vol. XXVI, Pt. I, 13.

country, the Confederate forces moved southward from the vicinity of Natchitoches and Shreveport and reoccupied the section south of Alexandria. The commanders of the forces concentrating in the country between Alexandria and the lower Teche were Major General Richard Taylor, Brigadier General Alfred Mouton, and Brigadier General Thomas Green. A detachment of men from Mouton's forces, under Major Sherod Hunter, captured Brashear City on June 23. Eleven siege guns, 2,500 stand of small arms, more than 200 wagons and tents, immense quantities of quartermaster and ordnance equipment, and 1,300 prisoners were reported captured by Major Hunter. On the next day 400 Federals surrendered to the forces of Brigadier General Green on Bayou Boeuf, near Brashear City.[33]

The Confederates were not so successful however in their next venture. After the affair of June 24, on Bayou Boeuf, General Green marched his forces toward Donaldsonville. At two o'clock in the morning of June 28, his little army of 800 men attacked the Federal garrison of about 600 men at Fort Butler at Donaldsonville. The fighting was most desperate, Green reporting, "Our men here used brick-bats upon the heads of the enemy, who returned the same." The attack was repulsed with 40 killed and 114 wounded in Green's party.[34]

Banks's decision to attack Port Hudson rather than join Grant at Vicksburg was disapproved in Washington. Halleck wrote him on May 25 that "the Government is exceedingly uneasy" over his separation from Grant, and added: "The success of such important operations on the Mississippi River should not be put in peril by the diversion of troops upon secondary operations. But I have so often called at-

---

[33] *Ibid.*, 223–26. General Taylor, speaking of the spoils of June 23, said, "For the first time since I reached western Louisiana I had supplies, and in such abundance as to serve for the Red River campaign of 1864." Taylor, *Destruction and Reconstruction*, 143.

[34] *Official Records*, Ser. I, Vol. XXVI, Pt. I, 227–30.

tention to this matter that it seems useless to repeat it." On June 3 Halleck again wrote to Banks: "The newspapers state that your forces are moving on Port Hudson, instead of co-operating with General Grant. . . . As this is contrary to all your instructions, and so opposed to military principles, I can hardly believe it true." On June 4 the following message was sent by Halleck to Banks: "I hope that you have ere this given up your attack on Port Hudson and sent all your spare forces to Grant." [35]

Neither Banks nor Grant was willing to send the other reinforcements. Banks wrote to Grant on May 28 that "we have ammunition, provisions, artillery, and cavalry, and want nothing but the men. . . . If it be possible, I beg you to send to me at least one brigade of 4,000 or 5,000 men." Grant replied, May 31, that Vicksburg was the vital point and his position there should not be jeopardized by any detachments whatever. "My arrangements for supplies are ample, and can be expanded to meet any exigency," he said. "All I want now is men." [36]

Confederate authorities were inclined to sacrifice Port Hudson for the sake of Vicksburg, at least for a while. Lieutenant General John C. Pemberton, Confederate commander at Vicksburg, ordered Major General Franklin Gardner, who was in command at Port Hudson, to bring 5,000 infantry with him to Vicksburg. This was on May 4. Gardner replied the next day that he would comply with the request or order "as soon as wagons return." On May 6 he

[35] *Ibid.*, 503 (letter of May 25); 534–35 (letters of June 3, 4). Banks replied to Halleck on June 18, asserting that his action in attacking Port Hudson was based upon a prior understanding with Grant and upon the advice of his officers who "knew it would be a source of great danger to New Orleans to leave a garrison of 5,000 men at Port Hudson, as many at Mobile, and a larger number in Teche country." He placed great stress on the point that sending forces to Vicksburg would "place New Orleans in immediate peril." *Ibid.*, 564–65. Halleck replied to this communication on June 27, saying, "The reasons given by you for moving against Port Hudson are satisfactory." *Ibid.*, 603.   [36] *Ibid.*, 519–20, 525–26.

ordered certain units of his command to proceed to Vicksburg and Jackson, Mississippi. On May 8, however, Pemberton sent this message to Gardner, who was at Osyka, Mississippi, on the way to Jackson: "Return with 2,000 troops to Port Hudson and hold it to the last. President says both places must be held." [37]

Had Banks not attacked Port Hudson when he did, it is most probable that it would have been evacuated and the long and bloody siege would never have occurred. General Joseph E. Johnston, who was in camp near Vernon, Mississippi, wrote to Major General Gardner, May 19:

> Lieutenant-General Pemberton has been compelled to fall back to Vicksburg and abandon Haynes' Bluff, so that your position is no longer valuable. It is important also, that all the troops in the department should be concentrated as soon as possible. Evacuate Port Hudson forthwith, and move with your troops toward Jackson, to join other troops which I am uniting. Bring all the field pieces that you have, with their ammunition and the means of transportation; heavy guns and their ammunition had better be destroyed, as well as the other property you may be unable to remove.[38]

Colonel John L. Logan, commanding the outposts at Port Hudson, wrote to Johnston on May 29, saying that Gardner had not evacuated the garrison because the works were already besieged when the order for evacuation was received. There was doubt of the ability of Gardner to get through the Federal lines. Logan asserted that Gardner intended to "come out, if possible," on the night of May 24, and

> . . . ordered me to place my forces so as to assist him, which I did. I think he found it impossible to cut his way through, and has, perhaps, concluded to remain to defend the place as long as he can, hoping to be relieved by re-enforcements. . . . Can we get re-enforcements? To relieve General Gardner is certainly

[37] *Ibid.*, Ser. I, Vol. XV, 1071, 1074, 1076, 1080.
[38] *Ibid.*, Ser. I, Vol. XXVI, Pt. II, 9.

very important, besides, I think it of great importance to hold our position at Port Hudson as well as the New Orleans, Jackson and Great Northern Railroad.[39]

Port Hudson was besieged by an army of perhaps 13,000 men, assisted by Federal gunboats and mortar boats under Farragut. The siege lasted forty-five days, with incessant and constant fighting on twenty-one days. The first general assault was made on May 27, and the Federals were repulsed with heavy losses. Banks reported that "the garrison was much stronger than had been represented, and the enemy was found able to defend his works at all points." According to Banks, his losses in the engagement of May 27 were 293 killed and 1,549 wounded.[40] A second general assault was made on June 14. The Federals gained ground and occupied a line within from fifty to two hundred yards of the Confederate line of fortifications. But this assault convinced Banks that his force was "unequal to the task of carrying the works by assault, and the slower, but more certain, operations of the siege were commenced." [41]

Disaster followed disaster for the Confederacy in July, 1863. Lee was repulsed at Gettysburg on July 3, Pemberton

[39] *Ibid.*, Ser. I, Vol. XXVI, Pt. I, 180. Colonel Logan commanded about 1,200 men in the vicinity of Clinton, Louisiana, whom he used to harass Banks's forces around Port Hudson. Logan repeated his plea to Johnston on June 7 for reinforcements for Gardner at Port Hudson. *Ibid.*, 181. George S. Denison wrote to Salmon P. Chase on July 15, 1863: "General Banks' private secretary informs me that Port Hudson would have been evacuated, if the investment had been delayed a few hours. The Rebel Commander had the order to evacuate from Johnston, in his pocket, and had commenced its execution when Banks appeared. This fact was not known until after the surrender." *Diary and Correspondence of Salmon P. Chase,* 396–97.

[40] *Official Records,* Ser. I, Vol. XXVI, Pt. I, 13, 16. Two Federal contemporaries were very critical of the operations against Port Hudson. Hoffman, *Camp Court and Siege,* 71, said: "There never was a more useless waste of life." Lieutenant Colonel Edward Bacon, *Among the Cotton Thieves,* 268–72, expressed the opinion that many lives were lost "to gratify the idiotic caprice" of officers.

[41] *Official Records,* Ser. I, Vol. XXVI, Pt. I, 14.

capitulated at Vicksburg on the fourth, and Gardner surrendered Port Hudson on the ninth. The surrender of Port Hudson included 5,500 prisoners, 20 pieces of heavy artillery, 5 complete batteries, 44,000 pounds of cannon powder, 5,000 stand of small arms, 150,000 rounds of ammunition, and 2 steamers. Soldiers and noncommissioned officers were paroled.[42]

Probably no two events of the Civil War combined to spell as great a disaster for the Confederacy as did the fall of Vicksburg and Port Hudson. No two rivers were so important to the Confederates as the Mississippi and the Red. Vicksburg and Port Hudson had assured the Confederates control of the Mississippi for more than 150 miles, and, what is more important, had protected the mouth of the Red River through which supplies of all kinds had flowed eastward from Western Louisiana, Texas, and Mexico. Now Federal forces controlled the Mississippi from its source to the Gulf and permanently separated the Confederate states of Arkansas, Texas, and most of Louisiana from their sister states east of the Mississippi. The mouth of the Red River was in Federal hands, and the granary of the West was closed to the Confederacy. One marvels now that Appomattox was still twenty-two months away.

The Louisiana military front was comparatively quiet for the remainder of 1863 after the fall of Port Hudson. The conclusion of the siege allowed Federal forces to move to Donaldsonville and Brashear City. Several thousand soldiers under Brigadier Generals Weitzel, Grover, and William Dwight made up the expedition. The Confederates, however, inflicted one defeat on this army before the recapture of Brashear City. Brigadier General Thomas Green and his Texas cavalry attacked the Federals under Weitzel and Grover on the Lafourche between Donaldsonville and Thibodaux on July 13. According to Green's report of the

[42] Reports of Major General Banks, *ibid.*, 55–56.

battle, over 500 of the Federals were killed and wounded, 250 were captured, and guns, ammunition, provisions, tents, wagons, and teams were taken by the Confederates. The Confederate loss in killed and wounded, Green reported, was less than fifty.[43] When the Confederate forces evacuated Brashear City they took with them considerable supplies, and ran railway engines and coaches into the bay. Heavy guns were dumped in the water.[44]

Early in September a Federal expedition under Brigadier General Marcellus M. Crocker marched from opposite Natchez, Mississippi, to Fort Beauregard on the Ouachita River at Harrisonburg. The fort was commanded by Lieutenant Colonel George W. Logan, who had at the time a force of only forty effective men. On learning of the approach of the Federals, Colonel Logan ordered the destruction of the works and evacuated the fort. After completing the work of destruction of the fortifications, destroying ammunition in the jail and courthouse and a gristmill, and burning fifty-seven bales of cotton marked "C.S.A.," the Federals returned to Natchez.[45]

The Teche country was the principal scene of military operations in Louisiana for the closing months of 1863. Early in October Federal forces under Major General William B. Franklin advanced from Berwick Bay to New Iberia. From that time till December 1, there were numerous skirmishes between the opposing forces in the country around New Iberia, notably at Grand Coteau, Washington, Vermilionville, Carrion Crow Bayou, and Vermilion Bayou. Probably the major engagement was at Grand Coteau on November 3, where each side suffered heavy losses. The

[43] *Ibid.*, 230–32. The Federal report of the engagement, however, placed their losses in killed and wounded at 270 and captured or missing at 183. See *ibid.*, 204–05, for report of Brigadier General Cuvier Grover.

[44] *Ibid.*, 15–16; Taylor, *Destruction and Reconstruction*, 145–46.

[45] *Official Records*, Ser. I, Vol. XXVI, Pt. I, 273–83.

War and War Measures

Confederate forces operating in these engagements were commanded by Taylor, ably assisted by Green and Mouton.[46]

South Louisiana had suffered much in 1863. Banks and his army had marched through the country on the way to Alexandria in April and May, seizing wagons, horses, cattle, cotton, and wreaking destruction. Then the country was reoccupied by the Confederates during the siege of Port Hudson in June and July. Next came the military operations of Generals Franklin and Taylor in October and November. A Confederate officer has left us this picture of South Louisiana in December, 1863:

> This section of country might have been termed the "Paradise" of Louisiana before the war; but alas, what a change has befallen it now! The houses are all deserted; occasionally you meet with a few old, faithful negroes, left by their owners to take care of their place until their return. Here you can behold mansion after mansion, including costly sugar-houses, now going to decay.[47]

A Federal soldier, writing to a Northern newspaper, told of the many handsome residences standing in ruins in Baton Rouge, and said "the city now looks ragged and desolate." Of another Louisiana town he said:

> Donaldsonville, a small town on the west bank of the river, some eighty-two miles above New Orleans, has paid dearly for its treason, as nearly every house has been destroyed. . . . Here, nothing but a heap of ruins marks the location of a once beautiful and flourishing town.[48]

[46] *Ibid.*, 332–95.

[47] J. P. Blessington, *The Campaigns of Walker's Texas Division* (New York, 1875), 153.

[48] From the New Bedford, Massachusetts, *Mercury*, quoted in the New Orleans *Daily True Delta*, December 12, 1863. For reports on the destruction of property in 1863 in the parishes of St. Landry, Lafayette, St. Martin, and St. Mary, see *Official Report Relative to the Conduct of Federal Troops in Western Louisiana During the Invasions of 1863 and 1864* (Shreveport, 1865), 5–63.

Louisiana in the Confederacy

Meanwhile, the authorities, civil as well as military, were making plans for a better defense of North Louisiana. In response to the recommendations of a conference of the governors of Arkansas, Louisiana, Missouri (Thomas C. Reynolds "representing" Missouri), and Texas, held at Marshall, Texas, in August, 1863, "Confederate Associations" were formed in each parish to unite the citizens in a "vigorous support of the Confederate and State authorities in defence of our families and homes." It was the duty of each Confederate association to keep alive "the fervid patriotism" of the people by frequent public meetings and "occasional" public speeches, by the dissemination of "accurate intelligence" of current events, and by the correction and prevention of exaggerated or false reports from the enemy's lines.[49]

The Confederate Association of Caddo Parish was organized in Shreveport on September 10. R. J. Looney was elected president and M. Estes secretary. On September 14 Looney announced the personnel of the committees. The following list of the committees will give some idea of the proposed activities of the "associations": (1) a committee on correspondence, (2) a committee to arrange meetings of the people and to procure speakers, (3) a committee to forward organization for public defense and obtain information as to arms and military supplies within the parish, (4) a committee to remove the women and children in case of invasion of the parish by the enemy.[50] Meanwhile, the work of placing Shreveport in a stronger position of defense, especially against a naval expedition, was undertaken. The labor on the defenses was done by Negroes requisitioned by Confederate authorities from the citizens of Bossier, Caddo, De Soto, Claiborne parishes, and Harrison County, Texas.[51] Exten-

[49] Shreveport *Semi-Weekly News*, September 25, 1863. For the work of the conference of governors at Marshall, see *Official Records*, Ser. I, Vol. XXII, Pt. II, 1004–10 and Ser. I, Vol. LIII, 892–94.

[50] Shreveport *Semi-Weekly News*, September 15, 1863.

[51] *Ibid.*, October 16, 1863. A public notice of Major H. T. Douglas, chief

160

sive fortifications were constructed at Shreveport. Forts armed with heavy guns were erected, and other earthworks were thrown up around the town.[52]

Henry Watkins Allen was inaugurated governor of Louisiana on January 25, 1864, succeeding Thomas Overton Moore. One of his first acts after his election to the governor's office was to make a "progress" through the state in order to arouse the people and to learn of his own problems. The state's new chief executive was a military figure, having served the cause faithfully at Shiloh and at Baton Rouge, where, as previously stated, he was severely wounded. He was still suffering from wounds and using crutches when he assumed the duties of the gubernatorial office. Allen had been promoted to the rank of brigadier general by President Davis.[53]

Governor Allen transmitted his first message to the Legislature on January 26. It was a long document touching upon many matters involving the welfare of the state. Only that portion of the message dealing with military affairs, however, is of concern here. He recommended that the governor be authorized immediately to call into the field a regiment of five hundred mounted men (to be increased to one thousand, if necessary) to be called the "State Guard." "In many of the border Parishes of this State," Allen said, "there is neither military nor civil law, and crimes are daily committed with impunity." Such a force was needed to arrest offenders against the laws. The message asserted that the "present militia law is a nullity, there being no method provided for its enforcement." Specific recommendations were made for a militia law with the following features: (1) enrollment of every able-bodied white male in the state between the ages of

engineer, in this issue of the *News* stated that the Negroes would be permitted to visit their homes at fixed periods "upon each owner obligating himself to return said negroes to the work at the expiration of their leaves of absence, or others in their stead."

52 O'Pry, *Chronicles of Shreveport*, 167.

53 Dorsey, *Recollections of Henry Watkins Allen*, 233–38.

fifteen and fifty-five, (2) provision for arming and equipping every enrolled man and for repairing the arms then in the hands of the people, (3) investment of the governor with full power to call out the militia, "provided they shall not be kept in the field longer than sixty days at a time." It was not intended, the governor said, that the militia should ever be called to the field as regular troops. "They are to be kept at home, and held in readiness for the purpose of checking the raids and incursions of the enemy, by land or water." [54]

The Legislature responded promptly to Governor Allen's request for authority to raise a state guard. He was empowered to raise a regiment or two battalions of mounted men, and to appoint all field and staff officers and company captains. Pay and allowance were fixed as the same as those for the cavalry of the Confederate army. This force was placed by the terms of the act "under the immediate control of the Governor, to act as conservators of the peace, and for the defence of the State." [55] Governor Allen informed the Legislature in January, 1865, that he had raised, equipped, and armed four companies under the authority granted to him in February, 1864. These companies, added to six state companies already in service, had formed two battalions of state troops. These battalions, he said, had participated in the battles of Mansfield and Pleasant Hill. They were mustered into the Confederate army on July 26, 1864, because the state had no depots of corn and provisions and no forage.[56]

The Legislature also responded to the recommendations of Governor Allen for a new militia law. The act, approved February 10, was an elaborate and detailed one, following

[54] Louisiana *House Journal*, 1864, p. 31; Shreveport *Semi-Weekly News*, January 29, 1864. The entire message was printed in the *Journal* and in the *Semi-Weekly News*.   [55] Louisiana *Acts*, 1864, p. 24.

[56] *Annual Message of Governor Henry Watkins Allen to the Legislature of the State of Louisiana*, January, 1865 (Shreveport, 1865). This message was printed by itself. A copy is in the Confederate Memorial Museum, New Orleans.

in the main the suggestions of the governor. It evidently greatly strengthened the militia system of the state. It provided, among other things, that all officers and soldiers convicted of having deserted the military service of the state "shall suffer death, or such other punishment as, by the sentence of a court-martial, shall be inflicted." The same penalties were prescribed for officers or soldiers "who shall be convicted of having advised or persuaded any other officer or soldier to desert the service of the State." [57]

The militia, however, did not remain subject to state authorities for long. On April 18, 1864, from Headquarters of the Army of Louisiana, at Shreveport, Governor Allen issued the following general order:

The Governor takes this method to thank the militia officers and men who have so promptly responded to his call. He will see that every man who has failed to comply with his order shall be arrested, and brought into camp. Citizen soldiers, our recent glorious victories have inspired our countrymen with hope and courage. Our cause is triumphant everywhere. We have vanquished the enemy on every field. Within the last forty days we have won ten victories. The Confederate Congress has so amended the law of conscription as to embrace the entire militia of the State, who will henceforth belong to the reserve corps of the army. You are therefore permanently discharged from the command of the Governor. He parts from you with much regret, and tenders to each and all of you his best wishes for your health, happiness and prosperity. [58]

Federal authorities had great plans for the conquest of Louisiana in 1864. Three armies totaling at least thirty thousand men were to co-operate in a campaign that was to

[57] Louisiana *Acts,* 1864, pp. 36–50.

[58] *Official Records,* Ser. I, Vol. XXXIV, Pt. III, 778. The Confederate Congress amended the conscription law on February 17, 1864, by extending the age limits to seventeen and fifty, which were the age limits of the Louisiana militia law. See *Public Laws of the Confederate States,* 1 Cong., 4 Sess., Chap. LXV.

culminate in an attack on Shreveport. Major General Banks was to move northward from New Orleans through Opelousas to the Red River at Fort De Russy near Marksville. Major General W. T. Sherman at Vicksburg, Mississippi, was to furnish not less than ten thousand men by way of the Mississippi and Red rivers to join Banks before Fort De Russy and, with the co-operation of Rear Admiral Porter's fleet, to capture the fort and open the way to Alexandria. Major General Frederick Steele, stationed in Arkansas, was to move at least ten thousand men toward Northwest Louisiana. The three armies of Banks, Sherman, and Steele were to appear at Shreveport on a day to be appointed beforehand.[59] The purpose of the Federal expedition, according to Banks, was to "defend Louisiana and Arkansas and form a base of operations against Texas." Banks expressed the opinion that "the occupation of Shreveport will be to the country west of the Mississippi what that of Chattanooga is to the east, and as soon as this can be accomplished the country west of Shreveport will be in condition for movement into Texas." [60]

A recent study of the Red River expedition of 1864 resulted in the conclusion that one motive of the campaign was to open up Arkansas, Louisiana, and Texas to trade. Banks had learned that the Confederate Government had cotton to the value of millions of dollars in those states. Naturally, if he could capture this cotton, the Confederate Government would be prevented from selling it. This expedition, there-

[59] Sherman to Banks, January 31, 1864, *Official Records*, Ser. I, Vol. XXXIV, Pt. II, 266–67. Sherman said: "The expedition on Shreveport should be made rapidly, by simultaneous movements from Little Rock on Shreveport, from Opelousas on Alexandria, and a combined force of gun-boats and transports up Red River." *Ibid.* See also Banks to Halleck, February 12, 1864, *ibid.*, 305, and Sherman to Steele, March 4, 1864, *ibid.*, 496–97. In this communication to Steele, Sherman said: "The moment Kirby Smith sees three columns all tending to Shreveport he will call for every man he has, and then decide to fight at Shreveport or save his army by retiring on Marshall, Texas. I believe he will do the latter."

[60] Banks to Halleck, January 23, 1864, *ibid.*, 133.

fore, might have an important bearing on hastening the end of the war.[61] Another object of the expedition was to secure to the Federals the uninterrupted control of the Mississippi River by driving any large Confederate forces from the vicinity of its western banks.[62]

The Confederate troops in that part of Louisiana west of the Mississippi were under the general command of Lieutenant General E. Kirby Smith, commander of the Trans-Mississippi Department, with headquarters at Shreveport. Directly under General Smith was Major General Richard Taylor, commander of the District of West Louisiana, whose headquarters were at Alexandria. Taylor's chief aides in the early months of 1864 were Major General John G. Walker and Brigadier Generals St. John R. Liddell, Alfred Mouton, and Camille Polignac, a native of France. General Liddell commanded the District of North Louisiana. Mouton commanded the Second Infantry Division, operating along the Ouachita River in the neighborhood of Monroe, and Polignac was a brigade commander at Harrisonburg in January, 1864. Taylor himself was in and around Alexandria, seeing to the establishment of depots and the strengthening of Fort De Russy below Alexandria. Major General Walker and his famous Texas Division were in the section between Fort De Russy and the mouth of the Red River.[63]

The Federal expedition was planned to start sometime after March 1. Major General Sherman wrote to Banks on

[61] Sarah Frances Ware, "General Banks's Red River Campaign of 1864" (M.A. Thesis, University of Texas, 1931), 5–6. Banks wrote to Lincoln, February 2, 1864: "There are in the State of Louisiana about 105,000 bales of cotton belonging to the rebel Government. . . . In Arkansas and Texas there is probably as much more, making at least 200,000 bales of cotton, the exclusive property of the rebel Government." *Official Records*, Ser. III, Vol. IV, 68–70.

[62] Halleck to Major General E. R. S. Canby, May 7, 1864, *Official Records*, Ser. I, Vol. XXXIV, Pt. III, 491–92.

[63] This paragraph is based upon various letters and orders in *ibid.*, Ser. I, Vol. XXXIV, Pt. II, 810–1107.

January 31 that it would require twelve feet of water on the rapids at Alexandria for boats to pass. This would be from March to June. "I have lived on Red River and know somewhat of the phases of that stream," he said. Banks wrote to Halleck on February 12 that the movement to Shreveport would begin about March 1. The troops were in good health and spirit, he said, and "I am confident of a successful result of the expedition." [64]

Early in March Rear Admiral David Porter of the United States Navy assembled a large fleet of gunboats at the mouth of the Red River. On the eleventh, ten thousand men of Sherman's army, under the command of Brigadier General Andrew J. Smith, in transports, arrived there. On March 12 the expedition of gunboats and transports started up the river. The first contingent of Banks's command began to move in the direction of Alexandria on the thirteenth, when the cavalry under Brigadier General Albert L. Lee left Franklin, Louisiana.[65] The Federals found the first obstructions in the Red River eight miles below Fort De Russy. They consisted of heavy piles driven into the earth and joined with heavy iron plates and chains. The obstructions were practically useless, and the Federals were able to destroy them and pass through. Fort De Russy, with 250 prisoners, several heavy guns, and considerable munitions of war, was captured by Brigadier General Smith's men on March 14. The route to Alexandria was open.[66]

The United States gunboats *Ouachita, Lexington,* and

[64] Sherman to Banks, *ibid.,* 266–67; Banks to Halleck, *ibid.,* 305.

[65] *Official Records, Navy,* Ser. I, Vol. XXVI, 24–25; *Official Records,* Ser. I, Vol. XXXIV, Pt. II, 598. Major General Frederick Steele, in Arkansas, was of the opinion that the forces of Banks were sufficient for the Red River campaign. On March 10, 1864, he wrote to Grant, "The forces under Banks will make Kirby Smith run without a battle." He wrote to Sherman the same day: "The force you send, joined to Banks' 17,000, can drive all the troops in Kirby Smith's department into the Gulf." See *ibid.,* 546–47, for both letters.

[66] Report of Rear Admiral Porter, *Official Records, Navy,* Ser. I, Vol.

War and War Measures

Eastport arrived at Alexandria on March 15, and the next morning a force of 180 men landed to occupy the town. Rear Admiral Porter, on the flagship *Black Hawk*, arrived a few hours afterward. Five Confederate boats managed to escape over the falls just before the arrival of the Federal gunboats. Porter, in reporting on the incidents connected with the capture of Fort De Russy and Alexandria, said:

The efforts of these people to keep up this war remind one very much of the antics of Chinamen, who build canvas forts, paint hideous dragons on their shields, turn somersets, and yell in the faces of their enemies to frighten them, and then run away at the first sign of an engagement. . . . It is not the intention of these rebels to fight.[67]

Federal troops reached Alexandria shortly after the arrival of the gunboats. Brigadier General Joseph A. Mower, of Andrew J. Smith's command, arrived on March 16, while Smith with the remainder of his men reached the town on the eighteenth. Banks's army had been delayed in South Louisiana by storms, and the first contingent of these troops did not enter Alexandria until March 20. The Confederate forces under Richard Taylor having moved up toward Natchitoches, Brigadier General Mower was sent in pursuit. He and his men surprised the Second Louisiana Cavalry and a battery of light artillery, at Henderson's Hill, on Bayou Rapides, March 21, and captured them at their campfires without firing a shot. The prisoners taken numbered 252.[68] Banks arrived at Alexandria on March 24 and made his headquarters there. The remainder of his forces, under Major General William B. Franklin, arrived on March 25 and 26. On April 2 Banks wrote to Halleck:

XXVI, 24–26; Report of Major General John G. Walker, *Official Records,* Ser. I, Vol. XXXIV, Pt. I, 598–601.

[67] *Official Records, Navy,* Ser. I, Vol. XXVI, 29–30.

[68] Report of Major General Andrew J. Smith, *Official Records,* Ser. I, Vol. XXXIV, Pt. I, 304–12.

Louisiana in the Confederacy

Our troops now occupy Natchitoches, and we hope to be in Shreveport by the 10th of April. I do not fear concentration of the enemy at that point. My fear is that they may not be willing to meet us there; if not, and my forces are not weakened to too great an extent I shall pursue the enemy into the interior of Texas, for the sole purpose of destroying or dispersing his forces, if in my power.[69]

Nathaniel Banks was not destined to enjoy the hospitality of Shreveport. Major General Taylor, who had retreated from Alexandria and then from Natchitoches just before the arrival of the Federal forces, decided to block the way to Shreveport. Surrounded by a group of able and daring officers, among whom were Major Generals Walker and Green, and Brigadier Generals Mouton and Polignac, he chose a site three miles southeast of Mansfield, which was forty miles south of Shreveport, for the fight. Here, on April 8, occurred the battle of Mansfield—next to the battle of New Orleans, 1815, the most famous battle fought on Louisiana soil.

The country around Mansfield is hilly and wooded. Taylor formed his line of battle in the edge of a wood bordering on an open field about one thousand yards wide. Emerging from the woods on the other side of the field and running across it in the direction of Taylor's army, was the Mansfield–Pleasant Hill road over which the Federal army was marching toward Shreveport. Taylor placed his troops facing south on each side of the highway and waited the arrival of the enemy. The first sign of battle was a skirmish between cavalry forces, and the Confederate cavalry was driven back. After some maneuvering which convinced Taylor that the Federal preparations for battle were incomplete, the Confederate

[69] *Ibid.*, 179–80. Banks wrote to Mrs. Banks from Natchitoches, April 4: "The enemy retreats before and will not fight a battle this side of Shreveport, if then." N. P. Banks Papers (Essex Institute, Salem, Massachusetts. Microfilm copy in University of Texas Archives).

War and War Measures

commander, a Louisianian, ordered Brigadier General Mouton, another Louisianian, to open the attack.

Mansfield was a hotly contested and sanguinary battle. While official reports of the number engaged vary widely, it is safe to say that at least thirty thousand men participated. Among those killed was the beloved Louisianian, Brigadier General Alfred Mouton. Major General Taylor, in reporting the engagement said, "The charge made by Mouton across the open was magnificent." Besides General Mouton, Colonel Leopold Armant of the Eighteenth Louisiana, Colonel James H. Beard and Major Mercer Canfield, both of the Crescent Regiment, Lieutenant Colonel William Walker of the Twenty-eighth Louisiana, and Lieutenant Colonel Sebron Nobel of the Seventeenth Texas were killed. "Seven standard-bearers," General Taylor reported, "fell one after another with the flag of the Crescent Regiment." [70]

During the night following the battle of Mansfield the Federal forces retreated to Pleasant Hill, twenty-two miles southeast of Mansfield. The Confederates followed, and on the afternoon of April 9 the battle of Pleasant Hill was fought. This battle is famous because both sides retreated immediately after the contest, which action did not prevent either commander from claiming a victory.[71]

It matters not whether Major General Banks won a victory or suffered a defeat at Pleasant Hill on April 9. His advance

[70] *Official Records,* Ser. I, Vol. XXXIV, Pt. I, 560–72, Report of Major General Richard Taylor; see also Evans (ed.), *Confederate Military History,* X, 135–43.

[71] Both Banks and Taylor reported that they ordered a retreat to rest the exhausted soldiers and to find water. These reports are most interesting. The student wonders, as he compares them, if he is reading about the same engagement. Banks says, for instance: "We had fought the battle at Pleasant Hill with about 15,000 against 22,000 men and won a victory. . . ." Taylor says: "With 12,000 men we had attacked twenty odd thousand. . . . We had driven them at every point, and but for the mistake and consequent confusion on the right we would have captured most of his army." General Banks's report is found in *Official Records,* Ser. I, Vol. XXXIV, Pt. I, 194–218; for Taylor's report, see *ibid.,* 560–72.

to Shreveport was stopped and his Red River expedition was turned into a retreat. On April 25 he and his army re-entered Alexandria; on May 13 they left Alexandria behind them, as they began their retreat to the Mississippi. A Federal soldier wrote: "The Red River campaign was over and nothing left to show for it but the great waste of men and money it had cost." [72]

The Federal army was delayed for more than two weeks at Alexandria on its march southward because the low stage of water in the Red River made it impossible for the fleet of boats to pass over the falls there. The army remained at Alexandria to furnish protection to the fleet. The falls were finally passed by the boats after a dam was constructed by the army. Lieutenant Colonel Joseph Bailey, army engineer, planned and directed the construction of the dam. Rear Admiral Porter, commenting on Bailey's work, said, "This is without doubt the best engineering feat ever performed." [73]

Major General Banks's Federal contemporaries were very severe in their criticisms of his operations at Mansfield and Pleasant Hill. Rear Admiral Porter, at Grand Ecore, wrote to General Sherman on April 14: "The army has been shamefully beaten by the rebels. There is no disguising the fact, notwithstanding the general commanding and his staff try to make a victory. Armies victorious don't often go back as this one has done." Writing to Secretary Gideon Welles on the same date, Porter said: "The army here has met with a great defeat, no matter what the generals try to make of it. With the defeat has come demoralization, and it will take some time to reorganize and make up the deficences in killed and

[72] Lawrence Van Alstyne, *Diary of An Enlisted Man* (New Haven, 1910), 342–43.

[73] Rear Admiral Porter's report, giving a realistic description of the passing over the falls, with actual photographs of the dam, is found in *Official Records, Navy,* Ser. I, Vol. XXVI, 130–35. The above quotation is taken from page 132. Colonel Bailey's report on the construction of the dam is found in *Official Records,* Ser. I, Vol. XXXIV, Pt. I, 402–04.

prisoners. The whole affair has been seriously mismanaged."
Porter closed his letter to Secretary Welles with this sentence:
"I enclose two notes I received from General Banks and
Stone. There is a faint attempt to make a victory out of this,
but two or three such victories would cost us our existence."
General Grant wrote to Halleck on April 25:

General Banks ought to be ordered to New Orleans and have
all further execution on Red River in other hands. I have just
received two private letters, one from New Orleans, and one
(anonymous) from the Thirteenth Corps, giving deplorable accounts of General Banks' mismanagement. His own report and
these letters clearly show all his disasters to be attributable to his
incompetency.[74]

Although the Federal soldiers failed to capture Shreveport,
the chief object of the expedition, they succeeded in dealing
the people of Central Louisiana a crushing blow by devastat-
ing the section. The indiscriminate destruction of property
of all kinds between Grand Ecore and Alexandria, while the
Federals were retreating, was probably not surpassed anywhere during the Civil War. Their line of march could be
traced by evidence of burned residences, barns, negro cabins,
smokehouses, and cotton gins. "Dead animals—horses,
mules, cows, calves, and hogs—slain by the enemy," said a
contemporary, "were scattered along the road." [75] A Louisianian's diary of 1864 helps the modern student to form a
picture of the scenes of three quarters of a century ago:

[74] Porter to Sherman, *Official Records*, Ser. I, Vol. XXXIV, Pt. III, 153–54;
Porter to Welles, *Official Records, Navy*, Ser. I, Vol. XXVI, 45–48; Grant to
Halleck, *Official Records*, Ser. I, Vol. XXXIV, Pt. III, 279. Halleck wrote to
Sherman, April 20: "Banks' operations in the West are about what should
have been expected from a general so utterly destitute of military education
and military capacity." *Ibid.*, 332–33.

[75] Blessington, *The Campaigns of Walker's Texas Division*, 266; see also
the report of Major General Richard Taylor, April 24, 1864, *Official
Records*, Ser. I, Vol. XXXIV, Pt. I, 580–81. General Taylor said: "The
destruction of this country [between Grand Ecore and Monett's Ferry, a
distance of forty miles] by the enemy exceeds anything in history. . . ."

Louisiana in the Confederacy

May 2 . . . Camp 10 miles from Mansfield. Houses all full of wounded soldiers. . . . May 3 . . . Make another early start. Mansfield a huge hospital. Quite a town. . . . May 5 . . . The battle field of Pleasant Hill shows some hard fighting. Dead horses graves trees torn and shot to pieces shows one of the desperate struggles of this unholy war. . . . May 7 . . . Start for Natchitoches. Cloudy. A desolate country, Campti Grand Ecore burned—also Colonel Hyams' and other places. Fences gone. Yankee graves on the road side. Stores and persons robbed. Church and Bishop dispoiled. . . . May 23 . . . Texans of Walker's Division driving off beef cattle. Between the Yanks and Confeds people in this section will be starved. So much for military rule. . . . June 9 . . . Reach Monroe a little after 12. Things look like all war places. Courthouse, R. R. bridge and depot and jail burned up. . . .[76]

Some of the acts of the troops were nothing less than petty vandalism. A resident of Loggy Bayou on Red River, approximately halfway between Grand Ecore and Shreveport, wrote this letter to the editor of a Shreveport newspaper, April 17, 1864:

On last Sunday, the 10th inst., the vandal yankee fleet made their appearance at this place, at about 2 o'clock, p.m. They commenced shelling in every direction. . . . As soon as the boat was made fast (the one that came nearest to my house,) about thirty of the vandals came into my yard and commenced a wholesale slaughter of poultries; they did not leave me a chicken to crow for day; killed hens that had been setting two weeks, and took eggs that had been set on for more than two weeks; broke open my smoke-house, took every piece of meat and two barrels of meal; went into the garden, took up every thing that could be used and destroyed that that could not be used; went into my shop, broke and destroyed all my tools; came into my house, took all the clothes that they wanted, took one gun and broke

[76] Diary of William H. Tunnard (MS. in possession of his granddaughter, Mrs. H. T. Gladney, Shreveport, Louisiana). For the destruction of property at Monroe, see report of Lieutenant Commander James P. Foster, U.S. Navy, in *Official Records, Navy*, Ser. I, Vol. XXVI, 236–37.

it to pieces and carried another off; yet I fared well to what some of my neighbors did. When I have more time, I may give you a history.

> In Haste,
> I am respectfully,
> One Who Suffered.[77]

Former Governor Moore wrote to a friend on June 27, 1864, that the Federals "did me all the injury they can, both my sugar mills and engines, and my engines to my gin and corn mill, were all broken to pieces before the torch was applied." His house in Rapides Parish was pillaged, and "we did not save as much as a blanket." "Not a hog, cow or sheep left," wrote Louisiana's "secession" governor, and added, "My places perfect wastes and very difficult to get anything to eat." [78]

The destruction of property by the Federal soldiers was not always with the approval of the commanding officers. At Alexandria, on April 27, Major General Franklin of the Federal army issued an order charging that the "advance" of the army from Grand Ecore to Alexandria had been "accompanied by indiscriminate marauding and incendiarism, disgraceful to the army of a civilized nation," and offered a reward of $500 for information leading to the conviction of parties guilty of incendiarism.[79]

It ought to be said, however, that not all the pillaging was

[77] Published in the Shreveport *News*, April 26, 1864. Rear Admiral Porter tells us why the Federal fleet did not continue the journey up Red River. "When I arrived at Springfield Landing I found a sight that made me laugh. It was the smartest thing I ever knew the rebels to do. They had gotten that huge steamer, *New Falls City*, across Red River, 1 mile above Loggy Bayou, 15 feet of her on shore on each side, the boat broken down in the middle, and a sandbar making below. An invitation in large letters to attend a ball in Shreveport was kindly left stuck up by the rebels, which invitation we were never able to accept." *Official Records, Navy*, Ser. I, Vol. XXVI, 60.

[78] Thomas O. Moore to Dr. Bartholomew Egan, June 27, 1864 (MS. in the Lavinia Egan Collection, Mount Lebanon, Louisiana).

[79] *Official Records*, Ser. I, Vol. XXXIV, Pt. III, 307.

the act of Federal soldiers. Confederates sometimes helped themselves to the property of citizens. Property was taken off by Confederate soldiers to use or to prevent it from falling into the hands of the Union army. A South Louisiana planter in December, 1862, complained of the lack of discipline and the disregard of private property among the troops of Brigadier General Mouton's command. "They have left on my plantation," he said, "devastation and desolation behind them." [80] A Federal soldier in March, 1864, wrote from Alexandria to the St. Louis *Republican:* "The rebels, when they left here, stripped the country districts of nearly everything of value that could be carried off." [81] Thus, the civilian population suffered at the hands of both armies. G. Purnell Whittington, who made a thorough study of war activities in Central Louisiana, said of Major General John G. Walker's Texas division:

Walker's troops were about as welcome as the Union Army to the citizens of the part of the State in which they operated. They committed almost as many depredations as the enemy, with the exception of General A. J. Smith and the 16th and 17th Army Corps that were loaned by Sherman for the second expedition. . . . These Texas men were good soldiers, brave and daring, and as fearless as one could desire, but they would confiscate property as badly as any Union soldier who ever served in this section.[82]

A considerable portion of Alexandria was burned on May 13, the day the Federals evacuated the town. The writer has no conclusive evidence to submit as to the responsibility for the burning of this town. Banks says that the rumor had been circulated in camp that Alexandria would be burned. Meas-

[80] Diary entry for December 19, 1862, Palfrey (William T. and George D.) Collection (Louisiana State University Department of Archives). An entry for September 22, 1863, reads: "We are now left at the mercy of the enemy, after being pretty well stripped by our own troops."

[81] Quoted in the New Orleans *Daily True Delta,* April 24, 1864.

[82] Whittington, "Rapides Parish, Louisiana—A History," in *loc. cit.,* XVIII (1935), 9–10.

ures were taken, therefore, he says, to prevent a conflagration. But on the morning of the evacuation, "a fire broke out in a building on the levee, which had been occupied by refugees or soldiers," said Banks, "in such a manner as to make it impossible to prevent a general conflagration." He said that he saw the fire when it was first discovered, and that the Federal soldiers "labored with alacrity and vigor to suppress the conflagration." A high wind and the combustible material of the buildings (according to Banks) made it impossible to check the fire.[83]

Lawrence Van Alstyne, a Federal soldier who was in Alexandria at the time, blames the burning of the town on jayhawkers who had assembled near Alexandria. "The Jayhawkers kept their promise to burn the place rather than have it go into the hands of the enemy again." [84] A Confederate soldier, who arrived in Pineville, across the Red River from Alexandria, on May 22 and remained there until June 4, said a decade later that Alexandria was burned by the Negro troops of the Federals.[85] Finally, to quote Whittington again:

These are the facts as they come down to us some 67 years after the event, and they clearly point to the fact that Alexandria was destroyed by the Union army under the command of General Nathaniel P. Banks. The actual work was done by the men of the 16th and 17th Army Corps under the command of General A. J. Smith; but had Banks tried he could have prevented the destruction.[86]

When the Federal army retreated down Red River below Alexandria, the forces of Major General Taylor pursued it;

---

[83] *Official Records*, Ser. I, Vol. XXXIV, Pt. I, 212.

[84] Van Alstyne, *Diary of An Enlisted Man*, 320.

[85] Blessington, *Campaigns of Walker's Texas Division*, 266, 267.

[86] Whittington, "Rapides Parish, Louisiana—A History," in *loc. cit.*, 38. For statements and affidavits of citizens of Alexandria concerning the burning of the town, see *Official Report Relative to the Conduct of Federal Troops in Western Louisiana During the Invasions of 1863 and 1864*, pp. 70–85.

and engagements occurred at several places, notably at Mansura on May 16, and at Yellow Bayou two days later. On May 19 the Union forces crossed the Atchafalaya, and the Red River expedition was at an end. Taylor, writing at Moreauville, near the Atchafalaya, on May 19, said: "The campaign may be considered as closed here, where it opened on the 12th of last March. It has been a most arduous one to me and to this army. The limits of human and equine endurance have been reached." [87]

Major military operations in Louisiana ended with the conclusion of the Red River campaign in May, 1864. Both the Federal and Confederate governments withdrew troops from the state to engage in campaigns elsewhere. There were occasional skirmishes in South and Southeast Louisiana when Federal scouting parties or other forces would advance from Brashear City, Baton Rouge, or some other concentration point. But no engagement involving a large number of men took place. One of the most successful of these minor expeditions of the Federals was sent out from Baton Rouge in October, 1864. The party consisted of one thousand cavalry under Brigadier General Albert Lee. They "visited" Clinton, Greensburg, and Camp Moore, captured fifty-one Confederates and more than two hundred horses and mules, burned a tannery and two thousand sides of leather, and destroyed a large amount of Confederate clothing and gray cloth.[88]

Important changes in personnel were made in each army. The Federal Government created the Military Division of West Mississippi, embracing the Department of the Gulf. Major General E. R. S. Canby assumed command of this new unit on May 11, 1864, with headquarters in New Orleans. Major General A. J. Smith, whose ten thousand men had been loaned to Banks for the Red River campaign, returned

[87] *Official Records,* Ser. I, Vol. XXXIV, Pt. I, 594–95.
[88] Reports of Major General Stephen A. Hurlbut and Brigadier General Albert L. Lee, *ibid.,* Ser. I, Vol. XLI, Pt. I, 880–82.

with his force to Vicksburg, which he reached on May 23. Banks remained in New Orleans until September, when he was succeeded as commander of the Department of the Gulf by Major General Stephen A. Hurlbut. Major General Simon B. Buckner of the Confederate army was assigned to command the District of West Louisiana in August. Richard Taylor, who had been promoted to lieutenant general, was relieved of duty in the Trans-Mississippi Department and assigned to command the Department of Alabama, Mississippi, and East Louisiana.[89]

[89] *Ibid.,* Ser. I, Vol. XXXIV, Pt. I, 6, 312; Ser. I, Vol. XLI, Pt. II, 1039, 1066, Pt. III, 297.

Chapter VI

Politics and State Finances

THERE WERE, IN effect, two governments and two administrations in Louisiana after the Federal occupation of New Orleans. The city passed under Federal military rule, and Confederate authority was never more than nominal there after April, 1862. What was true of New Orleans applied also, though not always in the same degree, to the territory adjacent to the city. Generally speaking, the parishes of St. Bernard, Plaquemines, Jefferson, St. John the Baptist, St. Charles, St. James, Ascension, Assumption, Terrebonne, Lafourche, St. Mary, St. Martin, and Orleans, along the Gulf coast from the Atchafalaya to Lake Borgne, and on either side of the Mississippi from the Gulf to Baton Rouge, were subject to Federal rule and lay outside the sphere of Confederate administration. For instance, they were excepted from the operation of President Lincoln's Emancipation Proclamation of January 1, 1863.[1] These parishes (except St. Martin) and the parish of East Baton Rouge were included in a Federal military draft in December, 1864.[2] These thirteen or fourteen parishes, therefore, were treated by the Federal Government as practically restored to the Union. From the viewpoint of the Confederate Government this territory was "unredeemed" Louisiana, subject in theory to Confederate laws but temporarily under enemy control.

[1] James D. Richardson, *Compilation of the Messages and Papers of the Presidents* (Washington, 1896–1899), VI, 158.

[2] *Annual Cyclopaedia*, V (1865), 508–09.

Politics and State Finances

Civil affairs in the "Union" portion of Louisiana will be discussed in a subsequent chapter. The purpose of this and the next chapter is to discuss the affairs of that section of the state under the government of officials acknowledging allegiance to the Confederate Constitution. The distinction, however, cannot always be maintained. In the first place, the distinction did not exist until almost the middle of 1862. In the second place, the fortunes of war resulted in the changing of "boundaries," and some parishes were "border" parishes, practically subject to dual control. Finally, economic conditions know no political boundaries, and it is not feasible to recognize any in discussing some subjects.

Politics of the ordinary sort took a vacation in Louisiana during the war. Political parties were virtually nonexistent, and election campaigns (with the possible exception of the election of 1864 in the Union section of the state) were tame affairs as compared to those of the ante-bellum days. The people had little interest in mere politics when their attention was fixed upon military movements which might mean devastation and ruin to themselves and their children.

According to the state constitution as amended in 1861, members of the Legislature were to be elected in November. Representatives were elected for two years, and state senators enjoyed a four-year term. The House was to consist of not more than one hundred nor less than seventy members, and there were to be thirty-two senators. The regular session of the Legislature was limited to sixty days. The governor's term was four years; he was to enter office on the fourth Monday of January following his election in November, and he was ineligible to succeed himself. The governor had the power of veto, and his veto could be overridden by a two-thirds vote of each branch of the Legislature.[3]

The first regular election in Louisiana in the Confederate era occurred on November 4, 1861. Certain officers, includ-

[3] *Journal of the Louisiana Convention,* 1861, pp. 298–309.

179

ing state treasurer, auditor, superintendent of public instruction, and state legislators, parish officials, and members of the lower house of the Confederate Congress were elected. The election campaign was very quiet, judging from newspaper records. Various announcements of candidates appeared in the columns of the press, and now and then a newspaper would speak a word in favor of some particular candidate. A few weeks before the election a Shreveport newspaper said: "Notwithstanding the election is now only two weeks off, there appears not the least excitement or interest felt about it. We most sincerely hope that the most honest and most capable (matters not what party they have heretofore acted with) may be selected to fill the various offices."[4] Down in New Orleans on the morning of November 4 the *Crescent* reminded its readers that it was election day, that the tickets before the people contained names of "good men and true, and no one can go wrong in making a selection"; however, the newspaper made special reference to the ticket of the Southern American party as "one that could hardly be improved upon." On the day after the election the *Crescent* remarked: "The election yesterday passed off very quietly—more quietly than any election which has taken place in the city for years past. We searched through the city for a single item of the kind usually occurring on election days without success."[5] The Shreveport *South-Western* of November 6 observed: "Last Monday the election for State and parish officers passed off very quietly."

Members of the Confederate House of Representatives were elected at this time to serve for a two-year term from February, 1862, to February, 1864. The representatives elected by the Louisiana voters were Charles M. Conrad, Lucius J. Dupre, Duncan F. Kenner, Henry Marshall, John Perkins, Jr., and Charles J. Villere.[6] The state Legislature elected Confederate

[4] Shreveport *South-Western*, October 23, 1861.
[5] New Orleans *Daily Crescent*, November 5, 1861.
[6] *Official Records*, Ser. IV, Vol. III, 1188.

Politics and State Finances

senators on November 28, 1861. On the first ballot the vote was as follows:

T. J. Semmes, of Orleans	51
J. P. Benjamin, of Orleans	45
Edward Sparrow, of Concordia	37
Alexander Declouet, of St. Tammany	30
A. S. Herron, of East Baton Rouge	19
A. Mouton, of Lafayette	18
D. F. Kenner, of Ascension	14
J. G. Olivier, of St. Martin	11
B. L. Hodge, of Caddo	10
T. Land, of Caddo	8

Edward Sparrow received 65 votes on the second ballot (62 were necessary for election) and was declared elected. On the fourth ballot Declouet received 50 votes, Benjamin 9, and Semmes 64. Semmes was declared elected.[7]

Opelousas, fifty-five miles due west of Baton Rouge, was chosen as the temporary residence of the state officials in May, 1862; and the Legislature was in session there in December, 1862, and January, 1863. An act of this session of the Legislature, approved January 3, 1863, said: "That the Seat of Government of the State of Louisiana shall be removed from Baton Rouge to the town of Shreveport, in the parish of Caddo, and there remain during the continuance of the war."[8] The first meeting of the Legislature in Shreveport was in May, 1863. This was an extra session, called by Governor Moore. Regular sessions of the Legislature were held in Shreveport in January of 1864 and 1865.

It became necessary, after the Federal invasion and occupation of a portion of the state, to amend the election laws. The second regular election of the war period was due to be in November, 1863. The Legislature, therefore, at the special

[7] These election figures are taken from the New Orleans *Daily Crescent* of December 2, 1861.

[8] Louisiana *Acts*, 1862–1863, p. 30.

181

session in Shreveport in May of that year, undertook to modify the election laws to correspond to existing conditions. According to an act approved June 12, in the approaching November election "every citizen of the State, who has not forfeited his citizenship by electing to adhere to the Government of the United States, and who shall be otherwise qualified according to law, shall be entitled to vote." With reference to the approaching election in November, the act also declared that "such election shall only be held in those portions of the State, not under the control of the United States or the army or armies thereof." [9]

A few days later the Legislature adopted a measure that declared vacant all district, parish, and municipal offices whose incumbents had at any time since January 26, 1861, taken an oath to support the Government or the Constitution of the United States, or had in any way declared allegiance to the United States, or had given aid, comfort, information or support to the United States.[10] Another act required any person "hereafter elected or appointed to any State, district, parish or municipal office" to take an oath that he had not, since January 26, 1861, taken an oath to support the Government or Constitution of the United States, nor given any aid, support or information for the benefit of the enemy. A similar measure provided for the taking of the same oath when a person offering to vote was challenged, or if the election commissioner was in doubt as to the voter's eligibility.[11]

Confederate authority in Louisiana began to wane in the last year of the war. When Banks invaded the interior of the state in 1864, and it appeared that his occupation was to be

---

[9] Louisiana *Acts*, Extra Sess., 1863, pp. 9–10. The "otherwise qualified according to law" referred, of course, to the requirements of the state constitution, which conferred the suffrage upon every free white male, twenty-one years old, who had been a resident of the state twelve months and of the parish six months, and who was a citizen of the United States on January 26, 1861. See the *Journal of the Louisiana Convention*, 1861, p. 299.

[10] Louisiana *Acts*, Extra Sess., 1863, p. 11.   [11] *Ibid.*, 11–12, 14.

permanent, many persons, as will be shown later, flocked to his camp and took the oath of allegiance to the United States. Desertions from the Confederate army also increased in the last months of the struggle. The authorities remaining loyal to the Confederate cause found themselves on the defensive and were forced to take stringent measures to maintain the cause which they held dear. The following oath required of commissioners of elections, included in an act of the Louisiana Legislature, adopted February 3, 1865, will give some idea of the condition of affairs:

I ——— do solemnly swear (or affirm) that I have not, at any time since the 26th day of January, 1861, given any aid, information or support to the Government of the United States, to any of its officers or soldiers, or to any other person for the benefit of the enemy, or denounced, accused, or betrayed before any of the United States authorities, any of my fellow-citizens on account of his or their loyalty to the Confederate States, nor have I at any time since the same date, either accepted or fulfilled any military, naval, civil or municipal, State or Federal office of any kind or degree under or by the authority of the United States Government, nor will I willingly permit any person known or suspected by me to have been guilty of the aforesaid disloyal acts, or any of them, to vote, without challenge, at any precinct in which I preside as one of the commissioners of election, so help me God! [12]

On the day following the adoption of the above act the Legislature passed a measure providing that when election commissioners were in doubt concerning the qualifications of a person offering to vote, the voter should be required to take the same oath prescribed for election commissioners, except, of course, that part pertaining to the actual duties of commissioners.[13]

Governor Thomas O. Moore was elected for a four-year term in 1859. He assumed the duties of the office in January, 1860. His term was to expire in January, 1864, and he was

[12] Louisiana *Acts*, 1865, pp. 23–24.   [13] *Ibid.*, 34.

not eligible to succeed himself. The election of November, 1863, therefore, was of more than usual interest, or should have been, since a new governor, as well as other state officers, and Confederate congressmen were to be chosen. State officials, other than governor and lieutenant governor, were eligible to re-election; and most of the administration were candidates to succeed themselves. The Shreveport *Semi-Weekly News,* in commenting on a "State Ticket" which it presented to its readers, said: "The names are familiar to all, and have been selected from the fact that they were the choice of the people before the present situation, and should be re-elected. We presume the ticket will give general satisfaction." [14]

The leading candidates for governor were Brigadier General Henry Watkins Allen and Colonel Leroy Stafford. Allen's home was in West Baton Rouge Parish, and Stafford was a resident of Rapides. Neither seems to have waged an active campaign and it appears to have been a case of the office seeking the man. A political notice in the *Semi-Weekly News,* signed "Many of All Parties," announced Colonel Stafford as a candidate for governor and asserted that Stafford was a veteran of Jackson and Lee, of twenty-three pitched battles, and "on seven of the bloodiest fields commanding his brigade." [15] The Alexandria *Louisiana Democrat* announced about three weeks before the election that General Allen was in town and added:

It is of course known to General Allen that the people of this State have now in prospect his elevation to the Gubernatorial chair. He will neither seek, nor decline the place. If his fellow citizens shall call him to this honorable position, he will not disregard their wishes, and if on the other hand they shall leave him in the discharge of his present duties, he will continue to serve the country as well as the wounds already received in that service

[14] Shreveport *Semi-Weekly News,* August 25, 1863.
[15] *Ibid.,* October 20, 1863.

Politics and State Finances

will permit. We say this by authority. We have expressed the belief that his administrative capacity, his known force of character, and his cool judgment admirably fit him for this high place.[16]

The result of the election was a landslide for Allen. The official count[17] of the ballots showed the following: Allen, 7,401; Leroy Stafford, 872; J. W. McDonald, 260; Benjamin L. Hodge, 21; Leonidas Polk, 26; John M. Sandidge, 3. Other officials elected were Benjamin W. Pearce, lieutenant governor; Henry D. Hardy, secretary of state; F. S. Goode, attorney general; Hypolite Perolta, auditor of public accounts; B. L. Defresse, state treasurer; W. H. N. Magruder, superintendent of public instruction.[18]

As mentioned previously, the election laws of 1863 provided that the election would be held only in that portion of the state free from United States military control. It is of interest to note in this connection that the House of Representatives on January 19, 1864, voted to seat those old members of the House who were present and who were from parishes in which it had been impossible to hold elections "in consequence of the presence of the enemy." The following were seated under the terms of this resolution: James Foulhouze of Plaquemines Parish, Robert Mott of Orleans, J. B. Robertson of St. Mary, E. F. Morehead of Ascension. Forty-eight members had been elected from twenty-nine parishes. Twenty-five was declared to be a quorum.[19]

We have now to consider Louisiana's fiscal policies subsequent to the Federal occupation of New Orleans and vicinity

[16] Alexandria *Louisiana Democrat*, October 14, 1863.

[17] The official election count as decided by the General Assembly. Louisiana *House Journal*, 1864, pp. 14–15.

[18] *Ibid.* The Congressional election and the issues involved are discussed in the chapter entitled "Relations with the Confederacy."

[19] *Ibid.*, 5. Evidently, nineteen parishes did not participate in the election. One senator, Thomas H. Weightman, representing the parishes of Ascension, Assumption, and Terrebonne, which were under Federal military control, served in this Legislature. See Louisiana *Senate Journal*, 1864, p. 1.

in 1862. If secession, new political alignments, and military preparations had created problems of no little importance, invasion and occupation of a portion of the state and constant military raids and expeditions into the interior, with much destruction of property, had increased and aggravated the difficulties.

It will be recalled that the Legislature in January, 1862, recognized the existence of an emergency by suspending the compulsory payment of state taxes, except licenses on trades, professions, and occupations, until February 1, 1863. This was to be repeated more than once. When the Legislature met in Opelousas, the property owner was no better off than he had been the year before. With a portion of the state, including the metropolis and the capital, under the military occupation of the enemy, and the rest of the state threatened, business in general was anything but prosperous. Accordingly, the Legislature in January, 1863, adopted another measure postponing the collection of state taxes. The act provided that the payment of state taxes "by compulsory process" be suspended until February 1, 1864, with the proviso, as in 1862, that the act did not apply to licenses on trades, professions, or occupations.[20] At the same time sheriffs and state tax collectors who had failed to "effect their final settlement" with the state for taxes and licenses were granted an extension of time. This act applied to taxes of 1860 and 1861 and to licenses for 1861 and 1862.[21]

Governor Moore, in his last annual message in January, 1864, told the Legislature that, because of the acts suspending the compulsory collection of taxes, the ordinary revenue of the state had not been "exigible for her expenditures." The taxes were accumulating each year and must ultimately be paid. "The people were never better able to pay their taxes than now," he said. He opposed, therefore, any further suspension of the collection of taxes. He recommended,

[20] Louisiana *Acts*, 1862–1863, p. 20. [21] *Ibid.*, 15.

moreover, that the issuing of treasury notes cease "as soon as practicable," since such a policy resulted in inflation.[22]

Governor Moore was the retiring executive, and his message probably had little weight with the Legislature. On January 25 he returned to private life, and Allen became Louisiana's chief executive. On February 9 the Legislature adopted the third tax moratorium, suspending the payment by compulsory process of all state taxes, except licenses on trades, etc., until February 1, 1865. The members of the Legislature evidently had some doubts about the ability of the Confederate military authorities to protect Shreveport from attack in the months ahead. This particular act contained the following provision: "Provided, however, if there should be no regular annual session of the Legislature previous to that time, February 1, 1865, then and in that event, the suspension of taxes herein provided for, shall continue until the next meeting of the Legislature thereafter." [23]

Early in 1865 the Legislature changed its tax policy and undertook to adopt more stringent measures for the collection of taxes. An act of February 4 declared it the duty of tax collectors to "proceed to collect the taxes provided for under existing laws." State assessments of taxes made for the years 1860, 1861, and 1864 "shall be collected during the year 1865." There were a number of exceptions, however, to the operation of the act. Persons who had paid any or all of their taxes for 1862 and 1863 should be relieved from the payment of that amount for the years 1860, 1861, and 1864. That is, such persons were to be credited on their tax statements for 1860, 1861, 1864, taken together, for the amount of taxes paid for 1862 and 1863. The act did not apply to taxable property within "that portion of the State held or occupied by the military authorities of the United States," or to lands

[22] Louisiana *House Journal*, 1864, p. 6; Shreveport *Semi-Weekly News*, February 2, 1864. Governor Moore's message was also printed separately. There is a copy in the Confederate Memorial Museum, New Orleans.

[23] Louisiana *Acts*, 1864, pp. 21–22.

formerly used for agricultural purposes, now abandoned by owners, or rendered unproductive by the loss of slaves. Collection of taxes upon all such property, except voluntary payments, was suspended until February 1, 1866. Furthermore, the act declared that the property of soldiers or sailors of the state or Confederate States should not be forfeited to the state, or seized and sold for taxes due, during the existence of the war.[24]

It is safe to assume that the state of Louisiana received very little revenue from taxes in the years 1862–1865. It was necessary, therefore, to depend upon the issue of treasury notes and the sale of bonds. The reader will remember that the first issue of treasury notes was authorized by the Legislature in January, 1862, to the amount of $2,000,000. This amount was issued.[25]

There was opposition and refusal to accept these notes on the part of some citizens. This was especially true after the fall of New Orleans, when the Confederate cause appeared to be less auspicious. At Opelousas, in July, 1862, Governor Moore issued several orders on the subject, one of which was a military order, under his authority as commander-in-chief of the militia. He directed the arrest of persons in Calcasieu and Vermilion parishes who had refused to receive state and Confederate treasury notes. Two persons were specifically named as guilty of the offense. "These parties and all others who thus refuse the aforesaid notes," an executive decree said, "are considered and are enemies to the Southern Confederacy and its causes and should be dealt with accordingly." A military order commanded the arrest and imprisonment of such persons, who, according to the order, should be required

[24] Louisiana *Acts*, 1865, pp. 54–55.

[25] Louisiana *House Journal*, 1864, p. 6; Shreveport *Semi-Weekly News*, February 2, 1864. Some revenue was obtained from the sale of public lands. See Treasurer's Office Records, State of Louisiana, 1859–1865. Records of the War Department, Confederate Records, Chapter 8, Vol. 125 (microfilm copy possessed by the writer).

to take the oath of allegiance and warned not to commit the offense again.[26]

State income for the year 1863 was derived almost entirely from the issue of treasury notes. Early in January of that year the Legislature adopted an act "For the Relief of the State Treasury." The governor was authorized and directed to have issued noninterest-bearing state treasury notes, in denominations of not less than $5 nor more than $100, to an amount not exceeding $20,000,000. These notes were made receivable in the payment of all state, parish, and municipal taxes, and all other public debts, as well as for the sale of public lands. They were made redeemable twelve months after a "definite treaty of peace between the Confederate States and the United States." [27] Governor Moore, as indicated previously, opposed the further issuance of treasury notes and recommended that the taxes be collected. The adoption of his recommendations would necessitate resort to the sale of bonds, he said, to supply the deficiency of revenue "occasioned by our inability to collect taxes in that portion of the State which is occupied by the enemy." [28]

Governor Allen on the day after his inauguration presented the Legislature with a message that was remarkable for its vigorous style, its reasonings, and the variety of its constructive recommendations. It deserves a special place of distinction among the state papers of Louisiana. There will be frequent occasions to refer to it later. The topic of interest here is Allen's discussion of the currency.

The governor approached the topic with two questions: "What Depreciates Confederate Money?" and "How is the Matter to be Remedied?" He began by saying that Confederate Treasury notes "are not so much depreciated as many seemed to think," and argued that contraction of the currency

[26] *Official Records,* Ser. I, Vol. XV, 772–73; Ser. II, Vol. IV, 804–05.

[27] Louisiana *Acts,* 1862–1863, pp. 29–30.

[28] Louisiana *House Journal,* 1864, p. 6; Shreveport *Semi-Weekly News,* February 2, 1864.

would not reduce the price of any one article then most needed. Scarcity of the article, not the abundance of currency, he contended, had raised the price of the former and had not depreciated the currency. Land and corn were about as cheap as before the war because there was plenty on the market, but Negroes and horses were about three times as high because they were very scarce, and nails and axes and cooking utensils were "almost worth their weight in gold" because they were not to be had at all. Corn was worth $2 a bushel; but the gallon of whiskey which it would make was worth $100, "not because the Confederate money is so bad, but because the bad whiskey is so scarce." Continuing the discussion with special reference to the remedy, Governor Allen said:

The only method, in my judgment, to benefit the currency is to follow the example that has been set us by Texas. Encourage manufactories of all kinds. Bend all your energies to the manufacturing of every article needed at home or in the field.

. . . Call into requisition every idle man and woman in the State, who wants work. If necessary take every fifth negro woman, and put her at the loom, and take every fifth negro man and put him into the shop, and, in a few short months, you will find a far different state of things. Ploughs and hoes, and axes, and cooking utensils, shoes and boots, and hats and clothing of every kind will all be as cheap as they were before the war began. Stock the market well with these necessary articles, and then Confederate money will buy as much as gold and silver did in former days.[29]

Evidently Governor Allen made use of high prices and the general discontent over a depreciated currency to approach a question which he considered of utmost importance—the encouragement of industry. That he did recognize a danger in inflation and was opposed to a continued policy of issuing

---

[29] Louisiana *House Journal*, 1864, p. 34; Shreveport *Semi-Weekly News,* January 29, 1864.

treasury notes is proved by his remarks in the latter part of his message. He was aware, he said, that there was too much Confederate money in circulation; and he hoped that there would be a curtailment. He recommended that Louisiana do her duty by calling in every dollar of state money, so that the currency would be uniform and there would be no "invidious comparisons" between state and Confederate notes. He advocated a law permitting persons holding state treasury notes to come forward in a given time and receive state bonds for the notes, payable in twenty years after peace was made, interest payable annually in Confederate Treasury notes. He also recommended that, when the state needed money, the governor be authorized to issue state bonds to be negotiated for the Confederate Treasury notes. "My object," he said, "is to withdraw entirely from circulation State notes, and in lieu thereof substitute those of the Confederacy."

Another recommendation of the message was that all corporations should be compelled to call in their issues of notes and redeem them in ninety days, and that the state treasurer be required to issue $500,000 in change notes, from ten cents up to a dollar. In this connection the governor remarked:

At present the merchants and shopkeepers, bakers and butchers, have on hand a large amount of uncurrent Parish paper, and the citizen who takes a journey through the State returns home with his pocket filled with this un-uniform currency. This should not be the case. . . . The change notes can be made redeemable at the Treasurer's office, in Confederate notes, when the sum of ten dollars is presented.[30]

The Legislature proceeded to enact several measures in line with Governor Allen's recommendations. The first of these acts, adopted February 8, authorized the governor to issue 6 per cent bonds to the amount of $10,000,000, interest payable semiannually. Bonds were to be made payable at

[30] Louisiana *House Journal,* 1864, p. 33; Shreveport *Semi-Weekly News,* January 29, 1864.

the expiration of not less than twenty nor more than forty years, at the discretion of the governor, provided that the amount payable in any one year should not exceed $1,000,000. Bonds were not to be sold for less than par.

The act provided also for the cancellation of state treasury notes. As the bonds were sold, the governor should "cause to be cancelled an equal amount of State treasury notes, then in the Treasury, equal to the amount realized from the sale or exchange of the said bonds." It was made the duty of the auditor and the state treasurer to create a sinking fund to meet the interest and the principal by crediting such a fund with 33⅓ per cent of the taxes collected. The sinking fund was to be invested in safe and well-secured bonds, bearing a rate of interest of not less than 6 per cent; and the "said fund is hereby declared sacred for the purposes contemplated by this act and shall only be applied thereto." [31]

The next of this series of acts authorized the governor to suspend the issuing of treasury notes when he thought it proper to do so. As soon as the sale of bonds provided funds sufficient for the needs of the treasury, the issuing of treasury notes was to cease "and the whole of them shall be cancelled." The act declared, however, that "nothing in this act shall prevent the re-issuing or compel the cancellation of any Treasury notes of denominations less than five dollars." [32]

Finally, the Legislature completed its strictly financial legislation by the adoption of an act authorizing and requiring the state treasurer to issue the sum of $300,000 in change treasury notes in denominations of twenty-five cents, fifty cents, and one dollar.[33] In connection with the change notes, Governor Allen in his message to the Legislature in January, 1865, said: "This well-timed supply of change has proved a great relief to the public, at small expense. The object of the law has been accomplished most admirably, since all local

---

[31] Louisiana *Acts,* 1864, pp. 11–12.   [32] *Ibid.,* 22.
[33] *Ibid.,* 72. The date of this act was February 11.

and corporation small notes have been withdrawn from circulation."[34]

Governor Allen opened the sale of state bonds on February 23, 1864. A bond sale notice was published in Louisiana (outside of Federal occupation) and Texas newspapers. Sealed bids were received, and the bonds were awarded to the highest bidder, "at the discretion of the Governor." According to the executive announcement, the sealed bids would be opened on the first Monday of every month until September 1, 1864.[35] But the sale of state bonds was disappointing. Governor Allen reported to the Legislature in January, 1865: "I have had occasion to sell only to the amount of $571,940." The proceeds of the sales were used to draw in state treasury notes, in accordance with the law.[36]

The withdrawal of a little more than one half million dollars of state treasury notes could not have had much effect in improving the situation in regard to a depreciated currency. Governor Allen soon realized that the sale of bonds would not prove a relief; and he adopted a method which, along with other constructive policies, has led a modern Southern editor to say: "Allen was the single great administrator produced by the Confederacy. His success in Louisiana indicates that he might have changed history to some extent if his talents could have been utilized by the Confederate government on a large scale."[37] Allen himself said of his method to improve the currency:

[34] *Annual Message of Governor Henry Watkins Allen*, January, 1865. Allen's message is found also in Louisiana *House Journal*, 1865, pp. 4–18. The Shreveport *Semi-Weekly News* of January 31, 1865, gives a résumé of the message.

[35] Shreveport *Semi-Weekly News*, February 23, 1864.

[36] *Annual Message of Governor Henry Watkins Allen*, January, 1865; Louisiana *House Journal*, 1865, p. 5; Treasurer's Office Records, State of Louisiana, 1859–1865. Records of the War Department, Confederate Records, Chapter 8, Vol. 125, p. 252.

[37] Article on Henry Watkins Allen by Douglas Southall Freeman in the *Dictionary of American Biography*, I, 193.

Louisiana in the Confederacy

When entering upon the duties of my office, I found the currency of the State very much depreciated. Farmers, merchants, butchers, bakers, mechanics, all refused to take it. Notwithstanding it was well known that the State was amply able to redeem her circulation, still her paper was in bad repute, and its exchangeable value daily declining. Much concerned at this, I earnestly sought a remedy. After mature reflection, I determined to establish a State Store, to sell cheap goods to the public, and to take payment in our depreciated currency. This has served a double purpose. It has drawn in from circulation a large amount of State notes, thus increasing the exchangeable value of the remainder, and has supplied our fellow citizens with articles of necessity, at prices comparatively moderate.[38]

Douglas S. Freeman said with reference to Allen's efforts to enhance the value of the currency: "By accepting Louisiana money at the state stores, he largely restored its value; and Confederate currency, almost worthless elsewhere, had purchasing power west of the Mississippi." [39]

Governor Allen told the Legislature that the state store at Shreveport had paid into the treasury from sales the sum of $425,249.61, besides giving to destitute wounded soldiers and to orphans and widows goods to the value of $22,159.50. The goods had been imported from Mexico and paid for in cotton. According to the governor's report the state had spent in his administration the sum of $6,247,979. A large proportion of the expenditures, he said, "is represented by valuable stores, advancing in market price, and more available than Treasury Notes to meet the future wants of the State." These goods consisted of cotton, sugar, "subsistence" stores, drugs, and medicines, amounting to $5,510,000, "all of which have been paid for." [40]

[38] *Annual Message of Governor Henry Watkins Allen,* January, 1865.

[39] Article on Allen in the *Dictionary of American Biography,* I, 191–93. See also Dorsey, *Recollections of Henry Watkins Allen,* 241.

[40] *Annual Message of Governor Henry Watkins Allen,* January, 1865; Louisiana *House Journal,* 1865, pp. 5–7. Sarah Dorsey says that in addition to the sales of $425,244.61 and the donations amounting to $22,159.50 "goods

Politics and State Finances

The establishment of a system of state stores was not only a means of restoring faith in the currency but was a part of a program to rescue the people of Louisiana from a terrible economic plight and to promote industry. The problems involved in this phase of the state's life deserve special emphasis.

---

to the value of $87,326.19 were transferred to the state departments, and army supplies, ordnance stores etc., to the amount of $627,816.60, had been turned over to the Confederate Government, making the transactions of this State store, since its inauguration, seven months before, amount to the gross sum of $1,162,551.90." Dorsey, *Recollections of Henry Watkins Allen*, 241.

Chapter VII

Social and Economic Affairs

THE WAR OF 1861–1865 was no exception to the rule that such conflicts disrupt the normal economic and social life of the people. This was particularly true of the South because the Confederacy was so unprepared to enter a martial conflict, and her territory was the stage for the drama. Louisianians, who were forced to make considerable adjustments in their economic life in the early months of the war, found themselves confronted with difficulties that tested human endurance when the state was invaded and occupied by armies of the United States. Scarcity of exotic commodities, a depreciated currency, confiscation of property and its destruction by troops and sometimes by civilian owners, the activities of guerrillas, and the demoralization among and desertion from the slave population—all combined to challenge the attention of the state and the individual.

Reference has been made to the general destruction of property in Louisiana by Federal soldiers. This fact should be recalled if we are to understand rightly the destitution of a portion of the population of Louisiana. A resident of St. Landry Parish wrote in January, 1864:

Our country I fear is destined to starve. The Yankees took all the corn. They took about 500 Barrels from me, nearly all Charley's, all from the Canal, took a good deal of sugar and molasses from me, all my horses, etc. I fear many now will have to move from the fear of starvation. Corn will soon be all gone.

Social and Economic Affairs

All the cattle, nearly all the hogs and sheep have been destroyed.

We can do nothing next year. All the fencing is gone. Many places all the buildings.[1]

A few months later (after Banks's expedition to North Louisiana) Governor Allen described the Red River Valley in these words:

From Mansfield to the Mississippi River the track of the spoiler was one scene of desolation. The fine estates on Cane and Red rivers, on bayous Rapides, Robert, and De Glaize, were all devastated. Houses, gins, mills, barns, and fences were burned; negroes all carried off, horses, cattle, hogs, every living thing, driven away or killed.[2]

With proper allowance for a governor's oratorical license, it can be safely said that the above picture is not greatly overdrawn. A Federal colonel reported the result of a fourteen-day expedition of his cavalry troop through Northeast Louisiana and Southeast Arkansas in January, 1865, as follows:

No squad of men, much less an army, can live anywhere we have been. The people have neither seed, corn, nor bread, or the mills to grind the corn in if they had it, as I burned them wherever found. . . . I have taken from these people the mules with which they would raise a crop the coming year, and burned every surplus grain of corn, and cannot imagine that one company of cavalry can obtain subsistence for more than thirty days in the whole country.[3]

---

[1] Alfred C. Weeks to Judge John Moore, January 13, 1864 (MS. in Weeks [David and Family] Collection, Louisiana State University Department of Archives).   [2] Dorsey, *Recollections of Henry Watkins Allen,* 279.

[3] Report of Colonel Embury D. Osband, U.S. Cavalry, *Official Records,* Ser. I, Vol. XLVIII, Pt. I, 805–06. There were exceptions to the general rule of scarcity of provisions, or perhaps Governor Allen's project of importing goods for the state stores was restoring "prosperity." Thomas Courtland Manning, at Alexandria, December 27, 1864, wrote to Thomas O. Moore: "This country is not as bad off as I supposed. Turkeys, eggs, etc., were abundant. A few days ago I dined at a friend's house with Commodore Semmes and a large party. The table groaned with a profusion of good things, and I am ashamed to say I ate until I made myself sick." On

Louisiana in the Confederacy

The people of some sections of Louisiana suffered much from the raids of lawless men, commonly known as guerrillas or jayhawkers. These companies were made up usually of recusant conscripts and deserters and ranged from fifty to five hundred men in membership, although most of the bands seem to have numbered less than two hundred. They raided and plundered homes of peaceable citizens and sometimes attacked whole communities, carrying off or destroying much property.

The country between the Mississippi and longitude 92° 30′ was especially cursed with the presence of jayhawkers. Reports of their depredations came from the parishes of Lafourche, Plaquemines, Point Coupee, St. Landry, Rapides, and Catahoula, and from the country between the Ouachita and the Mississippi. This part of the state was the richest and the most densely populated section of rural Louisiana. Much of this country was characterized by alluvial river-bottom lands and large plantations. It was also a country of bayous, lakes, and swamps, and offered natural protection to these lawless bands. With Federal control of the Mississippi and with Confederate lines in Central and West Louisiana, the guerrillas operated in the no man's land between. Both Federal and Confederate military authorities made efforts to capture or disperse these guerrilla forces, with little or no success. Judging from military reports, their numbers were augmented and the territory over which they operated was extended as the war was prolonged.[4]

The condition of communities subjected to frequent raids by these irregular, lawless bands must have been pathetic.

March 30, 1865, Manning wrote to Moore from Natchitoches: "I think I am very bad off, and yet I have never ceased using coffee, have an abundance of excellent bacon and corn beef and never sit down to my table without good biscuits and better eggbread." Thomas O. Moore Papers.

[4] See *Official Records*, Ser. I, Vol. XXXIV, Pt. II, 952–53, 962–67, 972–77; Ser. I, Vol. XLI, Pt. II, 593–94, Pt. III, 317, 402, 498, Pt. IV, 675, 901; Ser. I, Vol. XLVIII, Pt. I, 775, Pt. II, 220, 363.

Social and Economic Affairs

Horses, mules, arms, and personal property of any value whatever were usually taken, and cases of murder were not unknown. Governor Moore was the recipient of the following appeal from a community about forty miles south of Alexandria:

Bayou Chicot August 9th A.D. 1862

To His Excellency
(Governor of the State of La.)
Sir

I appeal to you in the name of the mothers, wives, and daughters, of Bayou Chicot and surrounding country; for protection against the insults threats and outrages of the Prairie Rangers. (Prairie Banditti would be a far more appropriate name.) We know not where to appeal for protection; since our Fathers Husbands and brothers are disarmed, if not to the Governor of our loved State. We could not fare worse were we surrounded by a band of Lincoln's mercenary hirelings. As often as that lawless band visits this part of the country; outrages of the deepest dye are daily committed in our midst by those whom we consider enemies to their country. Our homes are entered and pillaged of every thing that they see fit to appropriate to themselves. They do not as much as respect private rooms, but enter in spite of tears and entreaties; and turn up beds rip them open, search closets, break open what happens to be locked, in fact they leave no corner untouched. And if we appeal to the lawless wreches [sic] their reply is that they are but carrying out the orders of their (Captain Todd). (Who if justice was measured out to him not powder but rope would be administered.)

It is the general opinion of this community that ere the ending of this war that they will, after disarming the country, incite an insurrection or join the yankees, the first opportunity that offers. We hope that *Your Excellency* will inspect this matter closely, and remedy the terrible clamity [sic] that threatens this community. We can no longer clame [sic] protection from our Fathers, husbands, or brothers, the most of them are in the army and those that remain at home are disarmed. And if the evil is not corrected by the power of *Your arm*, civil and law martial, we will appeal to the public Journals, and hold the lawless band up to the execration of our glorious Confederacy.

If this appeal is not heeded by *Your Excellency,* then I say *God help us,* for we (the Ladies) must rely upon their own right arm, and I think that *Your Excellency,* will discover that soldiers do not all ware b [blank in MS.]

We beg and intreat you not to suspect this as having been written maliciously against Todd or our Country. It is written by a patriot in whose vans [sic] flow the blood of the Fathers of the revolution, and is written for the good of our community and the cause of our loved Confederacy.

Very Respectfully,
A Soldier's Sister.[5]

This section seems to have been the home of predatory bands. In February, 1864, Captain H. C. Monell of the Confederate army wrote from Opelousas, thirty miles from Bayou Chicot, of the raids in St. Landry Parish and asserted that the lawless bands were increasing in numbers daily. "It is no longer the case of a few isolated desperadoes; the entire community in the western part of the parish," he said, "is implicated in these organizations." Discontented whites, free Negroes, and slaves were joining them, and they were robbing the inhabitants "of everything of value." [6]

The state, as well as Confederate authorities, took steps to protect citizens against the raids of jayhawkers. The state militia was used to search the districts infested by the marauders. In February, 1864, the Legislature authorized the gov-

---

[5] Thomas O. Moore Papers.

[6] *Official Records,* Ser. I, Vol. XXXIV, Pt. II, 965–66. See also Shugg, *Origins of Class Struggle in Louisiana,* 179–80. There seems to have been much lawlessness in the Opelousas country before the war. It was reported in March, 1860, that St. Landry Parish was in the hands of vigilance committees and that Opelousas was "the headquarters of the basest scoundrels that ever disgraced the human form." Baton Rouge *Weekly Gazette and Comet,* March 7, 1860. This Baton Rouge paper, on May 15, 1860, said of the Opelousas country: "A terrible condition of society obtains there at this time. There are Vigilence [sic] Committees and counter Vigilence Committees, perpetrating outrages, too varied in nature and numerous to mention."

Social and Economic Affairs

ernor to raise a regiment or two of mounted men "to act as conservators of the peace, and for the defence of the State." Finally, as the last act of the Confederate era, the Legislature, February 4, 1865, authorized the Quartermaster General "to deliver to each member of the General Assembly, for the use of the inhabitants of the parish he represents, to enable them to defend themselves against predatory bands and jayhawkers, ten pounds of powder and one thousand percussion caps." [7]

When Federal gunboats began to move up the Mississippi, the Teche, and other streams, citizens of Louisiana destroyed thousands of bales of cotton to prevent the Union forces from acquiring this valuable property. The Mississippi at places between New Orleans and Vicksburg appeared to be on fire as the burning cotton floated along the surface. Contemporaries described such scenes at night as "a very beautiful sight." At one place an observer reported "volumes of smoke ascending on every side, for miles and miles, which marked the spots where the planters were burning their crops of cotton." [8] Even the people of Northwest Louisiana began to make plans for the destruction of cotton in the event of the approach of the Union army. As early as May, 1862, a meeting of the citizens of Caddo and Bossier parishes was held at Cotton Point, and it was resolved "that we cordially approve of the recommendations of his excellency, governor Moore, advising the cotton planters of the navigable streams of Louisiana to burn their cotton when in danger of falling into the hands of the enemy." A committee of eight persons was appointed to see that cotton was placed in "such a position as to be readily burned without endangering other property." [9]

[7] Louisiana *Acts*, 1865, p. 65.

[8] Dorsey, *Recollections of Henry Watkins Allen*, 281. See also Hoffman, *Camp Court and Siege*, 36–37.

[9] Shreveport *South-Western*, May 21, 1862. At a meeting at Bellevue in Bossier Parish it was resolved that "the owners of cotton on Red River or on Lake Bisteneau be requested to remove their cotton out of reach of the enemy by 5th June next." *Ibid.*, May 28, 1862.

Louisiana in the Confederacy

The possibilities of trade, however, were soon tempting the owners of cotton, and it was necessary for the military authorities to adopt stringent measures to prevent the traffic. Governor Moore, as commander-in-chief, issued an order on the subject, June 21, 1862. He asserted that he had received information that cotton had been shipped to New Orleans and that attempts would be made to sell it to the enemy. He charged that large quantities of cotton were on the banks of Bayou de Glaises, and on the Black, Ouachita, Trinity, and Tensas rivers within reach of the Federal forces. He ordered the colonels of militia of the parishes of Ouachita, Catahoula, Caldwell, Tensas, and Avoyelles to have such cotton burned immediately unless the owners moved it.[10]

In order to understand the position of the farmer it is necessary that we review the policies of the Federal and Confederate governments with regard to cotton. Naturally, with the establishment of the blockade the owner of cotton found the opportunities to dispose of his crop somewhat limited. He became more dependent upon government assistance in marketing his product. At the same time, under the rules of war the farmer found himself in an embarrassing position, since in this area the only outlet for cotton was through the Federal lines; and his own government opposed trade with the enemy. At times, therefore, he was hindered in his business by government policies. He found himself, many times, sorely pressed between conflicting policies of the two governments and even between the policies of civil and military officials of the same government.

Confederate military authorities, of course, insisted on destroying cotton that was in danger of falling into the hands of the Federals. This was but natural, since the object of the army was to win the war, and cotton surrendered to the enemy would have contributed to the enemy's resources. The Confederate Government realized the great wealth in cotton and

10 *Official Records*, Ser. I, Vol. XV, 761.

Social and Economic Affairs

in its efforts to finance itself adopted measures which directly involved that article. One of these measures was the so-called produce loan. This was an effort to obtain a domestic loan; and since specie was scarce, produce was acceptable to the Government. The measure, adopted on August 19, 1861, provided for a $100,000,000 bond issue. The Government issued 8 per cent bonds, a part of which were redeemable as early as January 1, 1864, and every six months thereafter. Agents of the Government were appointed to negotiate the loan with the planters, who were asked to agree to invest in these bonds the proceeds of the sale of a certain amount of cotton.[11]

On April 24, 1863, the Confederate Congress adopted another measure which directly concerned the cotton farmer. This act levied a tax in kind equal to one tenth of the agricultural products for the year 1863. This produce tithe was to be delivered to the post quartermasters by March 1, 1864. The cotton would then be transferred to the Confederate Treasury Department.[12] It was hoped to sell much of this cotton abroad for specie, but little success was had in shipping it. Some was used as collateral security in securing advances from foreign merchants. Much of the cotton destroyed in Louisiana on the approach of Federal troops was probably the property of the Confederate Government.

The Confederate authorities found it increasingly difficult to obtain supplies from their own people as the war continued. In order to overcome this difficulty, the Government resorted to the policy of impressments. This system would force the owner to sell his wares to the Government at fixed prices. Some cotton was acquired by the Confederacy in this way. Another Confederate policy along this line was the establishment of a cotton bureau in Texas to control the busi-

[11] *Statutes at Large of the Confederate States,* 177–83. John C. Schwab, *The Confederate States of America* (New York, 1901), 12–15, 26–27.

[12] *Public Laws of the Confederate States,* 1 Cong., 3 Sess., Chapter XXXVIII.

ness of exporting cotton to Mexico in exchange for merchandise.[13]

The Federal Government was interested in the question of cotton for obvious reasons. Although trading with the enemy was contrary to the theory of war, and the initial policy of the United States was to sever commercial intercourse with the South, that policy constantly changed; and there was an almost unrestricted trade near the end of the conflict.[14] A law of July, 1861, forbade all commercial intercourse with the Confederate States, with the exception that the President could license and permit trade in such articles and for such time as he thought best for the public good. This was called the license or permit system and was carried on under the direction of the United States Treasury Department.[15]

[13] Schwab, *The Confederate States of America*, 202–05, 266. The Produce Loan Office reported to Secretary Memminger, November 30, 1863, that the Confederate Treasury Department had purchased 106,793 bales of cotton in Louisiana for $6,739,762.13. *Reports of the Secretary of the Treasury of the Confederate States of America, 1861–1865*, p. 217.

[14] E. Merton Coulter, "Commercial Intercourse with the Confederacy in the Mississippi Valley, 1861–1865," in *Mississippi Valley Historical Review*, V (1919), 378; A. Sellew Roberts, "The Federal Government and Confederate Cotton," in *American Historical Review*, XXXII (1926–1927), 262–75. Professor Roberts says that the Federal Government "connived at a more or less corrupt domestic trade" in cotton, and he offers three excuses for such a policy: (1) Cotton was needed to keep Northern factories in operation. (2) "Cotton had to be doled out for French and English mills to prevent active interference by those governments in aid of the Confederacy and free cotton." (3) There was a desire to relieve the distress of the inhabitants of certatin districts under Federal military control.

[15] Coulter, "Commercial Intercourse with the Confederacy in the Mississippi Valley, 1861–1865," in *loc. cit.*, 379. Whereas Butler encouraged trade with the Confederates, Banks regarded the business with hostility and condemned the business as contrary to good military tactics. In a letter to Brigadier General William H. Emory, July 22, 1863, Banks expressed the opinion that the Confederates had constantly received munitions of war and other supplies from New Orleans. He thought the trade should be suppressed "absolutely and entirely." He recognized difficulties, however, in controlling the actions of Federal civil officers; and he made the charge that the War Department "seems to have transferred" to agents of the Treasury Department almost unlimited power upon the subject of trade. N. P. Banks Papers.

Social and Economic Affairs

Early in 1864 the Federal Government made its first explicit expression regarding a trade policy beyond the enemy military lines. Rules were promulgated by the Treasury Department and approved by President Lincoln. Any person in the Confederacy could bring his products to the Federal authorities and on taking an oath of allegiance to the United States might receive 25 per cent of the value in United States notes and a receipt for the remainder. If at the end of the war the owner could prove his consistent and continued loyalty, he might receive the balance of the payment.[16] A new law of July, 1864, was designed to eliminate the private trader and to place all necessary trade in the occupied territory under government agents. The President was deprived of power to grant permits. Congress evidently intended to stop the commerce between the Confederacy and the United States. This act, however, did not have the effect that Congress had anticipated. It threw the trade in cotton "wide open," for in September, 1864, the Treasury Department issued rules allowing any person who owned products in the Confederate lines to bring them to a government agency and receive three fourths of their market value in New York in greenbacks. These rules proved to be consistent with the act of Congress, to the amazement, it is said, of many of the lawmakers.[17]

The whole business of trading between the lines, especially the trade in cotton, whether under the license system or the system of government agents, was subject to great abuse; and perhaps in no other activity of the war of 1861–1865 was there so much corruption. Major General Banks, at New Orleans, wrote to Mrs. Banks, January 16, 1863: "I thank God every night that I have no desire for dishonest gain. I had one hundred thousand dollars offered me the other day to allow these people to 'continue' their commercial enterprises, but it was

[16] Coulter, "Commercial Intercourse with the Confederacy in the Mississippi Valley," in *loc. cit.*, 387. [17] *Ibid.*, 388–90.

no temptation for me." [18] Banks may have remained immune to temptation, but some of his contemporaries were not so high-minded. Rear Admiral David Porter, writing to Major General Sherman, October 29, 1863, referred to "an army of Treasury aids" appointed to carry out the regulations under the license system and said: "A greater pack of knaves never went unhung." Referring to the activities of the Treasury "aids" in enforcing the regulations governing the licenses, he remarked, "It is very much like setting a rat to watch the cheese to see that the mice don't get at it." [19]

Evidently all "knaves" did not wear civilian clothes. Indeed, Rear Admiral Porter's department seems to have had its share. A Federal army captain at Alexandria (with Banks's Red River expedition) wrote on March 19, 1864: "The navy is seizing all the cotton they can get hold of. Every gunboat is loaded with cotton, and the officers are taking it without regard to the loyalty of the owners. It looks to me like a big steal." [20] The army, too, found opportunities to trade—and to plunder—and some of the men yielded to the desire for personal gain. A Federal contemporary wrote:

Banks's Red River expedition was solely a cotton speculating raid. . . . Banks's expedition in the Teche country, General Washburn says, was organized for a similar purpose; but there, rumor had it, the speculators were more fortunate. Under threats of destruction of cotton and sugar, these products were transported in immense quantities to New Orleans, where a low price was offered the unfortunate owner, with a choice of acceptance or confiscation for disloyalty. I withhold the names of prominent officers whose fortunes were made while the soldiers were gulled, the owners defrauded, and the country's fame besmirched.[21]

[18] N. P. Banks Papers.

[19] *Official Records*, Ser. I, Vol. XXXI, Pt. I, 780–81.

[20] Captain Deming N. Welch to Colonel Samuel B. Holabird, *ibid.*, Ser. I, Vol. XXXIV, Pt. II, 654–55.

[21] Gordon, *A War Diary of Events in the War of the Great Rebellion, 1863–1865*, pp. 325–26. For a good discussion of this subject, see Landers, "Wet Sand and Cotton—Banks' Red River Campaign," in *loc. cit.*, 150–95.

Social and Economic Affairs

In spite of opportunities to trade, there was much cotton destroyed in Louisiana in 1864 when Banks advanced up the Red River Valley as far as Mansfield. Major General Taylor wrote Major General Walker in February, 1864, that no permission to trade with the enemy could be given. "My desire to alleviate the distress of the people," he said, "induced me to wink at the trade of a few bales for family supplies." Abuses of the privileges, however, were forcing him to "execute the law rigorously." Two weeks later Taylor informed Brigadier General William R. Boggs that he had given orders to burn all cotton likely to fall in the hands of the enemy. Taylor himself was instructed by Lieutenant General Kirby Smith to have all cotton east of the Ouachita and south of Alexandria, with certain exceptions, burned "as soon as you feel satisfied that the enemy will move in force." [22] In spite of such precautions, the Federals acquired much cotton at and near Alexandria in March and April, 1864, part by seizure and part by purchase. There was considerable dissatisfaction in military circles over the fact that citizens were willing to trade with the enemy. A Louisianian made the following entry in his diary on March 7, 1864:

Disaffection among our troops about trading with the Yanks. Lay down their arms. Good for our boys. What avails the war if we are to give the enemy cotton, what they need and what will injure us. No aid to the Yanks for Cotton is still king. Let us continue the contest on original principles and destroy every pound rather than give it to our foes though we starve and go naked. [23]

If the Federal forces were elated over the success in acquiring cotton at Alexandria, they were sorely disappointed with their harvest in the country immediately north of that place. A Federal officer with Banks's Red River expedition, writing from Grand Ecore on April 4, 1864, said: "The cotton on

[22] *Official Records*, Ser. I, Vol. XXXIV, Pt. I, 495, Pt. II, 939–40, 971–72.
[23] Diary of William H. Tunnard.

every plantation between a point near Alexandria and Natchitoches and beyond is reported burned by the enemy. The
fires were distinctly seen on plantations at a distance from the
line of route, while the cotton on fire showed plainly the
veracity of the reports." [24]

Governor Allen opposed the policy of burning cotton which
was exposed to Federal capture. In December, 1864, he
protested vigorously to Kirby Smith when Smith proposed to
carry out a policy of destruction. In the same month he
asked authority of Lieutenant General Buckner, commanding the District of Western Louisiana, to acquire and export
for the state of Louisiana cotton south of the Red River and
beyond the permanent military lines of the Confederate
forces and exposed to capture by the enemy. Buckner replied
on February 22, 1865, that "Every facility in my power will
be given you to carry out the purposes which you express in
your letter." [25]

While there are no statistics on the subject, it is known beyond doubt that the amount of cotton raised in Louisiana fell
off greatly in the years between 1860 and 1865. An authority
states that the cotton crop of the United States amounted to
more than four and a half million bales in 1860. There was
a gradual drop for each year thereafter, and the "crops of
1864 and 1865 probably did not exceed a half million bales." [26]
Louisiana, so much of which was overrun with Federal armies,
with consequent loss of horses, mules, implements, and slaves,
must have witnessed a marked decline in cotton production.

Slavery in Louisiana during the Civil War is a topic of no
little difficulty. Few, if any, generalizations can be made on
the subject. The problem here is to consider the institution

[24] Assistant Adjutant General George B. Drake to Lieutenant Colonel
Richard B. Irwin, *Official Records,* Ser. I, Vol. XXXIV, Pt. III, 35–36.

[25] Dorsey, *Recollections of Henry Watkins Allen,* 281–83; *Official Records,*
Ser. I, Vol. LIII, 1043.

[26] Schwab, *The Confederate States of America,* 279.

Social and Economic Affairs

as it affected the economic and social life of the state in the period covered by this study.

The slave population of Louisiana in 1860 numbered 331,-726, or 46.8 per cent of the total population. In thirty-one of the forty-eight parishes the slaves outnumbered the free inhabitants. In thirteen parishes (ten of which bordered on the Mississippi River) the ratio of slave to free population was more than two to one. In the district composed of the parishes of Carroll, Madison, Tensas, and Concordia, lying along the Mississippi from Arkansas to the Red River, the ratio of slaves to free people was more than six to one, the total population being 53,519 slave and 8,546 free. Orleans, which included the city of New Orleans, Winn, in North Louisiana, and Calcasieu and Sabine, both in extreme West Louisiana, were the parishes with the smallest percentage of slave population.[27]

In general, it can be said that the part of Louisiana (outside of New Orleans) which was subject to Federal occupation for most of the war period and the territory that experienced Federal raids and expeditions were inhabited by a relatively large slave population. For instance, in the territory covered by Rapides, Natchitoches, and De Soto parishes—the heart of the Red River expedition of 1864—the ratio of slave to free population in 1860 was 1.6 to 1. In fact, 59 per cent of the inhabitants of Louisiana outside of New Orleans, by the census of 1860, were slaves.

In Louisiana, as elsewhere in the South, slaves were of all kinds. During the strenuous days of the war some ran away at the first opportunity; some stole or destroyed the property of their masters and of others; but many remained loyal and peaceable to the very end. When the call to arms came and the husbands and fathers left to join the ranks of the Confederate army, the women and older men were left to manage

[27] *Eighth United States Census, 1860, Population,* 194.

the slaves. To the credit of the Negro race it should be said that their record in these years was relatively free of crime. In most cases the slave remained faithful to his mistress and master at least until the coming of the Federal armies. In many places, however, in order to help control the slaves, police patrols of men too old for the army were organized. Patrol boards exercised general supervision over the patrol work; the men elected their noncommissioned officers, and regular drills were held.[28]

When New Orleans and the surrounding territory were occupied by Federal troops in 1862, the slave population of South Louisiana was considerably affected. Since the Federal Confiscation Act of July 17, 1862, declared free the slaves of all persons in rebellion, and the War Department forbade the restoration to owners of those slaves who sought refuge within the Federal lines, Butler had ample opportunity to punish the "rebels" by treating their slaves as freedmen. Thousands of slaves deserted their owners and took refuge within the Union lines at Baton Rouge, New Orleans, and other places. Some planters, either unable to make them work, or to support them, or unwilling to keep them in idleness, directed their slaves to go to the Federals, perhaps for sustenance, with the hope of reclaiming them later. Butler, on July 19, 1862, because "certain persons" had ordered their slaves "to go to the Yankees," directed that all such declarations be considered acts of voluntary emancipation.[29]

So great was the exodus of slaves from the country to New Orleans that Butler was alarmed at the problem of taking care of them. On September 1, 1862, he wrote to Major General Halleck:

My commissary is issuing rations to the amount of nearly double the amount required by the troops. This is to the blacks. They

[28] See Whittington, "Rapides Parish, Louisiana—A History," in *loc. cit.*, XVII, 750; Alexander Pugh Diary, entries for July 14, 21, August 3, 10, 1861.

[29] Ficklen, *History of Reconstruction in Louisiana,* 117–19; *Official Records,* Ser. I, Vol. XV, 526.

Social and Economic Affairs

are now coming in by hundreds, nay thousands, almost daily. Many of the plantations are deserted along the coast, which phrase in this country means the river from the city up to Natchez. Crops of sugar-cane are left standing to waste which would make a million of dollars' worth of sugar.[30]

Many Negro slaves enlisted in the Federal army in Louisiana. The first Negro troops in the state were free Negroes, but by 1863 slaves were being admitted to the military ranks. In May of that year Major General Banks announced his plan to organize a *Corps d'Afrique,* consisting ultimately of eighteen regiments and representing all branches of the service. On August 17, 1863, Banks wrote to Lincoln that he had ten or twelve thousand Negro soldiers. "The regiments raised thus far," he said, "have been of great service in this department. I think it may be said with truth that our victory at Port Hudson could not have been accomplished at the time it was but for their assistance." In October Banks was writing to Secretary Stanton: "The number of black troops in this department is steadily increasing. I hope within a month or six weeks to add from 5,000 to 10,000 to their number." [31]

Although Lincoln's Emancipation Proclamation excepted thirteen parishes in South Louisiana, the Negroes in this section were actually nearer complete freedom than those within the Confederate lines. Perhaps it would not be incorrect to say that there was a *de jure,* but hardly a *de facto,* existence of slavery in these thirteen parishes. Many planters were persuaded to agree to pay wages to former slaves. Many "slaves" remained in New Orleans supported by the military

[30] *Official Records,* Ser. I, Vol. XV, 558.

[31] *Ibid.,* 716–17; Ser. I, Vol. XXVI, Pt. I, 688–89, 776; Ficklen, *History of Reconstruction in Louisiana,* 119–22. A planter of St. Mary Parish wrote in his journal, November 9, 1863: "A squad of federal soldiers this day marched suddenly into my corn field at Cypress Mort, where the hands were gathering corn and forced off without the opportunity of taking care of their families, thirteen of the negro men. . . . They afterwards released the three first named as too old for conscription." Palfrey Collection.

authorities. Some were servants for the officers of the Federal army in the city.[32]

Major General Banks published Lincoln's Emancipation Proclamation and called attention to the fact that portions of Louisiana were not affected. This general order, however, instructed military authorities that the laws of the United States forbade officers of the Army and Navy to return slaves to their owners. To prevent idleness and vagrancy among Negroes a "sequestration commission" was authorized to establish a yearly system of Negro labor at fixed wages or a proportion of the annual crop. Discipline and "perfect subordination" on the part of the Negroes were to be enforced by officers of the United States Government. Deserted fields were to be harvested and abandoned estates cultivated by the quartermaster's department of the Army.[33] This system of supervised labor, amended somewhat by subsequent military orders in 1864 and 1865, governed the relations between planters and Negro laborers in the Federal controlled section of Louisiana for the remainder of the war. It was reported that "During the year 1864, fifteen hundred plantations were worked by fifty thousand freedmen under the supervision of a Federal agent, who reported that on not more than one per cent of the plantations would the laborers fail to receive their full wages."[34] Some of the plantations were operated by the owners; others were managed by lessees, many of whom were Northern men. According to the Federal superintendent of free labor, the "old planters" dealt more fairly with the freed-

[32] Ficklen, *History of Reconstruction in Louisiana,* 119, 125; *Diary and Correspondence of Salmon P. Chase,* 316, 330.

[33] *Official Records,* Ser. I, Vol. XV, 666–67. George S. Denison thought that such a system was a return to slavery. He wrote to Chase about it on March 31, 1863, and after comparing the Negro problem under Butler and Banks said: "Slavery abolished by General Butler, I regard as completely re-established." *Diary and Correspondence of Salmon P. Chase,* 379.

[34] *Annual Cyclopaedia,* V (1865), 515. See also the report of Thomas W. Conway, superintendent of the Bureau of Free Labor, February 1, 1865, in *Official Records,* Ser. I, Vol. XLVIII, Pt. I, 703–10.

Social and Economic Affairs

men, paying them "more promptly, more justly, and apparently with more willingness than have the new lessees from other parts of the country," although "some few Northern men" treated the freedmen "better . . . than any others." [35]

Federal military control of the plantation system tended to become more strict and complete. By general orders of March 11, 1865, Major General Stephen A. Hurlbut directed that all contracts for plantation labor should insure the laborers "just treatment, wholesome rations, comfortable clothing, quarters, fuel, and medical attendance, and the opportunity for instruction of children," and wages of $10 a month for first-class male hands, $8 for first-class women workers, $3 for boys under fourteen, and $2 for girls. Hours of labor were limited to ten a day in the summer and nine in the winter, and the "afternoon of Saturday and the whole of Sunday shall be at the disposal of the laborer." Provost marshals in the parishes were charged with the general supervision and welfare of the laborers.[36]

Some planters, apparently, were not pleased with the system. Enforcement of the regulations caused much friction and almost chronic trouble between employers and the military authorities. Some provost marshals were influenced by political considerations, and special permits and fees encumbered the planters and sometimes ate up the profits.[37] The planters saw in the system many unnecessary restrictions and much "red tape." A. F. Pugh of Assumption Parish made the following observations in his diary:

March 28, 1865. I went to the sugar house today for the first time since January. I have purposely staid away to avoid talking

[35] Report of Thomas W. Conway, February 1, 1865, *Official Records,* Ser. I, Vol. XLVIII, Pt. I, 703–10.   [36] *Ibid.,* Ser. I, Vol. XLVIII, Pt. I, 1146–48.

[37] B. I. Wiley, "Vicissitudes of Early Reconstruction Farming in the Lower Mississippi Valley," in *Journal of Southern History,* III (1937), 444–45. Also, planters were often disturbed by visits of Federal officers in search of prospective Negro soldiers; and sometimes laborers, mules, and wagons were taken. *Ibid.,* 445–47.

to the negroes about a contract before I was ready to make one. I am now ready and had a talk with a few of them on the subject. It was not very satisfactory on either side.

April 5. Set up last night until 2 o'clock, preparing my contracts.

April 14. I have agreed with the negroes to pay them monthly wages. It was very distasteful to me, but I could do no better. Every body else in the neighborhood has agreed to pay the same and mine would listen to nothing else.[38]

The disgruntled lessee of Good Hope Plantation in Concordia Parish wrote to his business partner, May 11, 1865:

It will be impossible to get a correct report of our monthly proceedings and all the other little silly facts for the U. S. insane authorities. . . . Uncle Samuel is a kind obliging old gentleman to throw all these *wholly* superfluous obstacles and delays and petty annoyances in the way of his nephews—especially such deserving nephews as all lessees are. He is worse than Louisiana gnats. Had I better specify in the report the number of hump-backed and crooked leged [sic] ladies and gentlemen resident here? Are the pigs and fowls to be included among the "dependents" or the sore-backed angular horses and distorted lame mules?

Your gnat-and-government-stung partner
J. D. W.[39]

The military expeditions into Central and North Louisiana had a deleterious effect upon slavery in those sections. Some of the planters were wise enough to remove their slaves out of the way of the advancing army, taking them to the northwest corner of the state or to Texas. Many others had no such opportunity or failed to take such a precaution. When the Federal troops evacuated Alexandria and marched to Port

[38] Alexander F. Pugh Diary. There are several labor contracts and payrolls in the Louisiana State University Department of Archives. See especially the Good Hope Plantation Collection (A), and the Landry (Severin, and Family) Collection.

[39] J. D. Waters to G. Klapps, Good Hope Plantation Collection (A) (Louisiana State University Department of Archives).

Social and Economic Affairs

Hudson in 1863, planters found their slaves—if they were fortunate enough to find them—in a state of almost complete demoralization. A friend wrote to Governor Moore from Rapides Parish: "The arrival of the advance of the Yankees alone turned the negroes crazy. . . . All business was suspended and those that did not go with the army remained at home to do *much worse.*" Two weeks later the same correspondent was writing the governor that "Mr. Y. tells me you have 27 missing from Emfield—22 of whom are hands—and I think there are now eleven gone from Mooreland." [40] The experiences on many plantations were probably similar to those described by John H. Ransdell to Governor Moore in a letter of May 26, 1863, from Rapides Parish:

Things are just now beginning to work right—the negroes hated to go back to work again. Several have been shot and probably more will have to be. Chambers' down here—have been acting very bad—and the overseer and five or six others ran off since Friday last. On Sunday the most of those left were whipped and matters are getting on better now. All the furniture at Emfield was taken out of the house and taken to the negroes' cabins—and yesterday morning when I got there Y. was having it brought back. Old Frank and a number of others started too late—our cavalry turned them back—and now Frank says he never had any idea of going with them. The recent trying scenes through which we have passed have convinced me that *no dependence is to be placed on the negro* and that they are the greatest hypocrites and liars that God ever made.[41]

The white inhabitants of the section held by the Federal army were sometimes victims of the more or less lawless state of affairs. They were practically without power to aid or defend themselves, and the Federal army was not always a sure protection. Colonel Nathan A. M. Dudley of the Fed-

---

[40] John H. Ransdell to T. O. Moore, May 24, June 6, 1863. Quoted by G. P. Whittington, "Concerning the Loyalty of Slaves in North Louisiana," in *Louisiana Historical Quarterly,* XIV (1931), 491–93, 499–500.

[41] Thomas O. Moore Papers.

eral army wrote from Donaldsonville, in the Louisiana "sugar bowl," on August 2, 1863, that on the several government plantations in that vicinity, "stocked with negroes, from 100 to 250 each," there were no overseers, and the Negroes were destitute of subsistence and idle. "These negroes, in some instances," he said, "having procured mules and horses, ride from one plantation to another, threaten the lives of the few white inhabitants that remain, and commit various depredations, in some instances of a serious character." [42]

Many of the families in sections exposed to Federal raids moved with their slaves to the hill country of North Louisiana. A number of such groups moved from Madison and Tensas parishes to the vicinity of Mt. Lebanon, a thriving town in Bienville Parish, taking slaves and a portion of their household goods with them. When Vicksburg fell, many North Louisiana families, including a number from Mt. Lebanon, packed their wagons and started for Texas with slaves, mules, and cattle. Some of these went to the country around Marlin and Mexia, Texas.[43] The exodus of families and slaves was not without protest from those who remained. The editor of the Shreveport *Semi-Weekly News* commented on the situation in August, 1863:

Already do we hear of persons making preparations to leave this place with their negroes. This is patriotism—with a vengeance. How much better would it be for our cause, if every man with negroes would place himself at their head, and say that he had concluded to give a helping hand in driving back the destroy-

---

[42] *Official Records*, Ser. I, Vol. XXVI, Pt. I, 667–68. For the effects of the war on the "sugar bowl," see Walter Prichard, "The Effects of the Civil War on the Louisiana Sugar Industry," in *Journal of Southern History*, V (1939) 315–332. Professor Prichard says that the war "almost annihilated the sugar industry." R. W. Shugg says, "Of more than 1,200 large estates that harvested the cane of 1861, only 180 were struggling to get along in 1865." Shugg, *Origins of Class Struggle in Louisiana*, 193.

[43] Lavinia Egan, "History of the Egan Family" (MS. in the possession of Miss Lavina Egan, of Mt. Lebanon, Louisiana).

Social and Economic Affairs

ers of his peace. Future history could be read with great satisfaction by the next generation, if it chronicled the fact that on the approach of the enemy, A, B, and C, planters in the neighborhood, offered the service of their slaves to the military, and aided materially in driving back the invaders.[44]

The Federal Red River expedition of 1864, besides destroying real and personal property to the value of hundreds of thousands of dollars, added to the demoralization and further depleted the ranks of the slave population of Central and North Louisiana. Hundreds of slaves flocked to the Federal camps, and many enlisted in the Federal army.[45] Apparently, also, a new impetus was given to the exodus to Texas. William H. Tunnard, who was a member of a large party moving to Texas with slaves and livestock, while near Natchitoches in March, 1864 (Banks's army was at Alexandria), wrote in his diary:

March 26, . . . A very short journey. Trouble in crossing stock. 15 wagons buggies and carriages about 70 negroes sheep mules and cattle. Utter confusion—worse confusion. Awful tedious business this running from the Yanks. The pathetic and ridiculous combined. Sighs and tears, negro slang cursing, etc. blended.
[A few days later near Minden]
April 5. Awakened early by news of a general stampede in camp. Up and off with. . . . Chase and catch 11 negroes, two horses, 6 mules and ambulance. My pony gone. Still missing 14 negroes, 7 mules and 3 horses.
April 6. Clear and pleasant. Arrived after sun up from our negro hunt feeling completely used up. Preparing to leave camp once more minus many mules and negroes. So they go.[46]

[44] Shreveport *Semi-Weekly News*, August 25, 1863.
[45] Van Alstyne, *Diary of An Enlisted Man*, 292, 304.
[46] Diary of William H. Tunnard. Tunnard was on furlough from the army, evidently suffering from a wounded hand, as he says occasionally: "hand better." He did not go to Texas, but left the party near the Texas border and started toward the camp of his regiment.

Louisiana in the Confederacy

The state authorities were not unmindful of the problems and opportunities connected with slavery. When the Legislature was in session at Opelousas, it adopted an act in January, 1863, authorizing the governor to press into the service of the state to build fortifications and other works of public defense able-bodied male slaves from eighteen to fifty years old. The total number impressed at any one time should not exceed one half of the number of male slaves of those ages "belonging to any one person or persons, or under the charge of any person or persons." The owners of slaves impressed were entitled to wages of one dollar a day for each slave, to be paid in state or Confederate States Treasury notes.[47] It was under the authority of this act that slaves were impressed to work on fortifications on Red River, notably at Fort De Russy, Grand Ecore, and Shreveport.

Several measures pertaining to slaves were adopted by the Legislature at the session which began at Shreveport in May, 1863. Among them was one of June 17 that authorized slaveowners, or their agents, where more than thirty slaves were impressed from any parish, to select one person for every thirty slaves to give personal supervision over the Negroes in "all things affecting their health and comfort." Such supervisors were to be paid by the state. At the same time the Legislature appropriated $500,000 to pay owners for slaves lost by death or otherwise while employed on public works in Louisiana.[48]

Another measure of a different kind was inspired no doubt by the enlistment of slaves in the Federal army and by their acts of violence which followed the Federal march to Alexandria in the spring of 1863. This act of June 20 provided the death penalty for any slave convicted of bearing arms against the inhabitants or the government of the state or against the Confederacy, or convicted of engaging in any re-

[47] Louisiana *Acts*, 1862–1863, pp. 10–11.
[48] Louisiana *Acts*, Extra Sess., 1863, pp. 16–17.

Social and Economic Affairs

volt, rebellion, or insurrection. Another act of the same date provided that any slave accused of engaging in revolt, rebellion, or insurrection, or of encouraging others to do so, might be tried and punished in any parish of the state.[49]

Governor Allen was one of the first men of prominence in the Confederacy to advocate the use of slaves in actual combat service in the Confederate army. He publicly urged such a measure upon the Legislature and the Confederate authorities, recommending emancipation of all slaves placed in the army. As early as September 26, 1864, he wrote to Secretary James A. Seddon: "The time has come for us to put into the army every able-bodied negro man as a soldier. This should be done immediately. . . . I would free all able to bear arms and put them in the field at once. They will make much better soldiers with us than against us, and swell the now depleted ranks of our armies." [50] As is well known, the Confederate Congress authorized the use of slaves in the army a few weeks before the surrender of General Lee at Appomattox.

The exodus of planters' families and slaves received the attention of the Legislature. An act of February 3, 1865, legalized the removal of mortgaged slaves from the state when in danger of falling into "the hands of the enemy" upon application to the district judge and the granting of the necessary order, with the execution of a bond.[51] A similar act of the same date authorized administrators, curators, and executors of successions, and the tutors of minors, to remove the slaves and personal property of such successions and minors out of the state "when such property is in danger of falling into the hands of the public enemy." Administrators, etc., were required to make bond and give security before the removal of property. It was stated that the act was to take ef-

---

[49] The two acts discussed are found in *ibid.,* 27–28.

[50] *Official Records,* Ser. I, Vol. XLI, Pt. III, 774. See also Dorsey, *Recollections of Henry Watkins Allen,* 257.   [51] Louisiana *Acts,* 1865, pp. 14–15.

fect immediately and "remain in force during the existence of the present war." [52]

In a special message to the Legislature, January 27, 1865, Governor Allen recommended the passage of an act authorizing the governor to appoint "syndics" to operate abandoned plantations for the benefit of the absent owners.[53] The Legislature responded by an act of February 4 empowering the executive to appoint one or more syndics in each parish to take charge of and manage abandoned plantations, and to prevent their devastation. The syndics were to be remunerated from produce of the plantations at salaries fixed by the governor. Excess produce was to be sold and the proceeds paid into the state treasury for the benefit of the plantation owners.[54]

The act providing for the operation of abandoned plantations by the state is an example of the serious economic problems confronting the people in the last months of the war. It came too late to help to restore agriculture to a more prosperous condition—if, indeed, it could have had that result.

The story of fabulous prices in the Confederacy is too well known to require any lengthy discussion here. Louisiana, of course, was no exception. There, as elsewhere, high prices arose chiefly from a dual cause—scarcity of goods and a depreciated currency. Perhaps a few references to contemporary records will be of interest to the modern reader.

The ante-bellum South had been an agricultural district, dependent upon the outside world for its manufactured articles. Even such large cities as New Orleans were not built upon an industrial foundation. That city's wealth and population were due to its location on the Mississippi River, with its great import and export trade. It was, at least up to 1850 —when railroads began to affect the situation—the great port for the entire Mississippi River Valley. With very little man-

---

[52] *Ibid.*, 21. [53] Louisiana *House Journal*, 1865, pp. 40–41.
[54] Louisiana *Acts*, 1865, pp. 38–39.

Social and Economic Affairs

ufacturing of her own, the South found herself seriously handicapped by the disruption of trade with the industrial North
and by the partial, if not complete, severing of commerce
with Europe. When the supply of manufactured goods on
hand at the beginning of 1861 began to be used up, and military operations in some sections resulted in a certain amount
of destruction, articles of manufacture soon became conspicuous for their absence. Thus, a Louisiana girl wrote in her
diary in September, 1862:

Now, in present phraseology, "Confederate" means anything
that is rough, unfinished, unfashionable, or poor. You hear of
Confederate dresses, which means last year's. Confederate bridle
means a rope halter. Confederate silver, a tin cup or spoon.
Confederate flour is corn meal, etc. In this case the Confederate
carriage is a Jersey wagon with four seats, top of hickory slats
covered with leather, and the whole drawn by mules.[55]

The record of a newspaper, one of the few published without interruption in Louisiana throughout the war, is perhaps
a fair index to the scale of prices and the supply of articles of
manufacture. The Shreveport *News,* a daily, began publication on April 13, 1861, with John Dickinson as publisher and
editor. The subscription rate was $8 per year. The paper
continued as a daily until November. With the issue of
November 11, 1861, the paper became the *Semi-Weekly News*
with a subscription rate of $4 a year. The publisher gave two
reasons for the change to a semiweekly: poor health and the
fact that the town did not seem able to support a daily paper.
On December 2, 1862, Dickinson announced to his patrons
that "during my absence" another would have charge of the
columns of the paper. "Having not yet received the supply
of paper sent for," he said, "I have concluded to go in search
of some." The editor was back on the job on December 30,
having been successful in his quest for paper.

[55] Dawson, *A Confederate Girl's Diary,* 233. Reprinted with permission of
Houghton Mifflin Company, publishers.

Louisiana in the Confederacy

The annual subscription rate for the *Semi-Weekly News* by this time was $8, and a single copy sold for twenty cents. On March 10, 1863, the *News* made this explanation: "Last week we secured a small lot of paper for $900, or about 13⅛ cents a sheet. We notice this for the information of people who complain because they have to pay twenty cents for a paper in Shreveport, when in Richmond 10 cents is the price."

The *Semi-Weekly News* was more fortunate than many other Louisiana papers. Perhaps as an encouragement to its patrons and as a compliment to itself the *News* told its readers on the date of the above explanation of rates—March 10, 1863: "The *Avoyelles Pelican* is printed on wall paper, thus enabling its patrons in the course of time, to paper their rooms. . . . The *American Patriot,* Clinton, Louisiana, appears on leaves of a day-book or journal."

On August 14, 1863, the subscription rate of the *Semi-Weekly News* was raised from $8 to $12 a year. Two weeks later the paper made this announcement: "As we would much prefer not selling single copies of this paper we will commence today, charging fifty cents per copy." Early in September the announcement was repeated in these words: "The price of single copies of this paper is fifty cents, and no grumbling." [56] On November 27 the subscription rate went up to $20 a year, though single copies remained at fifty cents. Early in 1864 the publisher took the readers into his confidence and told them:

We paid last week, for common manilla paper, $220 per ream. Who can beat the figures? For the information of the unacquainted, we would state that 480 sheets constitute a ream. . . . We get fifty cents per copy for our papers when purchased by news-seekers, yet we would much prefer not selling a copy at one dollar and be compelled to supply the demand. [57]

[56] Shreveport *Semi-Weekly News,* August 28, September 8, 1863.
[57] *Ibid.,* February 9, 1864.

Social and Economic Affairs

Incidentally, on the day of this frank statement came the announcement that the subscription rate was raised from $20 to $30 a year. Evidently the publisher was about to exhaust the supply of paper on hand, for on February 26 he made this proposition: "We have a lot of Wall paper which we will exchange for white or colored printing paper. Who responds?" In less than two weeks the shortage of paper forced the publisher to make adjustments, and the *Semi-Weekly News* became the *News*, a weekly paper with a subscription rate of $15 a year. "We will reduce our prices as soon as we can obtain paper at reasonable rates," the publisher said in the issue of March 8, 1864, "as it is we would rather not receive any more subscribers."

But rates, in Confederate currency at least, were not reduced. The rate was increased on August 2, 1864, to $25 for six months and $15 for three months, indicating a drastic decline in the value of currency. On this day the publisher announced, "Persons who prefer paying in specie can have it at the rate of $6 per annum." On September 20 the rate for specie payment was reduced to $4, the charge for payment in currency remaining stationary.

Many other articles of manufacture, besides paper, continued to be scarce for the period of the war, though some things were obtained in increasing amounts in 1864 and 1865 from Mexico, particularly necessities, under Governor Allen's state store system. Provisions, too, in general, were scarce. Nearly all things sold for fabulous prices, chiefly because of the depreciated currency, which, however, seems to have had a higher value in Louisiana than elsewhere in the last few months of the war.

In February, 1864, Dr. Bartholomew Egan, superintendent of the state laboratory at Mt. Lebanon, purchased for his friend, former Governor Moore, thirty-four yards of cloth, a part of which he obtained in Shreveport. When sending the cloth, Dr. Egan wrote: "I am afraid I can procure no more of any description at present. . . . I paid fifteen dollars per yard for each kind, in all $510.00." [58] Prices in Shreveport in August, 1864, included the following: butter, $5 a pound; eggs, $5 a dozen; beans, $2.50 a quart; apples, 25 cents to 50 cents each; melons, $1 to $5 each.[59] A soldier, writing from "Starvation Hollow" near Alexandria, told of a week's stay in Shreveport and added, "I never became so tired of a place in my life. The fare at the hotel was meager and the prices exorbitant, $20 per day—fruits were in abundance. Melons were plentiful and in consequence I was never meloncholly." [60]

In December, 1864, E. W. Halsey wrote to Dr. Egan that he had had the state storekeeper at Shreveport to purchase two silk handkerchiefs for the doctor. "They cost seventy dollars each!" [61] he said. About the same time Thomas Courtland Manning, down at Alexandria, wrote to former Governor Moore, who was in Texas:

The improvement of the currency is gratifying as these military successes. Gold sold here last week at 14, and provisions are falling, but dry goods continue at unreduced prices. Mrs. A. who is selling out, offers a doz. cups and saucers at the moderate price of $300. I am reduced to three, all of my china and crockery having been stolen in the raid of '63, but if that is the price, I shall resort to tin cups or gourds.[62]

If necessity is the mother of invention, it is also the patron of discovery and the promoter of industry. It may, indeed,

[58] Egan to Moore, February 16, 1864, Thomas O. Moore Papers. A Confederate, J. D. Garland, near Harrisonburg, February 18, 1864, wrote his parents that "Socks sold here today at 10 and 12 dollars per pair." J. D. Garland Papers (Louisiana State University Department of Archives).

[59] Tunnard, *The History of the Third Regiment Louisiana Infantry*, 327.

[60] Frank Palm to Henrietta Lauzin, Aug. 21, 1864, Gras-Lauzin (Family) Papers (Louisiana State University Department of Archives).

[61] Halsey to Egan, December 8, 1864, Lavinia Egan Collection.

[62] Manning to Moore, December 27, 1864, Thomas O. Moore Papers.

Social and Economic Affairs

be the reviver of ancient practices. The war brought destruction, scarcity, high prices, and privation to Louisiana. It also presented the problem of overcoming difficulties and of finding ways to make adjustments. It tested the patience, the endurance, and the ingenuity of the people of the state. Just as suffering was not confined to the battlefields and the army hospitals, so, likewise, not all the acts of heroism and sacrifice nor all the great achievements were performed by officers and soldiers. Armies and a civilian population had to be fed and clothed; the sick had to be nursed and supplied with medicines; indigent families, especially those of absent soldiers, required assistance; and other matters pertaining to the common welfare, from the making of corn whiskey to the administering of justice in the courts, confronted the people and the public authorities.

Reference has been made in an earlier chapter to the revival of saltmaking in North Louisiana in 1861. This was necessitated by the blockade and by the Confederate Government's activities in salting great quantities of meat for shipment to the armies. Naturally, every possible source of salt was sought under such conditions. Salt licks which had scarcely been touched for twenty years were worked to full capacity during the war.

The Louisiana Legislature in January, 1862, withdrew from sale all public lands upon which were located salt springs, except lands along the Gulf coast. It was stipulated that any entry of such public lands during the existence of the war should be null and void. At the same time the Legislature granted to a Professor M. J. R. Thomassy, a French geologist, the exclusive right to use any salt springs or saline waters discovered or made available by him on lands belonging to the state, for the purpose of making salt. The right was not to apply to any salt spring or saline waters already used. Furthermore, this special grant was to become void

225

within six months after the passage of the act if the manufacture of salt had not commenced.[63]

The chief salt works of North (Northwest would probably be more correct) Louisiana were the Drake Salt Works on Saline Bayou in the western end of Winn Parish; King's Salt Works, also known as Castor Saline, in southwest Bienville Parish; Rayburn's Salt Works, about eight miles from the town of Bienville; the various works around Lake Bisteneau, a large lake lying in the parishes of Bossier and Bienville.[64] The land around Lake Bisteneau was claimed by the Confederate Government since it was an old lake bottom. No rent, therefore, was charged for saltmaking there. For this reason, as well as because of the purity of the salt, the Lake Bisteneau region came to be the greatest salt-producing site.[65]

The fame of the salt licks of North Louisiana spread far and wide during the Civil War, and men came from great distances with gangs of slaves to make salt. It was reported in January, 1862, that there were three hundred men engaged in saltmaking around Lake Bisteneau with an average production per man of six barrels per week.[66] Later the number of persons working at the Lake Bisteneau salines increased to more than one thousand. Numerous wells from ten to twenty feet deep were sunk. Platforms were built around the wells; the brine was pumped to the surface and then conveyed to the furnaces by troughs supported on forked

[63] Louisiana *Acts*, 1861–1862, p. 27, 84. Little is known of Thomassy's subsequent activity. In late 1862 or early 1863 a Frenchman named Thomassy appeared at Lake Bisteneau in Northwest Louisiana and began rather elaborate preparations for making salt by evaporation. His scheme was ridiculed by local residents. A band of Arkansas men arrived and a controversy between Thomassy and these men resulted in the departure of the Frenchman. Lonn, *Salt as a Factor in the Confederacy*, 74–75.

[64] Lake Bisteneau is located today in Bienville, Bossier, and Webster parishes.

[65] Lonn, *Salt as a Factor in the Confederacy*, 22, 48, 207. The writer is also indebted to Miss Lavinia Egan for the use of her manuscript entitled "The Salines of Bienville Parish."

[66] Shreveport *Southwestern*, January 29, 1862.

poles. Common iron washpots, kettles, and steamboat boilers were used for evaporating pans.

It is estimated that the Rayburn salt licks near Bienville yielded about one thousand bushels a day. The Confederate Government contracted with J. C. Weeks for all the salt he could make at Drake's Saline in Winn Parish at the rate of $10 a bushel, an agreement which Weeks probably regretted later when his neighbors were receiving as much as $15 a bushel for their salt. Some of this salt was hauled in wagons to the Confederate army at Monticello, Arkansas. Women whose husbands were serving in the Confederate army came in wagons, sometimes with ox teams, or on horseback, from great distances to the salt works of North Louisiana to get salt for their needs.[67]

The only new source of salt discovered during the war in Louisiana, or for that matter in the Confederacy, was the rock salt mine on Avery Island, near New Iberia. Salt springs had been worked intermittently on the island for more than half a century. Judge Daniel D. Avery, owner of the island when the Civil War began, attempted to increase the yield of salt from the springs. In the process of deepening the wells a bed of rock salt, clear as crystal, was discovered. This was in May, 1862. When the Confederate authorities learned of this valuable discovery, Major General Taylor was directed to furnish military protection and to promote the work of mining the salt. Pits were sunk by government agents, and a packing plant was established at New Iberia to cure meat. Great quantities of salt were shipped from Avery Island to points in the Confederacy. About five hundred men worked

[67] Lonn, *Salt as a Factor in the Confederacy*, 68–69, 207; Lavinia Egan, "The Salines of Bienville Parish." Miss Egan says of Rayburn's Salt Works: "A fee of 2½ bits per bushel was charged for the privilege of making salt and for the wood cut and consumed. At this rate, receipts are said to have amounted to about $375 per day, which would give a daily production of about one thousand bushels." Miss Lonn, too, places the daily production at Rayburn's at 1,000 bushels.

day and night in the salt mines, and the yield was over thirteen hundred bushels a day.[68]

This very valuable source of salt was under Confederate control for less than a year, for in April, 1863, Federal troops of General Banks's army advanced upon the salt works and took possession, destroying buildings, machinery, and six hundred barrels of salt ready for shipment. Federal authorities might not have known it, but a terrible loss was inflicted on the Confederacy when Avery Island fell to the boys in blue.[69]

Considerable efforts were made to discover mineral deposits in Louisiana during the last year of the war. The idea seems to have been part of Governor Allen's program to develop the resources of the state and to revive and promote trade and industry. In response to his recommendations, the Legislature, in February, 1864, adopted an act "To establish a Mining and Manufacturing Bureau for the State." The governor was authorized to have a thorough geological survey of Louisiana made and to select suitable sites for locating iron and lead furnaces and other works necessary to develop the mineral resources of the state. An appropriation of $500,000 was made to carry out the provisions of the act.[70] Soon after the passage of this act Governor Allen offered a reward of $2,000 to any person "who shall discover lead in the State of Louisiana, and make known the same to the Governor or his agents; provided it is found in sufficient quantities to justify the State in erecting furnaces, machinery, etc." [71]

Allen told the Legislature in January, 1865, that the state had been explored for deposits of lead and iron ore and only a little trace of lead ore was found. Several North Louisiana

[68] Lonn, *Salt as a Factor in the Confederacy*, 32–33, 70–71, 208, 222; Taylor, *Destruction and Reconstruction*, 114.

[69] Lonn, *Salt as a Factor in the Confederacy*, 192–93; *Official Records*, Ser. I, Vol. XV, 382, Report of Colonel William K. Kimball.

[70] Louisiana *Acts*, 1864, pp. 32–33.

[71] Shreveport *Semi-Weekly News*, February 23, 1864.

Social and Economic Affairs

parishes had iron ore in large quantities, he reported, but it was so "refractory" that he had not pursued the matter further. He had, however, purchased for the state one-fourth interest in the Sulphur Iron Works in Davis (now Cass) County, Texas, about ninety miles from Shreveport, for $50,000. The company, he said, "owns a valuable tract of land covered with inexhaustible beds of rich iron ore." The business was managed by a board of five directors, two of whom were appointed by the state of Louisiana. "I consider this purchase very fortunate," the governor said. "Already the stock is worth double the money stipulated." [72]

In an effort to stimulate the manufacture of cloth and to render assistance to families of soldiers and sailors the state authorities adopted a scheme of purchasing and distributing cotton and wool cards. The initial step was taken in the last year of Governor Moore's administration. In June, 1863, an act of the Legislature authorized the governor to draw as much as $500,000 from funds appropriated in January for the assistance of families of soldiers to buy cotton and wool cards to be distributed at cost to families of men in the military or naval service of the Confederacy, and to the families of deceased soldiers and seamen. Surplus cards might be sold to others for their own use at any price above cost as fixed by the governor and the state treasurer. [73]

Little or nothing seems to have been done, however, before the inauguration of Allen. That executive, with characteristic vigor, attacked the problem with enthusiasm and energy. He recommended to the Legislature in January, 1864, the appropriation of $1,000,000 for the purchase of cotton cards to be distributed among "the ladies of the State for personal use—in order that every white female in

[72] Louisiana *House Journal*, 1865, p. 6; *Annual Message of Governor Henry Watkins Allen*, January, 1865. A résumé of the message is found in the Shreveport *News*, January 31, 1865.

[73] Louisiana *Acts*, Extra Sess., 1863, pp. 22–23.

Louisiana, above the age of eighteen, shall receive a pair of cotton cards free of cost and charges." [74] The Legislature responded with an act of February 9, authorizing the governor to use state funds up to $700,000 to purchase cotton and wool cards to be distributed through police juries to families of soldiers and seamen, "Whether said officers, soldiers, or seamen be alive or dead" and to all indigent females above the age of twelve years. No more than two pairs, however, were to be distributed to any one family living together. [75]

Governor Allen took steps immediately to carry out the plan. He appointed agents and contracted with them for the purchase and delivery of cotton and wool cards. [76] By January, 1865, he was able to report to the Legislature that he had imported fifteen thousand pairs of cotton cards which he had sold to soldiers' families at $10 per pair. [77] The successful operation of the plan inspired the Legislature to adopt the following joint resolution on February 1, 1865: "Be it resolved. . . . That the Governor be requested to increase the importation of cotton and wool cards, so as to supply not only soldiers' families, but all the citizens of the State at a price merely covering cost and carriage." [78]

Steps were taken, also, for the manufacture of cotton cards within the state. In June, 1864, Allen appointed Josiah Marshall to superintend the erection and operation

[74] Louisiana *House Journal,* 1864, p. 32; Shreveport *Semi-Weekly News,* January 29, 1864. [75] Louisiana *Acts,* 1864, pp. 22–24.

[76] Contracts of the State of Louisiana. Records of the War Department, Confederate Records, The National Archives, Chap. 8, Vol. 134, pp. 21–35 (microfilm copy possessed by the writer). A contract between Allen and Leopold Levy, February 29, 1864, stipulated that Levy was to buy and deliver to Allen $40,000 worth of cotton and wool cards. *Ibid.,* 25. A good discussion of Governor Allen's work in this connection may be found in Chandler, "The Career of Henry Watkins Allen," 164–66.

[77] *Annual Message of Governor Henry Watkins Allen,* January, 1865.

[78] Louisiana *Acts,* 1865, p. 12.

of machinery at Minden for the manufacture of cotton cards.[79] A machine with a small amount of wire was obtained from Governor Joseph E. Brown of Georgia, and two machines and six hundred pounds of wire were procured from Virginia. This equipment was installed, and operations were begun at Minden.[80]

The importation of cotton cards, as well as other articles of manufacture, was effected through the purchase and exportation of cotton and sugar (mostly cotton) by the state. The governor appointed more than a score of agents to manage this business.[81] Most of the trade was carried on through Texas and Mexico; and Crockett, Navasota, San Antonio, and other Texas towns became bases of operations for the agents of Louisiana. Wagons, with Mexican and Negro drivers, crossed and recrossed the country between the Rio Grande and the Red River, exchanging Louisiana cotton and some sugar for Mexican and European commodities such as dry goods, medicines, tools, implements, paper, ordnance stores, and various other articles.[82] In this, as in all other matters, Governor Allen had the fullest co-operation and support of the Legislature. Indeed, Louisiana was most fortunate in the cordial rela-

[79] Contracts of the State of Louisiana. Confederate Records, The National Archives, Chap. 8, Vol. 134, p. 33.

[80] Louisiana *House Journal*, 1865, p. 7; *Annual Message of Governor Henry Watkins Allen,* January, 1865.

[81] Contracts of the State of Louisiana. Confederate Records, The National Archives, Chap. 8, Vol. 134, pp. 101–19, 134, 162. Names of agents and the amount of cotton purchased for the state by each in March–May, 1864, are found here. The agents are designated as "purchasing," "transportation," "purchasing and exporting," and "purchasing and importing" agents.

[82] Letters Received, Executive Department, State of Louisiana, 1860–1865. Records of the War Department, Confederate Records, The National Archives, Chap. 8, Vol. 131, pp. 59–87 (microfilm copy possessed by the writer). Emory Clapp, who seems to have been one of the most active agents, was stationed at Navasota. Communications from him, dated June 5 and November 5, 1864, are in *ibid.,* 71, 87. See also the excellent article on Henry Watkins Allen in the *Dictionary of American Biography,* and Dorsey, *Recollections of Henry Watkins Allen,* 238–39.

tions between the branches of the state government. In February, 1865, the Legislature lent its support to Allen's policy of supplying the needs of the people by the exchange of cotton for commodities. The act authorized him to purchase cotton belonging to citizens of Louisiana, export it, and "import the full value thereof, in such articles as in his judgment may be deemed necessary to supply the wants of the people of this State." [83] The Legislature, of course, was giving its approval to a *fait accompli*.

Medicines were obtained from two sources—from Mexico and from state laboratories established at Mt. Lebanon and Clinton. Governor Allen, in his first message to the Legislature in January, 1864, recommended the appropriation of $500,000 for the purchase of medicines to be distributed to the physicians of the state who should, "under bonds, be required to administer the same at cost and charges, to their patients." "I am receiving letters continually from the most respectable physicians," he said, "informing me that their patients are suffering for medicines. I cannot urge upon you too strongly this appropriation. The physicians ask it —all classes in the community call for it—humanity itself demands it." [84]

The Legislature responded with an appropriation as asked for. A dispensary was established at Shreveport. Large supplies of medicines were obtained from Mexico, and every

---

[83] Louisiana *Acts*, 1865, pp. 37–38. Governor Allen wrote to Dr. B. Egan, of Mt. Lebanon, February 15, 1865: "You speak in gratifying terms of the endorsement of my official acts by the Legislature. My intercourse with the members of the General Assembly, both official and social, was of a very satisfactory character. Their full approbation of my course and their cheerful action upon all of my recommendations will be remembered by me with grateful pride. I do not forget, however, that the measures which have won their approbation are those in which I have been aided and sustained by able and zealous assistants like yourself." Original letter in the Lavinia Egan Collection.

[84] Shreveport *Semi-Weekly News*, January 29, 1864; Louisiana *House Journal*, 1864, p. 33.

Social and Economic Affairs

portion of the state under Confederate control was supplied. Governor Allen reported in January, 1865, that great difficulties had been met but the medicines on hand were "amply sufficient for many months to come." "Every citizen of Louisiana," he said, "can now be abundantly supplied with medicines of all kinds." [85]

The state laboratories occupied an important place in Governor Allen's plans for aiding the citizens of Louisiana. In recommending to the Legislature, in his first message, the establishment of a mining and manufacturing bureau, including a laboratory for preparing indigenous medicines, he declared: "This is a great undertaking; but we are a great people, and should be equal to any emergency." The Legislature concurred with the governor and on February 11, 1864, authorized him to establish a state laboratory, "for the purpose of manufacturing, preparing and dispensing medicines," and appropriated $250,000 for that purpose.[86] Immediately, Allen undertook to put the act into effect. One of his first steps was the appointment of Dr. Bartholomew Egan as superintendent of the new laboratory to be established at Mt. Lebanon. When writing to Dr. Egan on February 24 to notify him of his appointment, Allen said:

These medicines when prepared are to be sent to different parts of the State and dispensed as the law requires. . . . You will purchase and put up such machinery as you may think proper, in order to meet the wants of the suffering. I have this matter much at heart and wish you to enter at once on the duties of your office. I suggest that you make your Headquarters at Minden and immediately advertise for indigenous barks, roots, herbs, etc.[87]

[85] *Annual Message of Governor Henry Watkins Allen,* January, 1865. Allen reported that medicines had been furnished citizens at about one third of the market price, to the value of $274,972, and that $13,790 worth of medicine had been distributed for charitable purposes.

[86] Louisiana *Acts,* 1864, p. 68. For Governor Allen's message, see Shreveport *Semi-Weekly News,* January 29, 1864, and Louisiana *House Journal,* 1864, p. 34.

[87] Lavinia Egan Collection.

Louisiana in the Confederacy

In March Allen authorized Dr. Egan to purchase the lands and buildings of the Female College at Mt. Lebanon and have the property "suitably fitted up." "I do not apprehend that the enemy will visit your town," he said, "and if they do they will not probably burn a medical Laboratory. In any event I deem it advisable to incur such risk. I desire you to expedite your preparations with all zeal and energy." [88]

Dr. Egan purchased for the state of Louisiana the Mt. Lebanon Female College and eighty-four acres of land for $6,400. One of his first acts was to address a circular to the people of Louisiana urging the extensive planting of medicinal plants. A machinist was employed and sent in search of machinery. The buildings were transformed into manufacturing laboratories. Most of the skilled workers were detached from the Confederate service, some of them being disabled for active war duty. A chemist, a manufacturer of castor oil, a distiller, a potter, two coopers, and an overseer of the turpentine operations were employed. Twenty-nine Negro men were impressed into service. In addition to these workers, a number of persons were employed to collect roots, barks, and medicinal herbs. [89]

The most needed medicines were turpentine, alcohol, pure whiskey, and castor oil. No difficulty was experienced in making turpentine, for the long leaf pine forests of North Louisiana furnished, according to Dr. Egan, "a pure article of spirits of Turpentine pronounced by every physician superior to the North Carolina Turpentine." An excellent brand of whiskey, also, was manufactured. Governor Allen wrote to Dr. Egan, November 24, 1864: "Accept my thanks for the second sample of the State whiskey. I find it improved in flavor, body and dimensions. Gentlemen of highly cultivated 'taste' pronounce it the purest and pleasantest domestic

[88] Allen to Egan, March 22, 1864, Lavinia Egan Collection.
[89] Report of Dr. B. Egan to Governor Allen, January 1, 1865. Dr. Egan's copy in the Lavinia Egan Collection.

Social and Economic Affairs

whiskey they have seen." [90]   This whiskey was manufactured
for medical purposes and was supplied to physicians.

J. W. Willis of Forest Grove, Louisiana, contracted with
Dr. Egan to raise castor beans and make castor oil.   Willis
had had experience in this work as superintendent of his
father's castor oil factory in Georgia.   He wrote to Dr. Egan
on January 21, 1865, that he was sending twenty-nine gallons
of castor oil, but added that "the oil is not as fair an article
as I would wish, which is owing to my not having the proper
fixtures for heating." [91]   Castor oil was made also at the State
Laboratory at Mt. Lebanon.   Although Dr. Egan reported
on January 1, 1865, that he had not been able to stimulate
the people sufficiently to cultivate medicinal plants and herbs,
the situation in regard to castor oil must have improved, for
he wrote to a friend after the war that he had "fortunately
procured the selfshelling seed and was about to make castor
oil enough when the war closed to supply the whole Trans-
Mississippi Department."   Opium, too, was made at Mt.
Lebanon from a native white poppy.   According to Dr. Egan,
the opium was "in its effects as far as I could see no way
inferior to the opium of commerce." [92]

On the day that Dr. Egan was appointed to superintend
the institution at Mt. Lebanon, Governor Allen authorized
Dr. Edward De Loney and W. D. Winter, state agent, to
establish a laboratory at Clinton in East Feliciana Parish to

[90] Lavinia Egan Collection.   This paragraph is based also on Dr. Egan's
report of January 1, 1865, referred to in the preceding citation, and on a letter
from Dr. Egan to Henry Boyce, president of the Alexandria and Arkansas
Railroad, August 23, 1870, *ibid.*

[91] Original letter in the Lavinia Egan Collection   Joshua Willis, father of
J. W. Willis, wrote to Dr. Egan on September 21, 1864, that a certain physician
had taken a bottle of castor oil to Shreveport as a specimen of manufacture
of J. W. Willis and had represented the oil as his own manufacture, and added:
"Dr. ——— and myself are church members and as this will involve a church
investigation, will thank you to send me . . . the certificate requested." *Ibid.*

[92] This paragraph is based on Dr. Egan's official report of January 1, 1865,
and on his letter to Henry Boyce, August 23, 1870, Lavinia Egan Collection.

manufacture and dispense medicines for the people of the state east of the Mississippi River. He gave them $10,000 to begin operations.[93] Allen reported to the Legislature in January, 1865, that this laboratory was operating successfully, although the work had been seriously interfered with by Federal raiding parties.[94]

Louisiana adopted a modified prohibition law during the war of 1861–1865. On June 20, 1863, the Legislature made it unlawful, for the period of the war, for anyone to distill within the state "any kind of grain, sugar, molasses or cane juice, into any kind of intoxicating liquors." Punishment for violation of the law was fixed at a fine of from $5,000 to $15,000, and imprisonment for from three months to one year. Informers were entitled to one half of the fine collected. The act empowered and instructed sheriffs to seize and detain any distillery or liquor manufactured in violation of the law.[95] This statute was warmly commended by Allen when he became governor in January, 1864. He felt, however, that further legislation was necessary, and he urged the Legislature to prohibit the importation or sale of intoxicating liquors except for medicinal purposes. In this connection he said:

There is still a crying evil in our midst. We are importing daily from neighboring States large quantities of alcoholic poison. The effect of this poison upon the community is most lamentable. . . . In the army it is worse—nine-tenths of the arrests and punishments are caused from intoxicating liquors. . . .

. . . The use of ardent spirits is a luxury; nothing more, nothing less; and our patriotic people will most cheerfully dispense with that luxury during the war. Besides, the trade now carried on in liquors is diverting a large capital into improper channels,

[93] Chandler, "The Career of Henry Watkins Allen," 170–71; Contracts of the State of Louisiana. Confederate Records, The National Archives, Chap. 8, Vol. 134, p. 97.

[94] Louisiana *House Journal,* 1865, pp. 7, 12–13.

[95] Louisiana *Acts,* Extra Sess., 1863, pp. 26–27.

Social and Economic Affairs

which, instead of being used for the good of the country, is flooding the land with poison, and death, and crime in all its horrid shapes.[96]

In this matter, at least, Governor Allen failed to win legislative concurrence. He was, however, very diligent in enforcing the law against the manufacture of liquor. He was impelled to do this by the necessity of preserving the supply of breadstuffs, sugar, and molasses for food, which was the chief purpose of the liquor-restriction law. On this subject he wrote:

All breadstuffs, sugar, and molasses are required for the army and for destitute families of soldiers. In many portions of Louisiana grain is already scarce. I daily receive appeals for assistance, and every surplus barrel will be needed during this and the coming year.[97]

Financial relief to indigent families of men in the military service was largely an undertaking of private persons and associations for the first year or two of the war. In addition to this form of aid many of the parishes appropriated funds for assisting those in need. But as the war was prolonged and the conscription acts increased the number of families deprived of the breadwinners, the problem of aiding the destitute became too great for private enterprise or for local governments. The state was forced to assume the responsibility. Louisiana accepted the challenge and adopted a liberal policy toward indigent families of soldiers and seamen. For the reader who is familiar with the history of the raising of an army by the United States in the World War, it should be pointed out that the selective draft of 1917 and 1918 did not deprive families of the one person upon whom they were

[96] Louisiana *House Journal*, 1864, pp. 31–32; Shreveport *Semi-Weekly News*, January 29, 1864.

[97] Dorsey, *Recollections of Henry Watkins Allen*, 243. See also Allen's reference to the subject of intoxicating liquors in his message of January, 1865, in Louisiana *House Journal*, 1865, pp. 7–8.

dependent. There was, therefore, no great social problem of feeding the families of soldiers. But the Confederate conscription acts took every able-bodied white man, except those in certain occupations and industries, regardless of the needs of his dependents. Dependent women and children were thus thrown on their own resources, except for the very small and often irregular pay which the soldier received.

The Louisiana Legislature at Opelousas, January 3, 1863, adopted a comprehensive scheme of relief with an appropriation of $5,000,000. Families of soldiers or sailors, who were citizens and residents of Louisiana at the time of entering the military service, in "necessitous circumstances, or [who] may hereafter become so," were entitled to receive payments from the state treasury as follows: five dollars a month for each child under twelve, ten dollars a month for the wife and "the like sum of ten dollars per month for the father and mother, and five dollars per month for each brother and sister under the age of twelve years, who are members of a family, dependent on such officer, soldier or marine, for a support and unable to support himself or herself." [98]

This remained the basic law on relief to soldiers' families. Subsequent acts merely filled in details or added new machinery to facilitate the operation of the law of 1863. For instance, an act of February 11, 1864, authorized the governor to arrange with Confederate officers for issuing provisions and other necessaries of life to those families entitled to such relief by the act of January 3, 1863. Confederate officers were to be paid for such provisions by the state authorities. At the same time the governor was authorized to purchase corn and other provisions from private individuals to supply families in districts where there was great scarcity.[99] Evidently, it was found that supplying women and children with state and Confederate Treasury notes was not sufficient to prevent acute distress. Speculators and an inadequate transportation

[98] Louisiana *Acts,* 1863, pp. 35–36.   [99] Louisiana *Acts,* 1864, p. 70.

Social and Economic Affairs

system, and perhaps other considerations, forced the state into the business of supplying food.

The task of administering relief was undertaken by Governor Allen with diligence and enthusiasm. The problem became an especially difficult and challenging one after Major General Banks's Red River campaign of March and April, 1864. Allen met the crisis with genuine sympathy for the sufferers and with a display of rare administrative skill. He appointed a number of relief commissioners to distribute provisions to the people of the state,[100] with instructions to sell supplies to persons able to pay for them and to give freely to the destitute.[101] Allen reported to the Legislature in January, 1865, that his agents had distributed 30,792 bushels of corn, 20,182 pounds of bacon, 59,965 pounds of flour, 62,195 pounds of sugar, and 700 beeves.[102] By this date $432,-882.94 had been drawn from the state treasury to issue provisions to families of soldiers and to indigent persons.[103] Some idea of the relief furnished by state bounty may be obtained from the following account of a Natchitoches newspaper in 1864:

No public notice has yet been taken of the State supplies of provisions furnished by Governor Allen to the destitute, and those in better circumstances, who had suffered by the Yankee invasion. His very prompt and liberal efforts in this way demand a public acknowledgment, which it is the object of this article to make. Vast good has been done in this and in the parish of Rapides, especially by this bounty. Early in May last, Governor Allen had loaded two boats with corn, bacon, flour and sugar, destined for this parish, without solicitation, and in anticipation of the wants of those who lived along the path of the enemy, . . .

[100] Summaries of reports of state agents for July–November, 1864, are found in Letters Received. Confederate Records, The National Archives, Chap. 8, Vol. 131, pp. 74–98. For instance, J. D. Strother distributed corn to the people of Winn Parish in July, 1864; and Joseph Pender and W. D. Godwin issued flour to soldiers' families in St. Landry in November.

[101] Louisiana *House Journal*, 1865, pp. 9–10.   [102] *Ibid.*

[103] Report of a special joint committee of the Legislature, *ibid.*, 36–37.

As much as near fifteen thousand pounds of flour, five thousand pounds of sugar, seven thousand pounds of bacon, and five thousand barrels of corn, were received, and either given to the destitute, or sold for such prices as they could afford to pay, to those who were able to pay. Along the line of march of the enemy from Mansfield to the mouth of Cane River, and along the river from above Campte [sic] to the same point, the enemy had taken or destroyed nearly every eatable thing, and what little they left, our own pursuing troops generally appropriated. Thus, those who had laid up abundant supplies for the season, suddenly found themselves deprived of their last ear of corn and pound of bacon by either one army or the other. Starvation literally stared this part of our population in the face, and the bounty of the State came very opportunely.[104]

Wounded soldiers were returning to Louisiana afflicted with permanent or temporary disabilities which made them unable to support themselves. Without government assistance they would have become a burden on the suffering families. In fact, many must have added to the already heavy load borne by the women. Governor Allen recommended to the Legislature in his initial message in January, 1864, that the state pay disabled men $11 a month. The Legislature responded by an act of February 10, 1864, entitled "An Act for the Relief of Sick and Wounded Soldiers." The measure provided for the payment of $11 a month, payable every three months, to every person entering the army or navy from Louisiana who was wounded or disabled in the state or Confederate military service to the extent of being unable to support himself with the necessities of life, and who had been honorably discharged from military service by reason of such disability. It was provided, however, that no person was to receive payment for any period of disability prior to the passage of the act. Two hundred thousand dollars was appropriated to carry out the law.[105]

[104] Dorsey, *Recollections of Henry Watkins Allen*, 279–80.
[105] Louisiana *House Journal*, 1864, p. 32. Shreveport *Semi-Weekly News*,

Social and Economic Affairs

Several hospitals for sick and wounded soldiers were maintained in Louisiana, and the Legislature was liberal in supporting these institutions. More than $100,000, for instance, was appropriated in 1863 for soldiers' hospitals at New Iberia, Greensborough, Natchitoches, and Monroe.[106]

Official acts of state officers and agencies do not complete the story of rendering assistance to the soldier or to his family. The personal touch of human sympathy was never lost, and private efforts and agencies of mercy never ceased to lend a helping hand. Louisiana women, like their sisters of other states of the Confederacy, labored in hospitals and relief stations to help the cause. A Texas soldier has left us this picture of October, 1863:

The court-house in Opelousas was made a hospital for our wounded, and there occurred a scene that melted into tears the most obdurate. It was the sympathy of the women. The ladies of Opelousas and its vicinity, young and old, Catholic and Protestant, came crowding in, and waited upon our men just as if they had been their husbands and brothers. Long will be remembered with heartfelt gratitude, by the Texas soldiers, the appreciative kindness and sympathy of the Louisiana ladies.[107]

In August, 1863, the ladies of Shreveport and vicinity opened a house on Edwards Street for the entertainment of soldiers passing to and from their commands. In the first ten days one hundred soldiers were fed and lodged and provided with rations for their journey. Citizens of Shreveport and Caddo and Bossier parishes donated such things as

---

January 29, 1864; Louisiana *Acts*, 1864, p. 30. Governor Allen made provision for many individual cases of distress from a contingent fund at his disposal. Wounded or destitute soldiers or mothers of such men were paid from $50 to $100 for expenses to travel home. One item of October 18, 1864, shows a gift of $200 to a woman for the expense of burying her child. See Contingent Fund, State of Louisiana, 1860–1865. Records of the War Department, Confederate Records, The National Archives, Chap. 8, Vol. 116 (microfilm copy possessed by the writer).

[106] See Louisiana *Acts*, 1862–1863, p. 26, and *Acts*, Extra Sess., 1863, p. 4.
[107] Blessington, *The Campaigns of Walker's Texas Division*, 145.

flour, meat, hominy, fruits, potatoes, and peas. A report of the treasurer of this Soldiers' Home for January, 1865, showed a cash expenditure of $870 with a balance of $1,713 in the treasury. Many donations of provisions and a cash contribution of $100 had been received during the month. The home had been visited during January by 535 soldiers, who were given 1,380 meals and 447 lodgings.[108]

Concerts and benefits of various kinds were given to raise money for relief causes. In October, 1863, the ladies of Shreveport gave a concert at the Presbyterian Church and raised $1,500 for the indigent soldiers' wives. In October of 1864 the Shreveport Glee Club gave "a grand vocal and instrumental concert," at the request of Governor Allen, for the benefit of the Missouri troops in the Trans-Mississippi Department. The sum of $5,000 was raised by this means. Shreveport ladies gave another concert in December, 1864, for the benefit of the Eighteenth Louisiana Regiment. According to the newspaper, the house was crowded to capacity and some were turned away. In the same month $3,517 and thirty-four pairs of socks were received as a result of two performances of a concert, one for the whites and one for the "darkies," at the Mansfield Female College. The concert was given for the benefit of the Missouri soldiers.[109]

[108] Shreveport *Semi-Weekly News*, August 28, 1863; Shreveport *News*, February 7, 1865.

[109] Shreveport *Semi-Weekly News*, October 6, 1863; Tunnard, *History of the Third Regiment Louisiana Infantry*, 329; Shreveport *News*, December 13, 1864.

Chapter VIII

Relations with the Confederacy

Anyone familiar with the history of the Confederacy is aware of the fact that the Confederate Government was confronted with and attacked upon the issue of state rights. There are those who believe that the insistence on their "sovereign rights" by the states of the Confederacy was one of the main causes of the failure of the movement for Southern independence. The extent to which this is true will probably never be determined. There is the danger of trying to make out a case for the Confederate Government and, consequently, of laying too much stress on isolated cases of controversies between state capitals and the Richmond government. The whole picture, with instances of co-operation as well as of controversy, is needed to give a balanced view.

It will be remembered that Louisiana sent six delegates to the convention which met at Montgomery, Alabama, on February 4, 1861, to form a provisional government for the seceded states. These delegates performed the mission and participated in the election of the president and vice-president of the Confederacy. They shared also in the labor of drafting the so-called permanent constitution of the Confederate States. It will be remembered also that the Louisiana secession convention of 1861 ceded to the Confederacy the former United States forts, arsenals, lighthouses, mint and customhouse in the state of Louisiana. On March 7 the convention authorized and instructed A. J. Guirot, state depository, to transfer to the Confederate Government the "bullion fund" of the mint and the money collected from custom duties at New Orleans after January 31, 1861. These transfers were made, and on March 14 the Confederate Congress adopted resolutions of thanks for the liberality of the state of Louisiana.[1]

There was some difficulty and apparently some friction at the beginning between Governor Moore and the Confederate authorities over military preparations. This was caused by the changing policies of the general government and by Governor Moore's desire to retain for state use part of the arms and ammunition captured with the Federal arsenal and forts. Later friction resulted from Governor Moore's belief that the defenses of Louisiana were being neglected by the Confederate authorities. While these differences seem to loom large on the records, it should not be overlooked that in the meantime regiment after regiment of Louisiana soldiers, long before Confederate conscription was practiced, were fighting in Virginia and Tennessee.

As related previously, the Confederate Congress adopted acts on February 28 and March 6 providing for the creation of a provisional army for the Confederacy. On March 8 Confederate Secretary of War Walker wrote Governor Moore concerning the acts of Congress and stated that since the organization of a regular army for the Confederacy must necessarily be slow, the main reliance of the general government at the time must be on the state forces then in service. He expressed the hope that Governor Moore would tender the Louisiana troops to the Confederate Government. The next day he appealed to Moore for 1,000 men for Pensacola and 700 for Forts Jackson and St. Philip.[2]

---

[1] *Journal of the Louisiana Convention*, 1861, p. 265; *Statutes at Large of the Provisional Government of the Confederate States*, 18. The "bullion fund" transferred amounted to $389,267.46; the amount of the customs was $147,-519.66.

[2] For both communications see *Official Records*, Ser. IV, Vol. I, 134–35. See

Relations with the Confederacy

When the Louisiana Legislature on March 15, 1861, authorized the governor to transfer the military forces of the state to the Confederate Government, Governor Moore immediately transmitted a copy of the act to Secretary Walker and indicated that he was complying with his request of March 9 for troops. At the same time the Louisiana executive put in a word for his own state by saying: "It is important, for the good of the service and especially with a view to the defense of the Mississippi and the approaches to the city of New Orleans, that an officer with the proper rank should without delay be placed in command of the Military Department of Louisiana." [3] In another communication Governor Moore wrote Walker that a small force of four companies of four-month men would be used to garrison Forts Pike, Macomb, St. Philip, and Jackson. Since the terms of enlistment of these men would soon expire, "I shall expect the Provisional Government of the Confederate States," he said, "to see to the proper protection of those forts." The forts, according to Moore, were inadequately garrisoned and "by no means in a proper state of defense." [4]

The seizure of the arsenal at Baton Rouge on January 10, 1861, resulted in the capture of 47,372 pieces of small arms and considerable gunpowder. On March 15 Governor Moore wired the secretary of war that he was ready to transfer arms and ammunition, and suggested that he send an agent to receive them. Walker accepted the offer, naturally, and sent an agent to Louisiana. When Captain William R. Boggs of the Confederate army appeared at Baton Rouge on March 26 to receive the arsenal for the general government, he found Adjutant General Grivot of Louisiana directing the removal of the serviceable arms to be retained as the property of the state. Boggs immediately wired Walker of this action, and

---

above, page 54 for the acts of the Confederate Congress, and page 55 for the acts of the Louisiana convention and Legislature on this subject.

[3] *Official Records*, Ser. IV, Vol. I, 172.　　[4] *Ibid.*, Ser. I, Vol. LIII, 636.

Louisiana in the Confederacy

Walker wired Governor Moore: "Are not all the arms and ordnance in your arsenal to be turned over to the Government?" Moore replied: "All except a sufficient supply for volunteer companies and militia, should the latter be needed." On March 28 he wrote to Walker:

Louisiana will keep arms only sufficient to arm the volunteer companies being organized throughout the State and to furnish the militia that might be called out in case of an emergency. I directed Adjutant-General Grivot to that effect. Should he have reserved more than I believe necessary for that purpose they will be immediately transferred. Ammunition and everything received from the United States that can be spared will be handed over to the Confederate States. Our interest and destiny are the same, and rest assured all that I can do to promote our success will be done.[5]

There were serviceable arms in the Baton Rouge arsenal when the Confederate authorities took it over. Governor Moore issued an order on the arsenal for arms on April 26. Captain John C. Booth, Confederate officer in charge of the arsenal, refused to honor the governor's order. Moore immediately wired a protest to Secretary Walker, saying, in part: "I have made no transfer to Government. . . . I want enough to arm all volunteers called for and some for the city, and must have them. . . . I cannot send men off unarmed." Walker ordered Captain Booth by wire to let Moore have arms and ammunition, and to Moore he telegraphed: "There is no need of any excitement. Whatever the arsenal contains is for the defense of the country." [6] On May 13 Captain

[5] *Ibid.*, 667–68, and Ser. IV, Vol. I, 171.

[6] These communications are found in *ibid.*, Ser. I, Vol. LIII, 675–76. It would appear, therefore, that the Confederate authorities had possession of the arms in the arsenal at Baton Rouge and surrendered them to Governor Moore on demand. In fairness to Governor Moore, it should be said that he seemed to be interested both in retaining arms for state defense and in seeing that Louisiana soldiers, when they left the state for service, should be equipped with arms. Louisiana regiments were leaving the state supplied by the state with arms from the Baton Rouge arsenal.

Relations with the Confederacy

Booth wired Major Josiah Gorgas, Confederate Chief of Ordnance, that Governor Moore had taken twelve hundred muskets, and added: "I have abandoned the arsenal. . . . The course of the Governor is astonishing." [7] A week later Governor Moore, who was trying to furnish the Confederacy with the troops that had been requested, wired Walker that the arming of any more regiments to leave the state depended upon the number of arms left in the arsenal. "I am emphatically unwilling to leave the State without sufficient arms for home protection," he said.[8]

While it would seem that Governor Moore was imbued with the spirit of local defense and was withholding or threatening to withhold arms from the Confederate Government, the fact remains that the state was fully equipping regiments for service elsewhere in the Confederacy. Moore did write to Secretary Walker on July 6, 1861, that "we ought not to be without arms when we may reasonably expect an invasion ourselves in the fall at furthest," and he made the claim that "our people have exceeded the number called for, more troops being in the field now from this State than were required to fill your requisitions." [9]

There were difficulties, too, in connection with furnishing troops. One disturbing element, at least to Governor Moore, was the fact that the Confederate authorities, who seemed

[7] *Ibid.*, 682.

[8] *Ibid.*, Scr. IV, Vol. I, 337. See also Frank L. Owsley, "Local Defense and the Overthrow of the Confederacy: A Study in State Rights," in *Mississippi Valley Historical Review*, XI (1925), 490–525.

[9] *Official Records*, Ser. IV, Vol. I, 422. Adjutant General Grivot, of Louisiana, wrote to J. P. Benjamin, then Confederate secretary of war, on January 28, 1862: "After having responded to the several requisitions made upon it, and placing into the field not less than 20,000 troops, all armed, the State finds itself at present without arms to supply the volunteer force organized by its citizens for its defense, as there are at present no less than 15,000 troops organized in companies, battalions, regiments, and of that number not more than 6,500 are armed, a large portion of which are the most miserable and unserviceable arms known in the civilized world; . . . ." *Ibid.*, Ser. I, Vol. LIII, 775.

none too certain of their own plans and needs in the early months of the war, expected the states to enlist and train troops and hold them in readiness for a call to be sent to a designated place. Governor Moore objected to this practice as being beyond the resources of the state. He insisted that the Confederate authorities receive and muster into the Confederate service the troops from Louisiana as soon as they were organized. As it was, the Confederate Government would not take charge of them until wanted for immediate service, and the state could not, for lack of means, according to Moore, keep them in camp to move at any moment. Of course, with the passing of time and the increasing need for more men in the armies of the Confederacy, this no longer remained a problem.[10]

The organization of regiments and the transfer to the Confederate service proceeded smoothly for several weeks. It will be remembered that on April 18, 1861, the secretary of war made requisition upon Louisiana for 3,000 soldiers for twelve months' service. This number was raised to 8,000 when a requisition for 5,000 additional men was made on April 21. Governor Moore immediately issued a proclamation calling for volunteers. On April 29 the First Regiment of Louisiana Volunteers under Colonel Albert G. Blanchard was transferred to the Confederate service and was ordered to Virginia. The Second and Third Regiments were mustered into the Confederate army on May 11. After the organization of the Fourth and Fifth Regiments on a twelve months' enlistment basis Governor Moore was informed on May 13 that "no more twelve-months volunteers will be received from Louisiana,"

[10] For Governor Moore's position see his correspondence with Secretary Walker and Attorney General Benjamin, April 23 and May 1, 1861, respectively, *ibid.*, Ser. IV, Vol. I, 235, 272. As an evidence of the fact that the Confederate Government was not certain of its needs at this time, the reader's attention is called to the words of the Confederate secretary of war to Governor Moore on May 3, 1861, when he wired: "It is impossible now to say when additional troops will be required." *Ibid.*, 276.

Relations with the Confederacy

but only enlistments for the war. The action of the Confederate War Department resulted from an act of the Confederate Congress of May 8, 1861, which authorized the President to accept volunteers to serve during the war, and from President Davis's preference for such enlistment to those for short terms because he believed the war would be a long one. Moore protested against applying the new policy to the Fourth and Fifth Regiments, whose men had been accepted and organized by the state for twelve months' service. After several weeks' delay the governor won his case as far as the Fourth Regiment was concerned, as Secretary Walker finally accepted it on a twelve months' basis. When Moore failed to get the Fifth Regiment accepted for one year he appealed to the men to enlist in companies for the war and gave them several days to consider the matter. At the end of the period the regiment was ordered disbanded, since no companies volunteered for the war. On the following day, May 26, Governor Moore received word that the Confederate authorities would receive the regiment for twelve months. It was necessary, however, to reorganize the Fifth Regiment, since many of the men were on their way home. The incident resulted in friction between state and Confederate authorities and created dissatisfaction among the soldiers involved.[11]

According to the report of the Confederate adjutant general's office, there were on September 30, 1861, sixteen regiments and seven special battalions of Louisiana troops in the Confederate service. One regiment was at Pensacola, Florida, under Major General Braxton Bragg, who had lived in Louisiana since 1856. Three regiments were in Tennessee, where Major General Leonidas Polk, the Louisiana bishop,

[11] *Ibid.*, Ser. IV, Vol. I, 295–96, 307, 316–17, 747–50. Governor Moore resented the action of the Confederate authorities in 1861 in attempting to raise volunteers in Louisiana without consulting him. He believed that proper courtesy and military efficiency required that troops should be raised only through the governor of a state. See *ibid.*, 194–95, and Frank L. Owsley, *State Rights in the Confederacy* (Chicago, 1925), 80–81.

was serving; and ten regiments were in Virginia, where General P. G. T. Beauregard, another Louisianian, was a corps commander in the Army of the Potomac. The Sixth, Seventh, and Eighth Louisiana Regiments participated in the memorable battle of Bull Run in July, and the Eleventh was in the battle of Belmont in Kentucky in August. By the middle of November, 1861, more than twenty-three thousand Louisiana troops were in the Confederate Army. According to Grivot, Louisiana adjutant general, all Louisiana troops had been fully armed and equipped.[12]

The fears of the state authorities concerning an attack on New Orleans and their pleas and complaints to the Confederate Government about what was considered the neglect of the defenses of the city and the state have already been mentioned.[13] Joined to the complaints of the lack of adequate measures of defense was the charge that Major General Twiggs, who assumed command of the Department of Louisiana on May 31, 1861, was unable to render acceptable service because of advanced age. Twiggs was born in 1790 and was therefore seventy-one years old.[14] Former Governor A. B. Roman, a distinguished Louisianian, wrote to President Davis on September 15, 1861, concerning the defenses of Louisiana and said that Twiggs was completely disqualified for the position which he held, since he was confined to an armchair by "infirmities." Walter G. Robinson, a citizen of New Orleans, wrote to Confederate Attorney General Benjamin, September 20, on the same subject and among other things said: "We want a competent officer in place of General Twiggs. He is not only too old, but physically incompetent." On the same day Governor Moore urged President Davis to send a commander to Louisiana who "with youth,

---

[12] The report of the Confederate adjutant general's office is found in *Official Records*, Ser. IV, Vol. I, 626–33; see also the report of the Louisiana adjutant general, November 22, 1861, *ibid.*, 747–55.

[13] See above, pp. 97–98.   [14] *Dictionary of American Biography*, XIX, 83.

Relations with the Confederacy

energy, and military ability" would stimulate activity and inspire confidence. On September 27 Benjamin and C. M. Conrad, a Louisiana member of the Confederate Congress, addressed the following letter to President Davis:

The undersigned, citizens of New Orleans, beg respectfully to represent that we have become satisfied, from the almost unanimous report of those who are best acquainted with General Twiggs, that advancing age has impaired his faculties to such an extent as to render it evident that he is incompetent to the command assigned him. We were not, perhaps, without influence in your selection of General Twiggs for that command. We are his friends and always have been, and it is with pain but with a sense of public duty that we feel compelled to solicit his withdrawal from an important command, which, at his advanced age, cannot be safely confided to him.[15]

Other complaints were made concerning the incompetence of Major General Twiggs. On October 5, 1861, Twiggs wired the secretary of war to send an active and efficient officer to relieve him, saying, "My health will not permit me to take the field." Two days later the War Department directed Major General Mansfield Lovell to proceed to New Orleans and relieve General Twiggs.[16]

Lovell was a comparatively young man, being but thirty-nine years old. He had graduated from West Point at the age of twenty and had served as first lieutenant in the war in Mexico. In 1858 he became superintendent of street improvements and deputy street commissioner in New York City. He resigned from the service of the city in September, 1861, to accept a commission as major general in the Confederate army.[17]

---

[15] Roman to Davis, *Official Records*, Ser. I, Vol. LIII, 739; Robinson to Benjamin, *ibid.*, 742; Moore to Davis, *ibid.*, Ser. I, Vol. VI, 740; Benjamin and Conrad to Davis, *ibid.*, Ser. I, Vol. LIII, 744.

[16] For Twiggs's wire to the Secretary of War see *ibid.*, Ser. I, Vol. LIII, 748. The special order, appointing Lovell to command at New Orleans is in *ibid.*, Ser. I, Vol. VI, 643.   [17] *Dictionary of American Biography*, XI, 441–42.

Louisiana in the Confederacy

The new Confederate commander in Louisiana was not without his critics. The fact that he was a Northern man who did not join the Confederate ranks until after the battle of Manassas caused some suspicion of his motives. It was charged that he had instructed Union soldiers during the first months of the war. Braxton Bragg thought that Lovell had been "bought" by the Confederacy. John B. Jones, at Richmond, wrote in his diary on February 2, 1862, that some Southern people "feared that New Orleans would be taken without firing a shot," since Lovell was in charge of the defenses. "He delivered lectures, it is said, last summer," Jones wrote, "on the defenses of New York, *in that city*." [18]

Naturally, Major General Lovell was severely condemned by Louisianians for the loss of New Orleans in April, 1862. The people of the state could not understand why the city should have fallen without stiff resistance by the soldiers under Lovell. He was blamed for this as well as for the passage of the forts by the Federal boats. Governor Moore wrote to President Davis, June 12, 1862:

The shock experienced by the fall of New Orleans was deadening. Our people were appalled. As usual on such occasions our people demanded a victim, and the industry and energy displayed by General Lovell previous to the fatal day were forgotten in the panic and terror inspired by an event as unexpected to the community as it was unfortunately unprovided for by him.[19]

J. B. Jones commented on June 25: "The people of Louisiana are protesting strongly against permitting General Lovell

[18] John B. Jones, *A Rebel War Clerk's Diary at the Confederate States Capital* (New York, 1935), I, 89, 108. For Braxton Bragg's opinion of Lovell, see G. P. Whittington, "Papers of Thomas O. Moore," in *Louisiana Historical Quarterly*, XIII (1930), 29–31. Gustavus W. Smith, from New York, March 5, 1861, wrote to General Beauregard concerning himself and Lovell and said that "propositions from either Mr. Davis or his military representative, his Secretary of War, would, if up to our standard (as we understand it), be favorably considered and in all probability accepted." *Official Records*, Ser. I, Vol. LIII, 129–30.　　　　[19] *Official Records*, Ser. I, Vol. XV, 753–54.

to remain in command in that state since the fall of New Orleans, and they attribute that disgraceful event, some to his incompetency, and others to treason." [20]

With New Orleans and vicinity in Federal hands, Louisiana west of the Mississippi was virtually separated from that portion of the state east of the river. Governor Moore lost no time in urging the Confederate authorities to organize the western section of the state into a military department and appoint a general to command. On May 8 he wired President Davis to this effect and added: "My personal preference is General Bragg; either he or General Price would please the people and the army." Davis replied immediately that a general to command the department would be sent "as soon as practicable." [21]

When Western Louisiana (Louisiana west of the Mississippi River, which is fully five sixths of the state's area, was referred to as Western Louisiana during the Civil War) was divided into two parts—that part north of the Red River attached to Arkansas and placed under Major General Thomas C. Hindman, and all south of the Red River attached to Texas under Brigadier General Paul O. Hébert—Governor Moore, July 25, 1862, made a vigorous protest to George W. Randolph, Confederate secretary of war Louisiana, he said, was "completely sunk out of existence," and the headquarters of Hindman and Hébert, at Little Rock and San Antonio, respectively, were both inaccessible to him. He requested that Louisiana west of the Mississippi be placed under one general whose headquarters should be in the state. Moore's wishes were soon to be fulfilled, for the Confederate War Department on July 28 assigned Richard Taylor to command

[20] Jones, *A Rebel War Clerk's Diary*, I, 135. Major General Lovell was freed from any serious blame for the fall of New Orleans by a Confederate Court of Inquiry in 1863. For conclusions of the Court, see *Official Records*, Ser. I, Vol. VI, 641–43.

[21] Moore to Davis, *Official Records*, Ser. I, Vol. LIII, 806; Davis to Moore, *ibid.*, Ser. I, Vol. VI, 888.

the District of Western Louisiana. Taylor arrived at Opelousas sometime in August.[22]

Conflicts arose over the seizure of state property by Confederate forces. Governor Moore wrote to General Beauregard, then in command of the Western Department, about the establishment of two military training camps in Louisiana and added:

I have no tents nor stores to supply the camps. I am shorn of everything I had. General Lovell's quartermaster has taken all that was brought out of New Orleans, and, after the fashion of that most conscientious class of officials, he admits that he has more than belongs to him, but declines to deliver any to my agent. Let me, therefore, in passing, ask and beg that in appointing a quartermaster to this place you will send not an honest one —that were asking an impossibility—but one that will not take more than half of what I may be able to get together. If what is taken from me were accounted for to the Confederate Government there would be no loss to the public, but————(?)[23]

In the latter part of June, 1862, a party of Confederate soldiers was sent to Alexandria by Major General Hindman. The troops, under the orders of their captain, seized the contents of a state warehouse. Guns, blankets, and clothing, property of the state of Louisiana, were taken. On July 8 Governor Moore sent a vigorous protest to Secretary Randolph, characterizing the affair as an unwarranted seizure of property and informing Randolph that a force of militia had been ordered to Alexandria to prevent a similar raid. Moore asked for the dismissal of two officers connected with the affair and said that "my marksmen may save you the trouble if they come again." On receipt of Moore's letter, Randolph issued a general order prohibiting seizure of state property.[24]

[22] For Moore's protest to Randolph, see *ibid.*, Ser. I, Vol. LIII, 819; for Taylor's appointment, see *ibid.*, Ser. I, Vol. XV, 789, 791.

[23] *Ibid.*, Ser. I, Vol. LIII, 812–13. This letter was dated June 11, 1862.

[24] *Ibid.*, Ser. I, Vol. XV, 773–75. Another case of seizure of state property which aroused Moore to make strong protests and led the entire Louisiana

Relations with the Confederacy

During the latter part of 1862 the opinion prevailed in Louisiana that the state was being neglected by the Confederate military authorities. This was due no doubt to the fall of New Orleans and to the dangers inherent in the occupation of that city by a Federal army. Many Louisianians believed that men of the state should be retained at home instead of being sent to Virginia and Tennessee. Governor Moore thought that the requirements of the Confederate Government, as far as Louisiana was concerned, should be reduced, since nearly one third of the state was in the hands of the Federals. On December 1, 1862, he demanded of President Davis that either Louisiana troops be returned to fight for their homes or others be sent "to prevent the utter ruin of this State." "What has been done for Louisiana?" he asked, and answered his own question by saying: "Nothing was done at New Orleans but sending a general there, and nothing more is being done now." As a result of such neglect the public mind was depressed, and a feeling of bitterness prevailed. Louisianians were discussing the question, he said, of how much better the state would have been defended had she retained her independence.[25] Richard Taylor, writing from the viewpoint of a Confederate officer, told somewhat the same story when he said:

I can assure you that at times I am almost disheartened by the want of patriotic feeling exhibited here. The people think or affect to think that our State has been neglected by the government at Richmond, and because soldiers are not sent to defend

delegation in the Confederate Congress to address a protest to the secretary of war was the seizure of arms and ammunition belonging to the state of Louisiana by Major General Earl Van Dorn in late June, 1862. See *ibid.*, 766–68, and Ser. I, Vol. LIII, 825–26.

[25] *Ibid.*, Ser. I, Vol. LIII, 836–37; see also Moore to Davis, June 2, 1862, *ibid.*, Ser. I, Vol. XV, 747–49. According to an official report, the number of effective troops under Major General Richard Taylor in the District of Louisiana was 6,882 in January, 1863. This was 2.1 per cent of the total number of effective troops reported for the Confederate army at that date. *Ibid.*, Ser. IV, Vol. II, 380.

them they are unwilling to do anything to defend themselves. In the lower part of the State this feeling is almost universal, and of course I as the representative of the government am abused on all sides for not accomplishing impossibilities.[26]

Because volunteering had fallen off, the Confederate Congress resorted to conscription in April, 1862, making all male citizens between the ages of eighteen and thirty-five, with certain classes of exemption allowed, liable to military service. Confederate authorities experienced some difficulties in enforcing the law in Louisiana. Some conscripts deserted at the first opportunity, and many failed to report for duty. Major General Taylor reported to Governor Moore in November, 1862, that it was "notorious" that a large number of deserters and recusant conscripts were to be found throughout the state and urged Moore to cause the arrest of all such persons. Governor Moore responded by ordering the arrest of all deserters and of all conscripts who had not reported.[27] According to Taylor, the parishes along the Mississippi River from Arkansas to the Gulf and the region along the Gulf coast were the sections in which it was most difficult to execute the conscript law. He tried the policy of authorizing persons of influence in these parishes to raise volunteer organizations. Meeting with little success, he sent cavalry to force the conscripts into camps of instruction.[28]

The situation in Louisiana, as elsewhere, did not improve when Confederate armies met with reverses in the field, Confederate soldiers went unpaid, and letters from home to the soldier in the ranks told of suffering among loved ones. In September, 1863, a Confederate scouting party reported some

[26] Taylor to Dr. James C. Egan (in Virginia), an undated letter in the Lavinia Egan Collection.

[27] *Official Records*, Ser. I, Vol. XV, 874. Ella Lonn, *Desertions During the Civil War* (New York, 1928), has an excellent discussion of the causes of desertions.

[28] Report of Major General Richard Taylor to Secretary Randolph, November 21, 1862, *Official Records*, Ser. I, Vol. XV, 872.

Relations with the Confederacy

twelve hundred or more conscripts and deserters secreted in
St. Tammany, Livingston, and Ascension parishes; Lieutenant General Kirby Smith at Shreveport was directing a
Confederate colonel to break up organizations of deserters
and conscripts collecting in Union Parish for the purpose of
resisting Confederate authorities.[29] From Alexandria on
October 12, 1863, Brigadier General Henry Watkins Allen
—soon to be governor—wrote to Secretary of War Seddon:
"Things over here look gloomy. . . . the people are desponding—very desponding. . . . The country here is full of deserters and runaway conscripts. . . . I am told they number
8,000—a terrible state of affairs." [30]

Disaffection and disloyalty to the Confederate cause were
found in civil life. Of course, in Louisiana, as elsewhere,
there were many who had opposed the secession movement.
Although such persons were in the minority and from the nature of things had to repress their true sentiments, there were
times and places when anti-Confederate feeling found expression. Such manifestation of opposition to the Confederacy tended to become more bold as the fortunes of war went
against the South and the prospect of Union victory grew.
The conscription acts, the Impressment Act, and the tax in
kind—each had its share in causing a growth of disloyalty to
the Confederacy.[31]

As early as April, 1862, Governor Moore was informed of

[29] *Ibid.*, Ser. I, Vol. XXVI, Pt. I, 313–14, Pt. II, 215. Assistant Adjutant
General Samuel S. Anderson at Shreveport wrote to Colonel Benjamin F.
Danley in Arkansas, November 5, 1863: "By sending a single company into
one of the parishes of Louisiana, 400 conscripts were obtained, only, however,
after shooting four of their number." *Ibid.*, Ser. I, Vol. XXII, Pt. II, 1057–58.

[30] *Ibid.*, Ser. I, Vol. LIII, 900 01; also Jones, *A Rebel War Clerk's Diary*, II,
86. Of course, not all deserters in Louisiana were Louisianians, though probably most recusant conscripts were. It was reported, for instance, in September, 1863, that an "unparalleled number of desertions" had occurred among
the Texas troops of General Richard Taylor's command. *Official Records*, Ser.
I, Vol. XXVI, Pt. II, 241. Taylor's army was in Louisiana at the time.

[31] See Georgia Lee Tatum, *Disloyalty in the Confederacy* (Chapel Hill,
1934), Chap. I, for a discussion of the causes of disloyalty to the Confederacy.

the existence of societies and clubs and secret meetings of "disloyal men" in the parishes of Natchitoches and Sabine. According to Moore, these groups had asserted a desire to restore the Union, denied connection with the Confederate cause, and had committed "sundry other acts of disaffection and disloyalty to the present Government." He directed the proper military authorities to ascertain the ringleaders and arrest them.[32] The following official report was made to General S. Cooper, Confederate adjutant general, on conditions in Arkansas and parts of Louisiana in December, 1863:

The condition and temper of the people were very unsatisfactory. Great dissatisfaction prevailed in many sections, and generally among the mass our success deemed almost a matter of indifference, and in many localities the advent of the enemy would be hailed as a relief. Major Johnson is of the opinion (and I fully concur with him) that much and perhaps most of this feeling is caused by the general disregard of all law or sanctity of private rights by the officers and men of our own army. In the matter of impressment is this peculiarly the case.[33]

The Louisiana Legislature adopted two measures in February, 1864, designed to punish disloyalty to the Confederate cause. The first act was entitled "An Act to Punish Persons for Harbouring Deserters." Any person harboring or concealing a deserter from the Confederate army, or who advised or aided a deserter to escape or conceal himself, was liable to imprisonment up to one year and to a fine up to $1,000. By the second act a penalty of from three months' to five years' imprisonment in the State Penitentiary was provided for any person convicted of (1) saying, printing, or writing any word or words, with the intention willfully and maliciously to subvert the Confederate or state government; (2) using any "ap-

[32] *Official Records,* Ser. II, Vol. II, 1422.
[33] Thomas E. Adams to General S. Cooper, January 29, 1864, *ibid.,* Ser. I, Vol. XXXIV, Pt. II, 921–22. Adams had traveled in the trans-Mississippi West with Major J. P. Johnson and was reporting for Major Johnson upon conditions in Arkansas and a portion of Louisiana.

pliances or influences" to prevent any person from enlisting in the military or naval services of Louisiana or the Confederacy; (3) adhering to, aiding, assisting, or supporting the constitution, laws, military orders or proclamations of the United States, "or any other pretended State Government created within the limits of this State, contrary to the constitution and laws of the same. . . ." [34]

It is doubtful that either of these acts had any salutary results. Confederate prestige and authority in Louisiana in 1864 were on the wane, and the acts referred to in the preceding paragraph constitute part of the proof. They were intended as medicines, so to speak, to cure a dangerous malady. But the disease would not be abated. When Major General Banks made his expedition up the Red River in March and April, 1864, many citizens of Central Louisiana came forward and took the oath of allegiance to the United States, and some white men enlisted in the Federal army. Among those who took the oath of allegiance were several men of prominence. In an editorial entitled "Returning to the Fold," the New Orleans *True Delta,* of April 8, 1864, said:

A Correspondent from Alexandria has transmitted to us the joyful intelligence of the return of two prominent men of Louisiana to the Union fold. We are always glad to welcome back the lost sheep, and are ever ready to slay the fatted calf at the return of each prodigal son.

The two prominent "prodigal sons," according to the *True Delta,* were John K. Elgee, who had served as chairman of the flag committee in the secession convention of 1861, and Lewis Texada, another Whig, who had been the Know-Nothing candidate for lieutenant governor in 1856. The *True Delta* said that the taking of the oath of allegiance to the United States by "several hundred" (probably an exaggeration) in

[34] Louisiana *Acts,* 1864, pp. 16, 74. These acts were adopted on February 8 and 11.

Alexandria "would indicate that the deluded victims of Slidell and Benjamin are returning to reason." [35]

The Confederate system of impressment was the source of much friction between the people and the state authorities on the one hand and the Confederate Government on the other. According to the law, prices that the Confederate Government would pay for commodities that it needed would be fixed by commissioners appointed by President Davis and the governor of the state. The system was designed to supply the army at reasonable prices. By this means the Government avoided paying the exorbitant prices which too often prevailed in the Confederacy. On the other hand, the system allowed the Government to fix the terms of exchange between the individual's property and the Government's steadily declining currency. The Government appropriated the commodities and paid the prices fixed by the commissioners—price schedules being made every two months.

One criticism of the Impressment Act was that it retarded production. The *Louisiana Democrat* (Alexandria), comparing the market prices and the impressment prices for flour and shoes in November, 1863, found flour selling for $100 per one hundred pounds whereas the government schedule allowed $12 for the same quantity; and shoes, because of the extreme scarcity of leather, selling for $40 a pair whereas the price fixed by the Government was $5. "Now who will make

[35] See also Flinn, *Campaigning With Banks in Louisiana*, 96; *Official Records*, Ser. I, Vol. XXXIV, Pt. I, 194–218 for Major General Banks's Report; Whittington, "Rapides Parish, Louisiana—A History," in *loc. cit.*, XVII, 549–51. Whittington named several other prominent men who took the oath of allegiance and followed Banks to New Orleans, one being C. W. Boyce who edited a Bell newspaper in Alexandria in the campaign of 1860. A friend wrote to former Governor Moore on July 7, 1864: "I rejoice to hear that Mrs. Moore did not take the oath and much regret to hear that so many of the citizens of Rapides have taken it." J. R. Mainor to Moore, Thomas O. Moore Papers. Doubtless many took the oath because they thought that the Federal occupation would be permanent, and they took this step to protect their property.

shoes," the editor asked, "if they are liable to have them seized as soon as completed at five dollars?"[36] Major General Taylor expressed the opinion in January, 1864, that the deficiency in subsistence and supplies for his army was artificially increased by the schedule of prices fixed by the commissioners. Corn was selling for $3 a barrel, but the Government was paying only about half that much. As a result, as Taylor saw it, farmers would declare they had no more corn than was necessary for their own use; "and the Government is now compelled to resort to impressment even for bread corn." Continuing, Taylor said:

This practice alienates the affections of the people, debauches the troops, and ultimately destroys its own capacity to produce results. Planters will hide much of their produce or remove it beyond our reach, and will assuredly in future plant no more than they themselves require.[37]

Another criticism of the Confederate compulsion policy was that impressments were often unnecessary, arbitrary, and illegal. Governor Moore in his last message to the Legislature in January, 1864, characterized the impressment law as "most unwise" and advocated its repeal. "Its effect," he said, "has been to oppress the citizens, and to afford idle and inefficient officers a means of obtaining without labor or trouble, that which could and ought to have been provided by their timely exertion and forethought."[38] A few days later Governor Allen assailed the way the Impressment Act was being executed, telling the legislators: "Confederate officers have, in a peremptory and insolent manner, taken the property, simply leaving their receipts for the same. This must be stopped. It shall be stopped." He recommended a law punishing by imprisonment in the penitentiary any person who

[36] Alexandria *Louisiana Democrat*, November 25, 1863.

[37] Taylor to William R. Boggs, chief of staff, January 21, 1864, *Official Records*, Ser. I, Vol. XXXIV, Pt. II, 902–03.

[38] Louisiana *House Journal*, 1864, pp. 8–9.

seized or impressed property contrary to the laws of Congress.[39] Allen complained also to President Davis concerning the arbitrary execution of the Impressment Act. Equipment and supplies of all kinds—horses, mules, wagons, slaves, and corn—had been taken by officers claiming to have the authority; in some cases no receipts had been given to the owners, and then payment was refused. In concluding, Allen said: "It is my sincere desire to act in the greatest harmony with your Excellency in the execution of the laws of Congress. But at the same time, my people must be protected in all their constitutional and legal rights." [40]

The Legislature adopted two measures in response to Governor Allen's recommendation. The first was a joint resolution of February 6 instructing the governor to use his most strenuous efforts with the military authorities of the Confederate Government to prevent the further illegal impressment of property and to effect the surrender of property unlawfully taken. The second measure provided that Confederate officers or other persons impressing private property in violation of the law should be liable to indictment before the district court of the parish in which the impressment was made and, if convicted, should be liable to punishment by a fine up to $5,000 and imprisonment up to six months.[41]

The Legislature protested also against what was considered the arbitrary and unnecessary seizure and "spoliation" of private property by Confederate military authorities on the plea of the possibility of such property falling into the hands of the enemy. A joint resolution was adopted, February 10, 1864, charging that such seizures caused "great unnecessary

[39] *Ibid.,* 32; Shreveport *Semi-Weekly News,* January 29, 1864.

[40] Quoted by Dorsey, *Recollections of Henry Watkins Allen,* 247. Other states also made complaints against the Impressment Act. For a resolution of the South Carolina Legislature, see *Official Records,* Ser. IV, Vol. II, 863–64; for the resolution of the Texas Legislature, see *ibid.,* Ser. I, Vol. LIII, 994–95.

[41] Louisiana *Acts,* 1864, pp. 8, 18. One cause of complaint was the impersonation of impressment officers.

suffering and destitution to many people" and authorizing the governor to protest to the military authorities or to take any other action against illegal seizures. On the same date the Legislature went so far as to provide punishment of from one to three years in the penitentiary for any officer or soldier or any other person "who shall seize, take or remove any species of property in this State, under any pretense whatsoever without the consent of the owner or agent, unless duly authorized and directed by the Governor. . . ." The act specifically stated, however, that it did not apply to the lawful execution of the Confederate Impressment Act, or any other act of Congress.[42]

Kirby Smith at Shreveport on December 28, 1864, wrote to Adjutant General Cooper that the scarcity of funds in his department had so seriously impaired the public credit that it was almost impossible to procure articles of prime necessity for the army, even by impressment. Impressment without the money to pay for the property impressed was so unjust and so illegal, according to Smith, that it excited a spirit of opposition among the people. The public credit was very low because the Confederate Government had "outstanding in the hands of citizens [presumably of the Trans-Mississippi Department] over $40,000,000 of certified accounts, some of these nearly of two years' standing." [43]

While the Legislature and Governor Allen seem to have been somewhat belligerent in their attitude toward the questions of impressment and seizures, they proved themselves cordial and co-operative in other matters affecting the Confederacy. For instance, on February 10, 1864, an act was passed granting the Confederate Government the right to make use of the timber on the public lands of the state for the period of the war. Moreover, a joint resolution was adopted on February 8, expressing confidence in President

[42] Louisiana *Acts,* 1864, pp. 57–58, for the joint resolution and the penal act.   [43] *Official Records,* Ser. I, Vol. XLI, Pt. IV, 1129–30.

Louisiana in the Confederacy

Davis and the Confederate military authorities and asserting Louisiana's "unfaltering determination to spare no expense of blood or treasure in defense of the Confederate States of America as a free and independent republic." [44]

Governor Allen was most loyal to the Confederate cause. His efforts to raise the value of the Confederate Treasury notes have already been referred to. Moreover, his efforts, in co-operation with the Legislature, to advance the economic life of Louisiana, to alleviate suffering among families of soldiers, and to aid men disabled in the Confederate military service were calculated to inspire hope and confidence in the cause of the Confederacy. He let no opportunity pass to appeal to the people for their wholehearted support of the war. On April 2, 1864, as Banks was moving up the Red River, he issued an executive proclamation from Shreveport, appealing to every man able to bear arms to come to the defense of home and fireside. It was a most eloquent appeal:

Come, then, as did the patriotic Greeks who defied the hosts of the Persian monarch. Come as did the heroes who left their ploughs standing in the field and gathered to the defense of Rome. Come as did the men of Bruce at Bannockburn. Come as did the soldiers of Israel's king who met and conquered the Philistines. Come, oh! come, as freemen born—as freemen who intend to live—as freemen who are resolved to die! . . . Ladies of Louisiana! I appeal to you by all you hold sacred in heaven or dear on earth to urge every man who can fire a gun to respond to this call. The enemy must be met. We will conquer him and you shall be free.[45]

The modern reader is tempted to smile when reading this message. But it must be remembered that a week later the Confederate forces turned back the armies of Nathaniel Banks and A. J. Smith at Mansfield and Pleasant Hill and saved Louisiana from complete conquest. Such a message

[44] Louisiana *Acts*, 1864, p. 30; *Official Records*, Ser. IV, Vol. III, 94.
[45] Quoted by the New Orleans *Daily True Delta*, June 1, 1864.

might have inspired the soldiers of Taylor, Mouton, and Polignac. Whatever the effect, this was not the last eloquent appeal of Henry Watkins Allen in behalf of the Confederacy. Early in 1865, at the request of Lieutenant General Buckner, he went to Mansfield and made an address to the demoralized soldiers. Three weeks after Lee's surrender at Appomattox, Governor Allen issued from his office in Shreveport a message to the soldiers of Arkansas, Louisiana, Missouri, and Texas and to the citizens of his own state of Louisiana, encouraging them to hope and to strive for final victory.[46]

Louisiana made a notable contribution to the civil life of the Confederacy. A. B. Roman, twice governor of the state, was one of the peace commissioners appointed by President Davis early in 1861 to negotiate with the United States for a peaceable separation. Pierre A. Rost was a member of the first mission sent abroad by the Confederacy. Early in 1861 he went to Europe with William L. Yancey and A. Dudley Mann to seek recognition and to make treaties with England, France, Spain, Russia, and Belgium. He worked at this task in London and Paris from April, 1861, to January, 1862, and later represented the Confederate cause at Madrid.[47] Judah P. Benjamin served in the Confederate Cabinet throughout the war, first as attorney general, then as secretary of war, and finally as secretary of state. He has been called "the brain of the Confederacy." [48] John Slidell, who was serving with Benjamin in the United States Senate when Louisiana seceded, was sent to the court of Napoleon III to seek to per-

[46] Dorsey, *Recollections of Henry Watkins Allen,* 295; Shreveport *Semi-Weekly News,* May 11, 1865.

[47] Owsley, *King Cotton Diplomacy,* 52–87, 300; *Official Records, Navy,* Ser. II, Vol. III, *passim.*

[48] James Schouler, *History of the United States of America Under the Constitution* (New York, 1894–1899), VI, 89. Schouler says: "Contemporaries had said at the outset that Toombs was the brain of this Confederacy; but that title, as events developed, belongs rather to Attorney-General Benjamin, the ablest, most versatile, and most constant of all Davis's civil counselors." Quoted with permission of Dodd, Mead and Company, publishers.

Louisiana in the Confederacy

suade France to recognize the Confederacy. While in France he negotiated the famous Erlanger loan for the Confederate Government.

The Louisiana delegation in the Confederate Congress was not without distinction. One of the group—C. M. Conrad—had served in the United States Senate and was secretary of war, 1850–1853, in the cabinet of President Fillmore. At least three of the delegation were college graduates. John Perkins, Jr., graduated from Yale in 1840 and later took a law degree at Harvard. Thomas J. Semmes, who served in the Confederate Senate, was also a graduate of the Harvard Law School, besides holding a degree from Georgetown College. He had served as United States district attorney in Louisiana in 1857–1858 and attorney general of Louisiana, 1859–1861, leaving that position to enter the Confederate Senate. Some idea of his ability may be gathered from the fact that he was elected president of the American Bar Association in 1886. Duncan F. Kenner was a graduate of Miami University (Ohio). After graduating from Miami he had traveled and studied in Europe.[49]

Among the Louisiana Confederate congressmen Duncan F. Kenner probably served with greatest distinction. He was chairman of the Committee on Ways and Means in the House of Representatives, 1861–1865. In 1864 he urged upon Benjamin, then serving as secretary of state, the sending of a special commission to Europe to offer Great Britain and France the abolition of slavery in return for recognition of the independence of the Confederacy. President Davis reluctantly agreed to the idea and sent Kenner as a sole commissioner with the rank of minister plenipotentiary. The mission was a secret one, and Kenner went to New York in disguise and sailed from there on February 11, 1865. The

[49] See articles on Conrad, Kenner, and Semmes in the *Dictionary of American Biography* and in *The South in the Building of a Nation;* for John Perkins, Jr., see Robert D. Calhoun, "The John Perkins Family of Northeast Louisiana," in *Louisiana Historical Quarterly,* XIX (1936), 82–85.

military situation at that time, however, destroyed European confidence in the Confederacy, and Kenner's mission failed.[50]

Although political campaigns of this period did not arouse much enthusiasm, the Congressional election of 1863 in Louisiana was not devoid of an issue; and there was at least one announced platform. In this race the candidates opposing the incumbents made an issue of the Confederate Exemption Law. The Confederate Congress adopted a measure on October 11, 1862, exempting from military service the owner or overseer of twenty or more slaves. This law was unpopular with the masses; and on May 1, 1863, Congress adopted another law on the subject, allowing exemption for one person for each farm or plantation the sole property of a minor, a person of unsound mind, an unmarried woman, or a person absent from home in the military service, on which farm or plantation there were twenty or more slaves. This act, too, had its critics, and it was subject to attacks in the campaign of 1863. The candidates of the opposition charged the members standing for re-election with supporting the law. Since Congress had acted in secret session, the incumbents maintained a silence on the question. It was charged that the law "made a broad and degrading line of distinction between the rich slave owner and the poor white man—between the silken son of pleasure and the hardy son of toil." [51]

The only political platform in the election of 1863 which the writer has been able to find was one issued jointly by Robert Mott and A. L. Tucker, candidates for Congress from

[50] James M. Callahan, *The Diplomatic History of the Southern Confederacy* (Baltimore, 1901), 260–67; Owsley, *King Cotton Diplomacy*, 550–61.

[51] Quotation from a letter signed "Americus" in the Shreveport *Semi-Weekly News*, October 30, 1863. For the Confederate exemption laws of 1862 and 1863, see *Public Laws of the Confederate States,* 1 Cong., 2 Sess., Chap. XLV, and 1 Cong., 3 Sess., Chap. LXXX. The Confederate Congress adopted a new exemption law on February 17, 1864, exempting "one person as overseer or agriculturist on each farm or plantation upon which there are now and were, upon the first of January last, fifteen able-bodied field hands, between the ages of sixteen and fifty." *Ibid.,* 1 Cong., 4 Sess., Chap. LXV.

the second and fourth districts respectively. These gentle-men—neither of whom was elected—announced the follow-ing principles: (1) continuation of the war until independ-ence was fully recognized; (2) opposition to exemptions from military service, especially exemptions based on property; (3) opposition to the principle of substitution in the army; (4) use of Negro labor in the army wherever practicable; (5) adequate pay for soldiers and immediate and permanent relief extended to their families; (6) free trade; (7) very strict naturalization laws; and (8) advocacy of every measure that would bring the currency to a specie standard.[52]

The election, as previously stated, passed off quietly. Those congressmen seeking re-election were returned to Richmond. Henry Marshall did not stand for re-election, and his place was taken by Colonel Benjamin L. Hodge. The voters were either satisfied with the records of their congressmen or in-different to politics.[53]

Congressman Hodge died in August, 1864, and Governor Allen called a special election for October 17 to fill the posi-tion for the unexpired term. The campaign seems to have been waged to some extent around the personality and policies of General Kirby Smith as Confederate commander of the Trans-Mississippi Department. General Smith and Major General Taylor had quarreled after the Federal Red River campaign of 1864, and the latter had assailed Smith for failure to reinforce him after the battles of Mansfield and Pleasant Hill. Taylor had wished to concentrate the Con-federate forces against the retreating army of Banks and de-stroy it. Smith, however, feared an attack on Shreveport by Major General Frederick Steele, who was in Arkansas. Tay-

---

[52] Shreveport *Semi-Weekly News,* October 13, 1863.

[53] The official MS. election returns are in the Executive Orders and Proclama-tions of the Governors of Louisiana, 1860–1865. Records of the War De-partment, Confederate Records, The National Archives, Chap. 8, Vol. 132, p. 136 (microfilm copy possessed by the writer).

Relations with the Confederacy

lor finally asked to be relieved of duties in the Trans-Mississippi Department.[54]

Richard Taylor was very popular in Louisiana. He seems to have been a man of engaging personality, cultured and forceful. Of course, the fact that he was a citizen of Louisiana and had made many political friends gave him a strong following. On July 6, 1864, M. C. Manning at Alexandria wrote to Braxton Bragg concerning the Smith-Taylor controversy. He gave Taylor credit for the success of the Confederate forces in Louisiana and condemned Smith, saying among other things: "His usefullness here is at an end, or, rather, it never had a beginning." He asked General Bragg to use his influence to retain Taylor in Louisiana and to relieve the state of Smith.[55] On July 9 Dr. Egan at Mt. Lebanon wrote to former Governor Moore:

Our people here are greatly chagrined at the loss of General Taylor's services. I do not pretend to know the merits of the difficulty between him and General Smith but I do know and the country knows that we cannot get a General who loves Louisiana more ardently or who could better use for her defence all the resources at his command.[56]

The bitter feeling between Smith and Taylor had a reverberation in the special election to fill Colonel Hodge's place in the Confederate Congress. Smith's feud with Taylor and probably his seeming continued inaction, together with the Confederate impressments, made him many enemies. At least, there was a definite anti-Smith faction in the election campaign. Henry Gray of Caddo Parish and John L. Lewis of Claiborne were candidates for the place in Congress. Lewis was charged by the opposition, whether justly or un-

---

[54] *Official Records,* Ser. I, Vol. XXXIV, Pt. I, 476, 488–548, 583–84, Vol. XLI, Pt. II, 990–91, 1066; Taylor, *Destruction and Reconstruction,* 176–90. For a defense of Kirby Smith, see Arthur H. Noll, *General Kirby-Smith* (Sewanee, Tenn., 1907), 236–50.

[55] *Official Records,* Ser. I, Vol. XLI, Pt. II, 992–93.

[56] Thomas O. Moore Papers.

justly the records do not reveal, with sustaining the military policy of Kirby Smith. A political notice signed "Many Voters" in the Natchitoches *Times* addressed this question to the candidates: "Do you endorse the military administration of General E. Kirby Smith in the Trans-Mississippi Department?" [57] The Shreveport *News* of September 6 said, "The question is important, for on the reply, depends the success of the candidate," and announced that Lewis supported Smith's policies. Judge E. Warren Moise at Natchitoches wrote to Thomas O. Moore on September 24, charging that Lewis sustained the military policy of Kirby Smith and said:

And are *you* going to support him? Is Rapides going to support him? Are you down there going to unite to send to Congress a man to uphold the character of Kirby Smith and to keep him at the head of things in Louisiana? By God! If you do—you deserve all you have suffered, and I have no sympathy for those who are the willing and knowing victims of his immeasurable stupidity. . . . Henry Gray is authoritatively announced. We know *his* opinion, and what we want now of all other things is to send to Congress a bitter opponent of Smith—and this we have in Gray.[58]

Henry Gray was elected by an overwhelming majority. Since Gray was known to the voters as an opponent of Kirby Smith, and since Smith was upheld by the Richmond authorities, the election may be interpreted as the expression of a declining confidence in the Confederate Government.[59]

[57] Quoted by the Shreveport *News*, September 6, 1864.

[58] Thomas O. Moore Papers. However, a letter from I. D. Harper at Shreveport, September 30, 1864, to T. O. Moore said: "The Shreveport News had no authority for stating that Col. Lewis endorsed Gen. Smith; the Col. was very much provoked about it." *Ibid.*

[59] The election returns (incomplete) are found in the Shreveport *News* of November 1, 1864. According to the incomplete returns Gray received 1,572 votes and Lewis, 673.

Chapter IX

Union Politics in New Orleans

PRESIDENT LINCOLN HELD the view that the union of the states was perpetual and that no state upon its own motion could lawfully withdraw. He maintained that the ordinances of secession were illegal and that the eleven Southern states never had left the Federal Union. The mass of the people in these states might be out of their proper relations with the Federal Government, but the states remained within the Union, and the citizens remained subject to the laws of the United States. Even though he could not always make a practical application of this view and was forced in many cases to recognize the Southern states as belligerents, he continued to hold to the ideal and took steps to re-establish the relations between the disaffected regions and the Federal Government as a logical result of his political philosophy.

Immediately after the Federal capture of New Orleans in 1862 efforts were made to promote the Union cause in the city. There were, of course, some Unionists who welcomed the Federal army and who formed the nucleus of a Federal party. In June Colonel (later Brigadier General) George F. Shepley was appointed military governor of Louisiana. In notifying Colonel Shepley of his appointment Secretary Stanton said that "the great purpose of your appointment is to re-establish the authority of the Federal Government in the State of Louisiana, and provide the means of maintaining peace and security to the loyal inhabitants of that State until

271

they shall be able to establish a civil government." Major General Butler was instructed to aid Shepley and to detail an adequate military force for the special purpose of a governor's guard, to act under Shepley's directions.[1]

Confederate courts ceased to function in New Orleans when the city was captured by the Federals. Judges either sought refuge within the Confederate lines or refused to hold court for the United States authorities. Consequently, provost courts were created, and military officers were appointed to hear and try criminal and civil cases. This system proved very unsatisfactory and inadequate, and it was decided to restore the regular court system. The old courts were opened by Shepley, and Union men were appointed judges.[2]

The courts set up by Brigadier General Shepley as military governor were municipal and state courts. What has been called the most extraordinary court of American history was created by executive order of President Lincoln in October, 1862. The main motive for the establishment of such a court was to provide for the settlement of controversies which were liable to result in international complications. This court was called "The United States Provisional Court for the State of Louisiana." Charles A. Peabody of New York was appointed judge of the court with power to appoint a district attorney and other court officials. He was to hear and to determine civil and criminal cases and to enjoy the powers and jurisdictions of district and circuit courts of the United States, and his judgment was to be final. Judge Peabody arrived in New Orleans in December, 1862, and opened the court on December 31. He ruled that members of the bar should take an oath that they would observe all constitutional laws of the United States, that they were practicing lawyers at the state

---

[1] Secretary Stanton to Shepley, June 10, 1862, *Official Records,* Ser. III, Vol. II, 141.

[2] Ficklen, *History of Reconstruction in Louisiana,* 92–93; Caskey, *Secession and Restoration of Louisiana,* 153.

courts, and that they would bear true and faithful allegiance to the United States Government.[3]

In the meantime, an election had been held in the First and Second Congressional Districts, and two congressmen were elected to represent that section of Louisiana in the United States House of Representatives. This election was ordered by Brigadier General Shepley with the permission of Lincoln before the President announced his well-known plan of reconstruction. In fact, as early as July, 1862, Lincoln had expressed his desire to have Louisiana resume proper relations with the Union. Writing to a friend on July 31, 1862, President Lincoln said:

Broken eggs cannot be mended; but Louisiana has nothing to do now but to take her place in the Union as it was, barring the already broken eggs. The sooner she does so, the smaller will be the amount of that which will be past mending.[4]

The election for United States congressmen was held not only by permission of Lincoln, but as a result of his very direct and urgent instructions. In a letter of November 21, 1862, to Shepley, Lincoln expressed annoyance at learning that nothing had been done about Congressional elections in Louisiana. "I wish elections for congressmen to take place in Louisiana," he said. ". . . And do not waste a day about it, but fix the election day early enough, that we can hear the result here by the first of January." Shepley was instructed to fix an election day in all the districts of the state, and "have it held in as many places as you can."[5] Moreover, Lincoln had very definite ideas concerning the proprieties of a Con-

---

[3] Ficklen, *Reconstruction in Louisiana*, 93–96; Charles A. Peabody, *The United States Provisional Court for the State of Louisiana, 1862–1865*, in *Annual Report of the American Historical Association for the year 1892* (Washington, 1893), 197–210; New Orleans *True Delta*, January 1, 1863; Caskey, *Secession and Restoration of Louisiana*, 153–56.

[4] John G. Nicolay and John Hay (eds.), *Complete Works of Abraham Lincoln* (New York, 1905), VII, 299–300, Lincoln to August Belmont.

[5] *Ibid.*, VIII, 80–81.

gressional election in Louisiana. His views were clearly expressed in another letter of this same day, November 21, 1862, to Shepley:

Dr. Kennedy, bearer of this, has some apprehension that Federal officers not citizens of Louisiana may be set up as candidates for Congress in that State. In my view there could be no possible object in such an election. We do not particularly need members of Congress from there to enable us to get along with legislation here. What we do want is the conclusive evidence that respectable citizens of Louisiana are willing to be members of Congress and to swear ot [sic] support the Constitution, and that other respectable citizens there are willing to vote for them and send them. To send a parcel of Northern men here as representatives, elected, as would be understood (and perhaps really so), at the point of the bayonet, would be disgusting and outrageous; and were I a member of Congress here, I would vote against admitting any such man to a seat.[6]

The election took place on December 3 and resulted in the choice of Michael Hahn and Benjamin F. Flanders for the seats in Congress.

Flanders was a native of New Hampshire but had lived in Louisiana many years. He was a successful businessman and had served as secretary and treasurer of the New Orleans and Opelousas Railroad. According to George Denison, agent of the United States Treasury Department in New Orleans, Flanders was an able man and was held in high esteem by all Union men in Louisiana.[7]

Michael Hahn was born in Bavaria in 1830. At an early age he came to the United States with his widowed mother and four other children. The family settled in New Orleans in 1840, and the mother died the following year. Hahn attended the public schools of New Orleans and then earned the LL.B. degree from the University of Louisiana in 1851. He

[6] Letter quoted in the New Orleans *True Delta*, December 18, 1863; also in Nicolay and Hay (eds.), *Complete Works of Abraham Lincoln*, VIII, 79.

[7] *Diary and Correspondence of Salmon P. Chase*, 307.

aligned himself with the Democrats, though he was opposed to the Slidell faction. He was an active supporter of Stephen A. Douglas in 1860, and after the election he canvassed the state against secession. When the Federals took New Orleans, he immediately pledged his allegiance to the United States.[8]

The credentials of Hahn and Flanders were presented to the United States House of Representatives just before Christmas, 1862. Objection was made in each case by Clement L. Vallandigham of Ohio, and the credentials were referred to the Committee of Elections. The committee reported, February 3, 1863, in favor of seating Hahn and Flanders, and the report was debated for several days. There were two main objections raised by the opposition. In the first place, it was argued that the election was called by a military governor and hence not in accordance with the laws of the United States or of the State of Louisiana. Much stress was placed on the danger of military power. Secondly, it was alleged that the people in New Orleans and the surrounding parishes were induced to send congressmen to protect their property in slaves. Daniel W. Voorhees of Indiana argued that the people reasoned that such an election would satisfy the President that Southeast Louisiana was not in rebellion and he would, therefore, except the area from his final emancipation proclamation. Hahn himself spoke to the House in defense of his claims. He claimed that a majority of the people of New Orleans and vicinity had always been loyal to the United States. The planter element of Central and North Louisiana, he charged, had led the state astray. These people, the state officers, and the minority in New Orleans, Hahn said, had coerced the loyal citizens into silence and a passive acceptance of the Confederacy. The vote on the report of the committee was taken on February 17, and the two Representatives from

[8] *Dictionary of American Biography*, VIII, 87–88. For Hahn's alleged Confederate connections, see Caskey, *Secession and Restoration of Louisiana*, 99–100.

Louisiana in the Confederacy

Louisiana were admitted to the United States House of Representatives by a vote of 92 to 44. They were able to enjoy the office for only fifteen days, since their terms ended with the expiration of the Thirty-seventh Congress on March 4.[9]

The reader will recall that Major General Nathaniel P. Banks arrived in New Orleans on December 14, 1862, and three days later relieved Major General Benjamin F. Butler in the command of the Department of the Gulf. It will be recalled, also, that Banks adopted a policy toward the inhabitants of New Orleans characterized by mildness in comparison with the regime of Butler.

While Butler was criticized and condemned by Southerners, Banks was somewhat of a disappointment to strong Union men in New Orleans. It was claimed that his mild policy was contributing to the growth of Confederate sentiments. George Denison wrote to Salmon P. Chase, February 12, 1863: "Banks' policy seems to be conciliatory and hesitating. He seems afraid of responsibilities. . . . I am not familiar with Banks' political history. Was he ever a Trimmer?" [10] Two weeks later Denison was writing to Chase:

This is less a Union City now than when Gen. Banks came here. There is more manifestation of disloyalty than at any time during the Summer. And the reason is that no punishment, or insufficient punishment, follows offenses. It won't do, you know, to be hard on a gentleman for exercising his constitutional right of abusing the United States. Judge Peabody of the Provisional Court, is also Provost Judge. Judge Peabody is a mistake. As Provost Judge, he is only a small magistrate. A man throws up his hat and hurrahs for Jeff. Davis in the street. Judge P. fines him five dollars. An enthusiastic rebel does not repent that price for so great a privilege. Butler would have sent the offender to Fort Jackson and neither he nor any acquaintance of his, would have committed the offense again.

The policy of conciliation, in whatever form, is useless, absurd

[9] *The Congressional Globe,* 37 Cong., 3 Sess., 144, 164, 695, 831–36, 1030–36.
[10] *Diary and Correspondence of Salmon P. Chase,* 358–60.

Union Politics in New Orleans

and hurtful, and whoever adopts it may justly be accused of expecting a nomination for the Presidency. . . .[11]

Perhaps the Confederate sympathizers in New Orleans were trying out Major General Banks somewhat as the boys of a generation ago used to try out the new school principal. At any rate, judging from the newspapers, there must have been quite a manifestation of Confederate feeling in New Orleans in the first few months of Banks's occupancy. Cases of "seditious conduct" and "seditious language" were frequently tried in the courts. "Hurrahing" for Jeff Davis, wearing "a rebel uniform," saying "There goes another Yankee," singing "The Bonnie Blue Flag," using "seditious language against the President of the United States," and publicly expressing devout wishes for the success of the Confederacy were among the offenses tried before the courts of New Orleans in the first three or four months of 1863.[12]

Federal military authorities and Union politicians took some steps toward cultivating and propagating Union sentiment in New Orleans, perhaps as a defense against what seemed to be a growing Confederate feeling. In March, 1863, the New Orleans school board adopted a resolution instructing the teachers in the public schools to make the singing of patriotic songs and the reading of appropriate passages

[11] *Ibid.*, 362. Banks's own comments on the condition of affairs when he assumed command at New Orleans may indicate some of the difficulties confronting him and explain some of his policies. On January 15, 1863, he wrote to Mrs. Banks: ". . . Everybody connected with the government has been employed stealing other people's property. Sugar, Silver plate, horses, carriages, every thing they could lay hands on. There has been open trade with the enemy. No attention has been given to military affairs. I have nothing to fight with—but a small force of raw men, poorly armed and much depressed in spirit." N. P. Banks Papers.

[12] See the New Orleans *True Delta* for January 5, 10, 14, 15, 16, 17, 24, 30, February 14, April 3, 11, 15 for these and other cases. The usual penalty was a fine of from $5 to $25. Two men who publicly expressed "devout wishes" for the success of the Confederacy were discharged by Judge Peabody and admonished not to "offend again in the same manner." See New Orleans *True Delta*, January 30, 1863.

from the addresses of patriotic men a part of the exercise of each day. According to a Union authority many of the pupils rose "in rebellion" and refused to sing national (Union) songs as requested by their teachers. About three hundred children who refused to join in the singing were expelled or withdrawn from the schools.[18] Brigadier General James Bowen, provost marshal general at New Orleans, issued an order, May 13, 1863, directing that all places of public resort, except churches, should fly the United States flag when open to the public. At all theaters where an orchestra or a band performed, a national air was to be played at the commencement and at the conclusion of the program. It was not proper, according to Bowen's order, to call for any music at a theater or opera which was not in the printed program. Any person or persons "persisting in calling for other music will be regarded as a disturber of the peace, and, as such, will be arrested." [14]

The seating of Flanders and Hahn by the United States House of Representatives must have encouraged the Unionists of the New Orleans area. They immediately busied themselves with plans for a complete restoration of the political machinery of Louisiana. Soon political parties were forming, and politics in the city and surrounding parishes took on new life.

The first real party to be organized was known as the Free State party. This party, as the name indicates, advocated the abolition of slavery. They held that Louisiana had committed suicide by adopting the ordinance of secession and that

[18] Emily H. Reed, *Life of A. P. Dostie; or, The Conflict of New Orleans* (New York, 1868), 47–50. The author quotes Dostie, a rabid New Orleans Unionist, as saying that the enrollment in the public schools of New Orleans was 8,000. This does not seem to be an exaggerated figure in view of the fact that the 1860 population of the city was 168,000.

[14] New Orleans *True Delta*, May 13, 1863. The prohibition against calling for music was of course designed to prevent the audience from calling for Southern airs like "Dixie." Just how successful the order was in this respect is not a matter of record.

consequently a new constitution was necessary. They proposed the election of a constitutional convention by those who swore they were citizens of the United States and had resided in the state six months. When the constitution was framed and ratified by the voters, the officers of the state should be elected.[15]

Another party which came to be known as the Conservative party was composed chiefly of planters who wished to revive the constitution of 1852 and to preserve the institution of slavery. A number of the leaders of this party had been adherents of the Confederate cause. The party advocated the holding of the regular biennial election in November, 1863, and in June sent a committee to see President Lincoln to obtain his consent to their plans. Lincoln's reply was conciliatory, but he failed to give his consent to such an election and even informed the committee that there were Louisianians who desired to amend the state constitution and who planned to elect a convention for that purpose.[16]

Evidently the President's sympathies were with the Free State party. He was in agreement with them on the question of slavery, and he seems to have suspected the motives of the Conservatives. He favored the idea of framing a new constitution for the state and gave his official sanction to the movement. On August 24, 1863, he directed Brigadier General Shepley to aid the loyal citizens of Louisiana to form a new state constitution and to re-establish civil government in conformity with the Constitution and laws of the United States. Shepley was instructed to cause a registration in each parish of Louisiana of all loyal citizens of the United States "as soon as it can conveniently be done after the people are relieved from the presence of the rebel troops." When this registration was made "as far as practicable," Shepley was to order an election for delegates to a convention of the "loyal

[15] Ficklen, *History of Reconstruction in Louisiana*, 45–46.
[16] *Ibid.*, 47–48; Caskey, *Secession and Restoration of Louisiana*, 75–77.

people" of Louisiana to form a constitution and re-establish a civil government in the state, "loyal to the United States." The basis of representation and other details for the election machinery were included in the instructions.[17] Naturally, such expressions as "as soon as it can conveniently be done" and "as far as practicable" gave General Shepley considerable latitude in appointing a time for taking the registration and holding the election.

Meanwhile, the Conservatives were going ahead with their plans for the regular election in November, 1863. A few weeks before the election day, officers of the party, styling themselves the "Executive Committee of Louisiana," issued an appeal to the loyal voters to participate in the election and assured them that the election would be approved by the Federal authorities. The leaders of the Free State party refused to countenance the movement, and Brigadier General Shepley issued an order forbidding the holding of the election.[18] An election was held, however, on November 3, 1863, in the parishes of St. Bernard and Plaquemines. Dr. Thomas Cottman, a New Orleans physician who had signed the Louisiana secession ordinance, A. P. Field, whose friends claimed he had always been loyal to the United States, and Joshua Baker were "elected" to the United States Congress, and Dr. John Leonard Riddell was chosen governor. The total vote cast in the election was probably less than five hundred.[19]

When the Thirty-eighth Congress convened on December 7, Field and Cottman answered the roll call.[20] On the nine-

[17] *Official Records*, Ser. I, Vol. XXXVI, Pt. I, 694–95. Also found in the N. P. Banks Papers.

[18] Ficklen, *History of Reconstruction in Louisiana*, 49; *Congressional Globe*, 38 Cong., 1 Sess., 411; *Diary and Correspondence of Salmon P. Chase*, 417–23.

[19] *Congressional Globe*, 38 Cong., 1 Sess., 411, 543; Ficklen, *History of Reconstruction in Louisiana*, 50; Caskey, *Secession and Restoration of Louisiana*, 85.

[20] *Congressional Globe*, 38 Cong., 1 Sess., 411–14, 543–47. When Thaddeus Stevens of Pennsylvania asked for the credentials of "the persons claiming to be Representatives from the so-called State of Louisiana," the clerk read a

teenth Schuyler Colfax, the speaker, "merely . . . for the information of the House," presented the resignation of Cottman as a member of Congress.[21] Perhaps Cottman thought it wise to allow Field, who had a better record for loyalty, to make a test case of the election. The House Committee of Elections reported unfavorably on Field's claim for admission on January 29, 1864, making the objection that the election was forbidden by the military governor and that the candidate hardly had a constituency, since he had received but 156 votes in St. Bernard and probably no more in Plaquemines.[22] As far as the committee was concerned, there was no question as to the loyalty of Field, but he was denied a seat in Congress on February 9 by a vote of 85 to 48.[23] Field spoke twice, making a spirited defense of his claim to a seat and of Louisiana's right to representation. "The loyal men of Louisiana, from the time of passage of the ordinance of secession," he declared, "have held that they were in the Union. . . . and we never dreamed that we had forfeited any right to the protection of this Government, or to our representation in this House."[24] In his final remarks this Louisianian said:

And now, Mr. Speaker, as I am about to take my leave of you and of the House, let me implore you to look kindly upon poor Louisiana. Guard her rights if you can. Protect her people who have been under military law for nearly two years, who have had

---

certificate of election from John Leonard Riddell, "Governor of the State of Louisiana," stating that Field and Cottman had been elected from the First and Second Congressional Districts respectively and that Joshua Baker had been elected from the fifth district "composed of the whole State of Louisiana." *Ibid.*, 5.

[21] *Ibid.*, **33.** On this occasion Colfax said, "The Chair finds on his table a communication dated 'Washington city,' signed by J. L. Riddell, not as Governor, but as Governor elect, of Louisiana, transmitting the resignation of Thomas Cottman as member of Congress. The Chair does not see the name of Thomas Cottman on the list of members." *Ibid.*

[22] *Ibid.*, 411.

[23] *Ibid.*, 547. Thaddeus Stevens of Pennsylvania had some doubts of Field's loyalty. *Ibid.*, 543. [24] *Ibid.*, 413.

no voice either here or elsewhere in their own government. Look upon her kindly, protect her if you can, and give her at least some right to be heard, if not now, at least in some future time, upon this floor.[25]

While the faction responsible for the election of Cottman and Field was waiting upon the decision of the United States House of Representatives, plans were made by others for the election of administrative officers of the state. These plans were in accordance with the program of President Lincoln. To be sure, the Federal authorities in New Orleans had not proceeded with the registration of "loyal citizens" with the dispatch with which President Lincoln had desired, and he became impatient as early as November, 1863. Lincoln wrote Banks on November 5 that he had understood for at least three months that a registration was being taken in Louisiana preparatory to the election of a constitutional convention, but he had just been informed by a prominent citizen of New Orleans, who was then in Washington, that nothing had been done. "This disappoints me bitterly," Lincoln said, "yet I do not throw blame on you or on them." Banks was urged to "lose no more time," and was told not to wait for more territory but to go to work and "give me a tangible nucleus, which the remainder of the State may rally around as fast as it can, and which I can at once recognize and sustain as the true State government." [26]

On December 8, 1863, President Lincoln made an official announcement, which has come to be known as Lincoln's Plan of Reconstruction. The announcement contained a

[25] *Ibid.*, 544–45.

[26] N. P. Banks Papers. There seems to have been some friction between Banks and Shepley, at least from Banks's viewpoint, as he resented Shepley's authority in New Orleans. George S. Boutwell, United States congressman from Massachusetts, wrote to Banks on December 21, 1863, that in an interview with Lincoln the President expressed great confidence in Banks. Lincoln said, according to Boutwell, that he had never intended that anyone in the Department of the Gulf should exercise command independent of Banks; Shepley had been appointed to relieve Banks of "drudgery." *Ibid.*

promise of amnesty and a plan of civil government for the Southern states. With the exception of certain classes of Confederates, all Southerners might be restored to civil rights upon taking an oath of allegiance to the United States. When in any of the seceded states citizens equal in number to not less than one tenth of the votes cast in the state in the presidential election of 1860 and qualified to vote by the election law of the state at the time of secession should take the oath of allegiance and organize a civil government, the President would recognize it as the true government of the state.

Little or no time was lost in Louisiana in setting in motion the political machinery needed to create a civil government that might answer the specifications of the President of the United States. Brigadier General Shepley was by this time holding registrations of loyal citizens in line with the instructions from Washington in August, 1863. On January 11, 1864, Major General Banks, as military commander of the area, issued a proclamation to the people of Louisiana on the subject and in the beginning said:

In pursuance of authority vested in me by the President of the United States, and upon consultation with many representative men of different interests, being fully assured that more than a tenth of the population desire the earliest possible restoration of Louisiana to the Union, I invite the loyal citizens of the State qualified to vote in public affairs, as hereinafter prescribed, to assemble in the election precincts designated by law, or at such places as may hereafter be established, on the 22nd of February, 1864, to cast their votes for the election of State officers. . . .[27]

According to Banks's proclamation the following officers were to be elected: governor, lieutenant governor, secretary of state, treasurer, attorney general, superintendent of public instruction, and auditor of public accounts. The oath of allegiance prescribed by President Lincoln's Proclamation and

[27] New Orleans *True Delta,* January 12, 1864; also found in *Official Records,* Ser. III, Vol. IV, 22–23.

the Louisiana constitutional requirements were to constitute the qualifications for voters. Articles IV and V of Banks's proclamation announced that members of a constitutional convention would be elected in April and that arrangements would be made for the early election of members of Congress.

The proclamation was the starter for a first-class political campaign. Political clubs, meetings, parades, and conventions demanded the attention of the voters. The cry of "Rally! Rally! Rally!" appeared more than once in the columns of the *True Delta*. The Pioneer Lincoln club announced its rallies in the press under the caption "Hurrah for Abraham Lincoln." Other clubs were organized, and one announcement said: "Come one, come all! and see the right man in the right place. The next governor will be present at a meeting of the Working Men's Loyal National League." [28] A Young Men's Union association was formed in New Orleans for the purpose "of securing the election of worthy and patriotic men to office, and for the purpose of defeating the aspirations of those who are unfit for civil positions." A membership fee of $50 was charged. One New Orleans citizen wrote to the editor of the *True Delta* that he was interested in electing good men to office and considered himself a first-rate judge of fitness for civil positions, but he could not spare fifty dollars "as the price of that exciting pastime." He proposed, therefore, a "slight reduction of their terms in my behalf—say to thirty-four dollars and seventy-five cents." This communication was signed "One Who Has Not the Fifty." [29]

A Union meeting was held in Baton Rouge on January 19. "The Star-Spangled Banner" was played by a United States military band. Colonel R. T. Posey was the main speaker; and, although he spoke an hour, he kept his audience "spell-

[28] New Orleans *True Delta*, January 16, 21, 28, 1864.
[29] *Ibid.*, January 23, 1864.

bound," if we are to believe the news report. He charged that James Buchanan acted as if he were a traitor to the flag of the Union. He paid a similar compliment to General Twiggs for surrendering a Federal arsenal in Texas and "portrayed in a feeling manner old Sam Houston, with tears in his eyes, as he beheld the destruction upon which the enemies of Texas and the Union were determined." [30]

The purpose of most of these rallies was to elect delegates to a Free State nominating convention called for February 1 by a committee of the Free State party. When the convention met in New Orleans, the political ambitions of certain men were too great to secure harmony. Its proceedings were characterized by much wrangling and the wildest disorder, due chiefly to the presence of contesting delegations from some of the parishes. The *True Delta* said on February 2: "While the tumult was the highest and a dozen members were yelling like New York firemen, high above them all could be heard the shrill soprano of the president, crying 'order, order.'" [31] The dissension within the convention resulted in one faction bolting and retiring to another hall, where they nominated candidates to their liking. The bolters nominated B. F. Flanders for governor; Michael Hahn was the nominee of the rump convention. J. Madison Wells, a planter of Rapides Parish and a neighbor of Thomas Overton Moore, was nominated for the office of lieutenant governor by both conventions. This would indicate that the division was the result of factional politics rather than of any fundamental differences in principles. George Denison wrote to Secretary Chase: "We have therefore two Union candidates in the field. The only distinction I feel able to make is, that one is a Banks and the other an Anti-Banks party." Denison added

---

[30] *Ibid.*, January 24, 1864.

[31] New Orleans *True Delta* of February 2 gives an account of the report of the committee on credentials and the subsequent disorder.

that he was following General Banks's lead and was supporting Hahn.[32]

The Conservatives entered the campaign with a complete
list of nominees headed by J. Q. A. Fellows, candidate for governor. Naturally, their hopes of success were brightened by
the division of the Union party. Ficklen designated the three
tickets in the field as "Administration" (supported by Banks),
"Flanders," and "Conservatives." [33]

The campaign waged by the three factions lacked none of
the elements or excitement of a regular peacetime contest.
Rallies were held in New Orleans, Baton Rouge, Donaldsonville, Thibodaux, and smaller towns. Such slogans as "Rally,
Sons of Freedom," "Abraham Lincoln, The Friend of the
People and Liberty," and "The Workingmen, The Strength
and Sinew of Our Greatness" were prominently displayed in
parades and at rallies. Mud slinging and whispering campaigns were not lacking. George Denison wrote on February
19: "As I predicted, the political contest has become quite
bitter, as all such contests do, which spring from local questions, and personal prejudice. . . . Public meetings,
speeches, music and processions prevail every night." [34]

While the political campaign was getting under way in and
around New Orleans, the Legislature up at Shreveport was
condemning the whole movement as a "direct violation of the
principles of liberty" and as a step to "supplant the regular
Constitutional Government of the State, and rear in its stead
a mock government, existing by the suffrage of a military
despotism." It was resolved, therefore, by the Legislature on
February 10:

That all persons whatsoever, residing in that portion of the
State of Louisiana now occupied by the military forces of the

[32] *Diary and Correspondence of Salmon P. Chase,* 430; New Orleans *True
Delta,* February 2, 1864.

[33] Ficklen, *History of Reconstruction in Louisiana,* 61.

[34] *Diary and Correspondence of Salmon P. Chase,* 430–31; New Orleans *True
Delta,* February 13, 14, 1864.

United States Government, or which may hereafter fall under their power, are hereby warned against lending any aid or countenance, directly or indirectly, to the organization of a State Government in the wrongful and illegal manner proposed in the proclamation of Major General N. P. Banks, of the United States Army, and they are hereby notified that any aid or countenance given by them to this wicked and nefarious scheme, will subject them to obloquy and disgrace, and render them liable to the pains and penalties of treason.[35]

General Banks issued an order on February 14 setting forth the qualifications for voting in the coming election. Every free, white male twenty-one years of age who had lived in the state twelve months and six months in the parish in which he offered to vote, who was a citizen of the United States, and who had taken the oath of allegiance prescribed by President Lincoln on December 8, 1863, was entitled to vote in the election of February 22.[36]

The result of the election was a victory for the Administration ticket headed by Michael Hahn for governor and J. Madison Wells for lieutenant governor. The total vote cast numbered more than eleven thousand, which was well over the one tenth required by Lincoln, since the state's vote in the presidential election of 1860 was about fifty thousand.[37] The voters in this election included 808 soldiers of the Federal army stationed in and around New Orleans (including 108 at Fort Barrancas, Florida). Though some of the soldiers may have been Louisiana Unionists enlisted in the United States military forces, the evidence is conclusive that Northern soldiers cast ballots in this Louisiana election.[38]

[35] Louisiana *Acts*, 1864, p 54

[36] New Orleans *True Delta*, February 14, 1864; Ficklen, *History of Reconstruction in Louisiana*, 62.

[37] Ficklen, *History of Reconstruction in Louisiana*, 62, gives the returns for the election. J. Q. A. Fellows ran second in the gubernatorial race. George Denison thought Fellows might have been elected had Banks not required the proclamation oath. *Diary and Correspondence of Salmon P. Chase*, 431.

[38] N. P. Banks Papers, for the election returns. These returns show votes

Louisiana in the Confederacy

Major General Banks was pleased with the conduct and presumably with the results of the election. He wrote Lincoln on February 25 that the election was conducted with "great spirit and propriety" and "there is no sounder basis for a State government than is presented by this population." About two weeks later he was writing to Halleck, describing in glowing terms the inauguration of Hahn which occurred on March 4. "I have never witnessed such a spectacle elsewhere," he said, "and never conceived it possible that in this state a popular demonstration of such magnitude and friendly spirit to the Government could be attained. It is impossible to describe it with truth." [39]

Louisiana, which had experienced two administrations since April, 1862—a Federal military regime in and near New Orleans and a Confederate state administration in the remainder of the state—was now for the last year of the war to have two rival civil governments, each claiming to be the government of the state and the agency of the people.

When Michael Hahn was inaugurated on March 4, he was a governor without a legislature and apparently without a constitution. But Major General Banks was an experienced politician, and these adjuncts to a state government were on the program. Elections and conventions seem to have had a special appeal for the general who was a former governor of Massachusetts and who had been speaker of the United States House of Representatives. A few days after Hahn's inaugura-

---

at the army posts in the vicinity of New Orleans, including 131 soldier votes in the city. A "list"—in the Banks Papers—dated January 28, 1864, contained the names of "citizens" eligible to vote in the February 22 election at Fort St. Philip. The list indicated the name, military rank, and residence of each eligible soldier or officer. For instance, the name of a colonel whose residence was in New York, a captain whose home was in Maine, and the names of several lieutenants from Maine, Vermont, and Massachusetts were on the list of eligible persons. Such persons, perhaps, had "lived" in Louisiana twelve months, and hence were declared qualified to vote in the state.

[39] Banks to Lincoln, *Official Records*, Ser. III, Vol. IV, 133–34; Banks to Halleck, March 6, 1864, *ibid.*, Ser. I, Vol. XXXIV, Pt. II, 512–13.

tion Banks ordered the election of delegates to a constitutional convention. The first proclamation with instructions for holding the election was issued just before he set out on the Red River campaign. Evidently he expected to conquer the whole state, for provision was made for delegates from all forty-eight parishes with a total membership of 152. One section of the proclamation read: "Any Parish not now within the lines of the army shall be entitled to elect delegates as herein specified, at any time before the dissolution of the convention, should such parish be brought within the lines of the army." [40] While he was at Alexandria contemplating a victorious march up the Red River Valley to Shreveport, Banks issued another order on the subject of the election. By this order, elections were to be held early in April at Alexandria, Opelousas, Marksville, and Harrisonburg to choose delegates from the parishes in which these towns were located. Citizens expelled from other parishes for devotion to the Union were to be allowed to vote if they were qualified to vote in the parish of their legal residence.[41]

The convention assembled on April 6 in Liberty Hall in New Orleans. The secretary of state reported to the convention that ninety delegates were qualified for membership, sixty-three from Orleans Parish and twenty-seven from fifteen parishes in the vicinity of New Orleans. Eighty-two delegates answered the roll call on the opening day. When the committee on credentials reported on the second morning, two delegates from Avoyelles Parish and four from Rapides were admitted.[42]

[40] *Ibid.*, Ser. III, Vol. IV, 170–72; also published in the New Orleans *True Delta*, March 16, 1864.

[41] *Official Records*, Ser. III, Vol. IV, 209. The election in New Orleans and vicinity was held on March 28, the day before the above order was issued. An election was held in Alexandria with about 300 votes cast, and four delegates were elected. Whittington, "Rapides Parish, Louisiana—A History," in *loc. cit.*, XVIII, 21–22. Evidently an election was also held at Marksville, since delegates from Avoyelles Parish were admitted to the convention.

[42] *Official Journal of the Proceedings of the Convention for the Revision*

Louisiana in the Confederacy

The convention was in session for nearly four months. When it adjourned in late July, it had framed a new constitution for the state. The most striking features of the new constitution, perhaps, were those pertaining to the institution of slavery. Slavery was abolished and prohibited "throughout the State," and the Legislature was prohibited from passing any law recognizing the right of property in man. The Negro was not given the right to vote, but the way was paved for limited Negro suffrage by the article empowering the Legislature to "pass laws extending the right of suffrage to such persons, citizens of the United States, as by military service, by taxation to support the government, or by intellectual fitness, may be entitled thereto." [43] Article XIV of the new constitution conferred "the right of voting" on every white male, twenty-one years old, who was a citizen of the United States, a resident of Louisiana at least twelve months preceding an election and three months a resident in the parish in which he offered to vote.[44]

The convention provided for an election in September at which the electorate would vote on the constitution and elect members of the General Assembly. The new constitution provided for representation of the whole state in the General Assembly, whereas nearly two thirds of the parishes were within the Confederate military lines. This anomalous situation is illustrated by the provision that the election of members of the Assembly was to be held "in all the parishes where

---

and *Amendment of the Constitution of the State of Louisiana* (New Orleans, 1864), 3–6. Cited hereafter as *Journal of the Louisiana Convention of 1864.* George Denison did not regard the delegates very highly. Several days after the election he wrote to Chase: "I regret to say that the character, ability and standing of the Delegates is not such as could be wished. There are a few excellent men elected, like Judge Durell, Judge Howell, Dr. Bonzano, and Mr. Brott—but the majority of them are of little account." *Diary and Correspondence of Salmon P. Chase,* 435–36.

[43] *Journal of the Louisiana Convention of 1864,* pp. 74, 130, 173. The vote on the article abolishing and prohibiting slavery was 72 to 13.

[44] The constitution is found in *ibid.,* 173–84.

the same may be held" and in other parishes "as soon as it may become practicable." [45]

On the day of adjournment the convention, by a vote of 68 to 8, adopted a resolution denouncing the Louisiana Ordinance of Secession as a "perverted theory of State rights," brought about in the interest of slavery and based upon an "unfounded assumption of State sovereignty." The doctrines of state rights and state sovereignty were declared to be "utterly subversive of our form of government, and tending to confusion, anarchy and national destruction." It was declared that the Ordinance of Secession "is, and has always been null and void." [46]

It must not be thought that the people of New Orleans and vicinity were enjoying civil government as the result of the election of state officers and a convention. The area was still conquered territory, and supreme authority was vested in the commander of the military forces. Governor Hahn was invested with the powers exercised by Brigadier General Shepley but was made subordinate to the Federal Government in their application. At the same time the commander of the Department of the Gulf, with headquarters in New Orleans, continued to issue orders in matters purely civil and political.[47] In fact, it was difficult to distinguish between political

---

[45] *Ibid.*, 173.

[46] *Ibid.*, 168–69. Banks wrote to President Lincoln, July 25, 1864: "The Constitutional Convention adjourned today. It has been in session 108 days. The Constitution it presents to the People is the best that this country has produced, and considering the circumstances under which it has acted no State can present a higher claim to the respect and support of the country." N. P. Banks Papers. Lincoln examined a copy of the Louisiana constitution of 1864, and on August 9 he wrote to Banks, saying, "I am anxious that it shall be ratified by the people." Nicolay and Hay (eds.), *Complete Works of Lincoln*, X, 185–86.

[47] Ficklen, *History of Reconstruction in Louisiana*, 63, 74. For a controversy between Major General S. A. Hurlbut (Banks's successor) and Governor Hahn over the municipal government of New Orleans, see *Official Records*, Ser. I, Vol. XLI, Pt. IV, 734–38.

and military affairs, although it was clear that the civil government was subordinated to the army.

That the army was in politics, that the military administration was influenced by political considerations, and that there was much corruption in both civil and military affairs are apparent from the records. Major General David Hunter in New Orleans wrote to General Grant, May 2, 1864:

> The Department of the Gulf is one great mass of corruption. Cotton and politics, instead of the war, appear to have engrossed the army. The vital interests of the contest are laid aside, and we are amused with sham State governments, which are a complete laughing-stock to the people, and the lives of our men are sacrificed in the interest of cotton speculators.[48]

George Denison, viewing the situation as a civilian, was no less critical than General Hunter when he wrote on June 17 that the convention stood no higher than Banks himself in public estimation. It was very commonly remarked, he said, that the members of the convention were making fools of themselves. "The few intelligent men among the members are entirely lost sight of," he continued, "in the great mass of inexperience and vulgar ignorance." According to Denison, the convention was held in contempt by nine tenths of the people.[49]

The character of this politico-military regime was not enhanced by the election of September 5, 1864, when the constitution was adopted and members of the General Assembly and representatives to Congress were chosen. The evidence indicates that many persons voted who were not entitled to vote and that in some places the election was restricted to the military post.[50] In May, 1865, a citizen of Point Coupee

[48] *Official Records*, Ser. I, Vol. XXXIV, Pt. III, 390.

[49] *Diary and Correspondence of Salmon P. Chase*, 439. See Ficklen, *History of Reconstruction in Louisiana*, 76–77, for the extravagance of the convention and for cases of fraud in connection with the expenditures. See also Caskey, *Secession and Restoration of Louisiana*, 135–37.

[50] According to the *Annual Cyclopaedia*, IV (1864), 479, the constitution

Union Politics in New Orleans

wrote to Major General Banks that the people of his community could not "respect the late Legislature or its acts," since the election of the state senator had been confined to an army post (Morganza) and the people knew nothing of the election. "They had no part or lot in it," he said, and the senator "has not one single constituent." [51] Moreover, if we are to believe Banks's successor in the Department of the Gulf, the military regime of Banks furnished transportation, military protection, and money to certain candidates for electioneering purposes.[52] Also, somebody must have been ingenious enough to work out a system of absentee voting, for the editor of the *Louisiana Democrat* at Alexandria wrote in the columns of his paper on October 5, 1864:

In reading an old New Orleans paper of the 22nd ult., we came across the list of elected Senators and representatives to the Banks-Hahn Legislature of this State. The following are put down from Rapides: . . . As a matter of curiosity we would like to know at what precincts the election was held, and how many votes cast.

The Legislature, elected on September 5, met in October. There was nothing particularly striking in the work of the

---

was ratified by a vote of 6,836 to 1,566. Acting Governor J. Madison Wells on May 3, 1865, issued a proclamation stating that nearly five thousand persons were registered as voters in New Orleans who did not possess the qualifications required by law to become voters in the state and declared the books of the registrar of voters closed and all current registrations null and void. A new set of registration books was opened on June 1, 1865. *Annual Cyclopaedia*, V (1865), 509.

[51] *Official Records*, Ser. I, Vol. XLVIII, Pt. II, 537. See also *Annual Cyclopaedia*, V (1865), 509. A report in the N. P. Banks Papers entitled "Recapitulation of the votes of soldiers cast in the Louisiana Election of the 5th of September, 1864," shows that a total of 1,178 votes were cast at five army posts, namely, at New Orleans, 568; Baton Rouge, 13; Carrollton, 57; Port Hudson, 179; Morganza, 361. A special report in the Banks Papers shows that the election at Morganza was held in the regimental camp, where the election commissioners were two captains and a lieutenant.

[52] Major General S. A. Hurlbut to Lieutenant Colonel Christian T. Christensen, October 25, 1864, *Official Records*, Ser. I, Vol. XLI, Pt. IV, 233–34.

body. Several steps were taken in an attempt to resume normal relations with the Federal Government. One of the first of these was the election of United States senators on October 10. Charles Smith was elected to fill the place vacated by Benjamin, and R. King Cutler was elected to John Slidell's seat.[53] On October 31 all laws in force regulating the selection of electors for President and Vice-President were repealed, and the electors were chosen by joint ballot of the two houses on November 8. This action was taken, it was stated officially, because the time intervening was too short, "in the present unsettled condition of the interior of this State," to give full notice of a popular election. The act provided that henceforth electors would be chosen by popular vote.[54]

In January, 1865, the Legislature instructed the Louisiana senators and requested the representatives to "use all their influence and cast their votes in favor of the proposed amendment to the Constitution of the United States, forever prohibiting slavery in all the States and Territories." On February 17 the proposed thirteenth amendment to the Constitution was ratified by the Legislature at New Orleans. This act was accepted by the Federal Government and was virtually the only recognition of the Banks-Hahn government accorded

---

[53] *Acts Passed by the General Assembly of the State of Louisiana*, 1864–1865 (at New Orleans) (New Orleans, 1865), 8–9. Dr. J. V. C. Smith, prominent physician and a member of the New Orleans sanitary commission (by appointment of Major General Banks), wrote to Banks—who had returned to the North—on October 15, 1864, that the people of the New Orleans area were surprised and indignant at the election of United States senators by the Legislature. He quoted Dr. A. P. Dostie, an ardent New Orleans unionist, as saying King Cutler was "an escaped rogue" from Indiana, who murdered the king's English. Disgust and dissatisfaction, Smith said, prevailed in circles where he moved. But since "they are in only for the short term, a higher grade of intellect and educational preparations may be selected for their successors." N. P. Banks Papers.

[54] *Acts Passed by the General Assembly of Louisiana*, 1864–1865 (at New Orleans), 4.

by the Thirty-eighth Congress.[55] The Louisiana electoral votes in the presidential election of 1864, for instance, were rejected on the ground that states in rebellion were not entitled to representation in the Electoral College.[56]

Congress had at least one other opportunity at this session to pass upon the status of the Union government of Louisiana. In the election of September 5, 1864, five representatives to the United States Congress, M. F. Bonzano, A. P. Field, W. D. Mann, Robert W. Taliaferro, and T. M. Wells, were chosen. Thus, when the Thirty-eighth Congress convened in December, two senators and five representatives from Louisiana were seeking admission. The Senate Committee on the Judiciary, to which was referred the credentials of Charles Smith and King Cutler, reported a resolution declaring that the United States recognized the government of the state of Louisiana "inaugurated under" the convention of 1864 "as the legitimate government of the said State."[57] The resolution was debated at length, but it did not reach the stage of a final vote. Although there was some support for seating the Louisiana delegations, neither house took definite action before adjournment in March; and, consequently, the Louisianians were not admitted to membership.[58] Because of an assault

[55] Ibid., 40, 42; Ficklen, History of Reconstruction in Louisiana, 92. Dr. J. V. C. Smith, New Orleans physician, wrote to Banks on March 18, 1865: "The legislature is a byword and a reproach to the intelligence of the age. You, were you here, I am quite sure, Cromwell like, would have driven the members out of the hall long ago." N. P. Banks Papers.

[56] Congressional Globe, 38 Cong., 2 Sess., 533, 608, 618. When the Senate Committee on the Judiciary reported a resolution denying the eleven seceded states representation in the Electoral College, Senator John C. Ten Eyck of New Jersey offered an amendment to strike out of the preamble to the resolution the word "Louisiana," thus making an exception in the case of that state. Ten Eyck's proposal was debated at length on February 1, 2, 3, 1865, and defeated by a vote of 22 to 16. Ibid., 533–37, 548–62, 574–82.

[57] Ibid., 903. For the debate on this resolution, see ibid., 1011, 1061–70, 1091–99, 1101–11, 1126–29.

[58] Congressional Globe, 38 Cong., 2 Sess., 2, 5, 8, 756, 1395; Caskey, Secession and Restoration of Louisiana, 156–57.

upon William D. Kelley, representative from Pennsylvania, committed on January 20, 1865, Field was convicted by the House of a breach of the privilege of that body. He was arraigned before the bar of the House on February 22 and reprimanded by the speaker.[59]

Louisiana added another name to her roll of governors before the end of the war; and the last one, strange to say, was the only governor of the war period who was a native of the state. Thomas O. Moore was born in North Carolina, Henry Watkins Allen in Virginia, and Michael Hahn was a native of Bavaria. When Hahn resigned in March, 1865, after his election to the United States Senate by the Louisiana Legislature (the Union Legislature at New Orleans, of course), he was succeeded by Lieutenant Governor J. Madison Wells of Rapides Parish. Wells had been a slaveholding Unionist, and it was claimed that he had been forced to leave Rapides Parish because of his Union sympathies. As governor he adopted a policy of conciliation toward his erstwhile Confederate opponents. He came into conflict with leaders of the radical Union faction of Louisiana and was called by one leader of that group "the John Tyler of the Free State party." [60]

[59] *Congressional Globe*, 38 Cong., 2 Sess., 371–75, 971–74, 991.
[60] Reed, *Life of A. P. Dostie*, 183; Ficklen, *History of Reconstruction in Louisiana*, 104–05.

Chapter X

The End of the War

THE WAR WAS practically over in Louisiana before the end of 1864. In fact, there were no major military engagements in the state after the retreat of Banks from North Louisiana in May of that year. The Federal Government seemed to be satisfied to hold New Orleans and immediate vicinity while concentrating its main forces in Tennessee, Georgia, and Virginia. The Confederate authorities, nevertheless, realized the necessity of retaining some troops in Louisiana to protect the northern and western portions of the state from a possible Federal expedition from New Orleans or from Arkansas. Moreover, the Confederate army west of the Mississippi remained there for the reason that Federal control of the river made it impossible to transfer any large number of men to the east side. There were early in 1865 at least forty thousand effective Confederate troops in the Trans-Mississippi Department. The department was commanded by General Kirby Smith with headquarters at Shreveport, where the executive offices of Louisiana were located.[1] Though there were no major military engagements, there was considerable activity in 1865 on the part of small detachments of Federal troops in

[1] See Smith's letter of March 7, 1865, to President Davis concerning the strength of his department, *Official Records*, Ser. I, Vol. XLVIII, Pt. I, 1411. President Davis desired that troops be sent from the Trans-Mississippi Department to Virginia, but General Smith doubted that it could be done with the Mississippi carefully guarded by Federal ironclads. In fact, efforts to get troops across in July and August, 1864, had met with failure. *Ibid.*, 1411, 1418.

the section immediately west and northwest of New Orleans, especially around Thibodaux, Brashear City, and Donaldsonville. Federal scouting parties were frequently sent out from these points to drive out or to capture Confederate recruiting or foraging parties. Minor skirmishes occurred at such points as Bayou Goula, Lake Verret, Bayou Teche, and Grand Bayou. The Federal lines apparently did not extend farther than Morganza, in Point Coupee Parish, about thirty miles south of the mouth of the Red River. West and northwest of this point the state was under Confederate control.[2]

The chief points of concentration for the Confederate forces in Louisiana in the last months of the war were Opelousas, Alexandria, Minden, and Shreveport. Brigadier General Joseph L. Brent commanded the troops in the section between Opelousas and Alexandria. This force was engaged in obtaining provisions from South Louisiana and in forming the first line of defense against the Federals at Donaldsonville and at Brashear City. The District of West Louisiana was under the command of Lieutenant General Buckner with headquarters at Alexandria. Just before the end of the war Buckner was made chief of staff in the Trans-Mississippi Department, and Major General Harry Hays was placed in command of the District of West Louisiana. Besides General Brent, Major General Thomas J. Churchill and Major General John H. Forney were assisting General Buckner. Churchill's and Forney's troops were stationed in the vicinity of Shreveport and Minden.[3]

The most spectacular affair in the closing weeks of the war was the exploit of the Confederate ram *W. H. Webb*. This boat was fitted up at Shreveport and left that place on April 7 under the command of Lieutenant Commander Charles W.

---

[2] Reports of expeditions and skirmishes in Louisiana in the months of January–May, 1865, are found in *ibid.*, Ser. I, Vol. XLVIII, Parts I and II.

[3] This paragraph is based upon various reports, etc., *ibid.* See also Arndt M. Stickles, *Simon Bolivar Buckner, Borderland Knight* (Chapel Hill, 1940), 256, 263–65.

The End of the War

Read, the destination being unknown to the crew. At Alexandria the boat was loaded with cotton and supplied with pine knots for fuel. Early on the morning of April 23 the *Webb* left Alexandria for points south, and it arrived at the mouth of the Red River at half-past eight that evening. The Confederate ram carried the signal lights ordinarily used by Federal boats, and consequently it succeeded in passing the United States squadron near the mouth of the Red River. At Donaldsonville, however, the identity of the *Webb* was revealed, and General Banks at New Orleans was notified of the boat's approach. Banks sent the following note to Brigadier General Thomas W. Sherman, commanding the defenses of New Orleans, on the morning of April 24: "Information is received that a rebel ram passed Donaldsonville this morning. The dispatch is dated 9:20 A.M. If the report has foundation it must be their intention to run the mouth of the river. You will be in readiness for any movement of that kind if it should occur." [4]

A few miles above New Orleans the *Webb* raised the United States flag at half mast, increased her speed to about twenty-five miles an hour, and prepared to race by the city. New Orleans was reached at noon, and Federal boats were waiting for the arrival of the enemy. In spite of the Stars and Stripes the *Webb* was recognized and was fired upon by the Federals. Three shots struck the *Webb,* but no great damage was done; and the Confederate ram raced down the Mississippi loaded with some 250 bales of cotton and a quantity of turpentine and rosin. The Gulf and a foreign port were the destination points of the boat which had only recently left Shreveport.

The Mississippi had been entered, New Orleans had been passed, and the Gulf was not far away. There were, of course, Forts Jackson and St. Philip to the south, but the officers hoped to run by the forts at night. Just as the prospects of

[4] *Official Records,* Ser. I, Vol. XLVIII, Pt. II, 169.

success seemed brightest, the Federal sloop of war *Richmond* was encountered. The order was given to turn the boat around and start back up the river, but at this moment a pursuing gunboat made its appearance, and the *Webb* was trapped. After a few moments' hesitation the *Webb* was run ashore and set on fire by her own crew, twenty-five miles south of New Orleans. The crew escaped into the woods and swamps, separating into small groups the better to avoid capture. One group of fifteen, however, was captured by the Federal forces.[5]

The last months of the war in Louisiana were days of despair and demoralization for the population acknowledging allegiance to the Confederacy. Search as we may in the records, the picture, with little to brighten it, is a tragic one. If the soldiers had been more active, if the enemy had been threatening to conquer the state, and if a real campaign had been waged, more than likely the morale of both soldier and civilian would have been higher. As it was, there was no real test to bring out the best in the people. Times were exceedingly hard, and news from Georgia, South Carolina, and Virginia was most discouraging. There is no wonder, then, that men became disheartened and that a spirit of hopelessness and indifference prevailed among the rank and file.

Louisianians continued their movement into Texas, where conditions were reported to be better and where one was farther from the military lines of the enemy. Thomas O. Moore moved to Crockett, Texas, in the latter part of 1864. On January 3, 1865, his friend Robert C. Hynson wrote to him from Alexandria that

It is all excitement here for the last few days, what is to be the result God only knows. I think I shall fix up and endeavor to remove what few negroes I have left, say 12 to 15—look out for a comfortable little place for me with plenty of house room

[5] The story of the *Webb,* from official reports, is found in *ibid.,* Ser. I, Vol. XLVIII, Pt. I, 203–07, Pt. II, 169–72.

The End of the War

if any such to be found and let me know the chance—Chambers started Friday and Mr. Wells on Sunday last, 2 inst., Ransdell I hear leaves this week, and in fact almost everyone is going, if the Yankees could be kept off, we cannot live here for our own men, they will not let us live, but destroy everything we can make.[6]

Between the demands of the Confederate forces, the demoralization among the slaves who remained, and the raids of small bands of Federals, with the consequent destruction of property, the civilian population of certain parts of Louisiana suffered severely in the closing months of the war. Northeast Louisiana was especially open to attacks by Federal raiding parties from east of the Mississippi. A Federal expedition from Memphis, Tennessee, in late January and early February, 1865, penetrated into the country around Mer Rouge, Bastrop, and Monroe, destroyed much property, and captured more than one hundred Negroes, besides many horses and mules. Two hundred thousand bushels of corn were burned near Mer Rouge. The commander of the expedition reported to his superiors that "the corn being burnt by us, and the horses and mules most thoroughly hunted up and taken possession of," the Confederates could not possibly "this season or during the next year subsist anything more than a scouting party" between the Mississippi and the Ouachita rivers.[7]

Discouragement, discontent, and insubordination prevailed among Confederate forces in Louisiana in 1865. This condi-

[6] Thomas O. Moore Papers. Assistant Adjutant General Joseph F. Belton at Shreveport wrote to Major General John A. Wharton at Nacogdoches, Texas, January 25, 1865: "It has become necessary to withdraw the cavalry of the District of Arkansas from the Red River Valley into Texas. General Buckner is sending his cavalry to the rear. In order to save the country from being consumed by the host of mounted men in the service, the commanding general will soon be forced to reduce their number by at least one-half." *Official Records*, Ser. I, Vol. XLVIII, Pt. I, 1344.

[7] Report of Colonel Embury D. Osband, *Official Records*, Ser. I, Vol. XLVIII, Pt. I, 68–72.

tion resulted chiefly from lack of pay and scantiness of rations, which prompted an ever-increasing number of desertions. It was reported that desertions were occurring daily around Alexandria in January, 1865, although deserters were treated with rigor and several executions a week occurred. A deserter who left Alexandria on January 25 reported to the Federals at Morganza that "Louisiana troops are discouraged and are deserting daily, some going to Mexico, some to the Federal lines. They have not been paid for more than a year." [8] A Confederate soldier wrote from near Alexandria on February 12 that "Every night as many as 6 and sometimes 12 soldiers desert from the Infantry and go home or with the Yankees. The plan of shooting still goes on—and as many as 5 and 6 are sent to their long accounts every week." Writing from the same place on March 1, this soldier said, "The state of things now in this Dept. approaches nearer to mutiny than anything I can say. Our food is the poorest of beef and musty meal—our corn for our horses—and heavy duty. . . . The affairs are badly managed—yes—in a horrible condition." [9]

Federal military authorities were not unmindful of the demoralized state of the Confederate forces, and they sought to reap advantage from the situation. Major General Canby of the United States Army at New Orleans on March 3 issued general orders which promised good treatment to deserters from the Confederate army and other persons who might seek refuge within the Federal lines. Neither deserters nor resigned or discharged officers or soldiers would be forced into the Federal military service. If they were needed they would receive remunerative employment in some department of the army, and if not needed in the army they would be aided in finding other employment. Those whose homes were within the enemy's lines and who did not desire employment would

[8] Report of Lieutenant Myron Adams, Jr., *ibid.*, 728.

[9] Letters of February 12 and March 1, 1865, Frank Palm to Miss Henrietta B. Lauzin, Gras-Lauzin (Family) Papers.

be furnished with transportation to Cairo, Illinois, or to some other point within the loyal states. Serviceable horses and arms of those who came would be purchased at a fair price.[10]

Already there was "talk" of reconciliation with the Union, and the Shreveport *News* of February 14 discussed the matter editorially. According to the *News*, the question of "reconstruction" had been "mooted from time to time by gentlemen heretofore of high standing and character." The *News* condemned the idea in the following language:

Nothing will more dishearten our troops, who have been battling through four long years for the great principles of national independence, than to learn that the people at home, who have experienced none of the hardships and privations which those who fight for our liberties have undergone, have the unblushing affrontery to openly advocate the reunion of the States.

The news of the surrender of General Lee on April 9 was not calculated to strengthen the declining morale of the men and women west of the Mississippi. The leaders realized the necessity of encouraging the army and the populace to remain steadfast in the cause. On April 21 Kirby Smith at Shreveport issued a stirring appeal to the soldiers of his department, saying in part: "The crisis of our revolution is at hand. Great disasters have over-taken us. The army of Northern Virginia, and our Commander-in-chief are prisoners of war. With you rest the hopes of our nation, and upon your action depends the fate of our people." The soldiers were told, "You possess the means of long resisting invasion," and were encouraged to hope for succor from abroad. They were urged to continue the struggle, to stand by the colors, and to maintain discipline, with the promise that the great resources of the Trans-Mississippi Department "will secure to our country terms that a proud people can, with honor, ac-

[10] "General Orders No. 30," *Official Records*, Ser. I, Vol. XLVIII, Pt. I, 1062–63.

cept, and may, under the Providence of God, be the means of checking the triumph of our enemy and of securing the final success of our cause." [11] President Davis, who at this time was in North Carolina on his flight from Richmond, was planning, in case he found no prospect of a successful resistance east of the Mississippi, to cross to the Trans-Mississippi Department and there continue the struggle.[12]

General Smith's message was read to the troops on dress parade at Shreveport on April 24. A Federal scout who was present reported:

The effect of this order upon the troops was marked in the extreme. The men instantly became dejected. Mutiny and wholesale desertion was openly talked of. This soon gave way to a general apathy and indifference, but through all could be seen by a close observer that the Army of the Trans-Mississippi was in spirit crushed.[13]

Governor Allen and a group of prominent Louisianians issued a call for a public meeting at Shreveport on Saturday, April 29, for the purpose of considering "the wants and conditions of the country, and of suggesting such measures as may be necessary to encourage our people and promote the success of our glorious cause." According to a newspaper report, the meeting was attended by thousands, probably two thousand of whom were soldiers; and the exercises lasted from eleven in the morning to four in the afternoon. Among those present were Governor Allen; General Kirby Smith; Lieutenant General Buckner; Major General Sterling Price; Brigadier Generals Harry Hays, Evander McNair, and Alexander T. Hawthorn; Thomas C. Reynolds, whom Confederate authorities recognized as governor of Missouri; Judge Ochiltree of

---

[11] *Ibid.*, Ser. I, Vol. XLVIII, Pt. II, 1284; also published in Shreveport *Semi-Weekly News*, April 22, 1865.

[12] Jefferson Davis, *The Rise and Fall of the Confederate Government* (New York, 1881), II, 696–97.

[13] Report of C. S. Bell, *Official Records*, Ser. I, Vol. XLVIII, Pt. II, 393–403.

The End of the War

Texas; and other prominent men. Allen, Hays, Hawthorn, Ochiltree, and three colonels spoke to the assemblage, asserting that the war was not lost, and that the South should continue the struggle; they appealed to the people to remain loyal and to support the leaders.[14] One Confederate officer at Shreveport wrote to another officer, April 29: "Mass Meeting today. Thayee and I listened awhile. Sun was hot audience cold and speeches as far as we heard good in their way. Ochiltree was to speak. Possibly he will arouse them. Allen's remarks abounded in poetic imagery."[15]

On May 8 General Kirby Smith received Lieutenant Colonel John T. Sprague of the United States Army at headquarters in Shreveport. Colonel Sprague presented his host with a communication from Major General John Pope, U.S.A., stationed at St. Louis. The message from Pope was a request to General Smith to surrender the Confederate forces under his command upon the same terms that General Lee had accepted. Pope pointed out that the armies of the United States were now available for operations in the Trans-Mississippi Department; and the Confederate commander was told that "by prolonging a contest, now manifestly hopeless for any of the purposes for which it was inaugurated," he would be responsible for unnecessary bloodshed and devastation. "Wisdom and humanity alike require that this contest, under the circumstances," said Major General Pope, "be brought to an end without further suffering or shedding of blood."[16]

Kirby Smith rejected the proposal to surrender upon the

[14] Shreveport *Semi-Weekly News*, May 4, 1865. The meeting probably had little effect on the mass of the people. J. C. Wise at Shreveport wrote to Thomas O. Moore on May 8: "The clouds thicken around us from every quarter, every countenance is filled with gloom and despondency." Thomas O. Moore Papers.

[15] Major William H. Thomas to Major John Reid, April 29, 1865, Confederate States Army Collection (B), 1852–1865 (Louisiana State University Department of Archives).

[16] *Official Records*, Ser. I, Vol. XLVIII, Pt. I, 186–87.

terms submitted, saying the terms "were not such as a soldier could honorably accept." He did not believe that an army which was not immediately threatened could "afford to surrender as prisoners of war." He did, however, make counterproposals to Lieutenant Colonel Sprague. He proposed that military resistance to the United States Government should cease in the Trans-Mississippi Department upon the condition that the United States authorities grant immunity from prosecution for past acts to all officers, soldiers, and citizens of the department; that the Confederate officers and soldiers be permitted to return to their homes with transportation furnished as far as practicable; and that all officers, soldiers, and citizens who desired might be permitted to leave the country, with or without their arms. "Many examples of history," he said, "teach that the more generous the terms proposed by a victorious enemy the greater is the certainty of a speedy and lasting pacification, and that the imposition of harsh terms leads invariably to subsequent disturbances." [17]

Meanwhile, Governor Allen had come to the conclusion that the time had come to surrender. He saw that subjugation was inevitable, and, like the gallant Lee, he wished to avoid the useless loss of life. He called on Kirby Smith and offered to go to Washington to seek reasonable terms of surrender for the trans-Mississippi region.[18]

General Kirby Smith's reply to Lieutenant Colonel Sprague was made on May 9. On the same date he addressed a letter to the governors of Louisiana, Texas, Arkansas, and Missouri (Thomas C. Reynolds), requesting them to meet him in conference in order to take action "touching such important matters as are not embraced in my powers as commanding general and as may conduce to the common defense and welfare." This step was necessary, he said, since Richmond had been evacuated and it was impossible to confer with the President. Smith admitted that there was little probability of successful

[17] *Ibid.*, 191–93.   [18] Dorsey, *Recollections of Henry Watkins Allen*, 288.

resistance east of the Mississippi; but his own army, he said, "yet remains strong, fresh and well equipped," and the seat of the Confederate Government "may be transferred to the western side of the Mississippi." [19]

The conference of governors was held at Marshall, Texas, on May 13. Governor Pendleton Murrah of Texas was ill and was represented by Guy M. Bryan as agent of the state of Texas. The executives advised General Smith to accept the following terms of peace: that the Confederate forces in the Trans-Mississippi Department be disbanded, and that officers and men return to their homes, freed from all disabilities and restored to the rights of citizenship; that guarantees be given that no officer, soldier, or citizen should be prosecuted in any court for offenses committed against the United States during the war; that permission be granted to all persons to leave the department, with their arms and effects, unmolested, and go to any foreign country; that the existing state governments be recognized until conventions could be called to settle all conflicts between the people of the states; that all military authority be surrendered to the several states; and that each state should retain _____ [sic] number of men to preserve order and protect life and property.[20]

Governor Harris Flanagin of Arkansas, Governor Reynolds of Missouri, and Guy M. Bryan of Texas requested Governor Allen to visit the United States authorities with a view of making a complete pacification of the Trans-Mississippi Department. "You are fully possessed of the views of each of us in writing," they said, "and we confide in your patriotism and ability. Trusting to your judgment, we will sustain your engagements in the premises." [21] Lieutenant Colonel Sprague, however, did not see fit to allow Governor Allen to accompany him into the Federal lines, reporting that "I did

---

[19] *Official Records*, Ser. I, Vol. XLVIII, Pt. I, 189–90.
[20] *Ibid.*, 190–91.   [21] *Ibid.*, 191.

not feel at liberty to give a safeguard to the governor of a rebel State." [22]

The morale of the soldiers was going from bad to worse; military order had given way to chaos. Contemporary accounts agree that the army in gray was virtually demobilizing and disbanding itself while the leaders were consulting over peace terms. At Alexandria on May 5 Brigadier General Brent reported that the demoralization of the garrisons of Forts Randolph and Buhlow, across the Red River from Alexandria, "is still progressing" and that there were nearly fifty desertions on the night of May 4. The deserters took arms and ammunition with them. "From representations made to me," General Brent said, "I think the temper of the greater part of the troops of the garrisons is such as to forbid the belief that they can be relied on." [23] About two weeks later, May 17, Assistant Adjutant General David F. Boyd, also at Alexandria, wrote to Colonel L. Amedée Bringier of the Seventh Louisiana Cavalry:

The fact can no longer be concealed that the whole army and people, with scarce an individual exception, are resolved to fight no more, and to break up the army at all hazards. All is confusion and demoralization here, nothing like order or discipline remains. Heavy desertions and plundering of Government property is the order of the day. There are but eighty-six men at the forts. All the commands of every arm of the service at and near Alexandria are destroyed . . . in a word, colonel, the army is destroyed and we must look the matter square in the face and shape our actions (personally and officially) accordingly.[24]

Similar scenes were being enacted in the vicinity of Shreveport. According to Sarah Dorsey, conflicting rumors of General Smith's determination to fight and of Governor Allen's resolution to surrender produced a general confusion; and the soldiers became alarmed and "began to disband by hun-

---

[22] *Ibid.*, 188–89. [23] *Ibid.*, Ser. I, Vol. XLVIII, Pt. II, 1294–95.
[24] *Ibid.*, 1310.

The End of the War

dreds in open daylight." Army officers no longer had power to control the soldiers, who blamed their arrears in pay "to the carelessness, negligence, cupidity, or rascality of the quartermasters." Many of the men robbed government stores and depots, justifying their acts on the ground that they had a right to the property since the government was indebted to them for back pay.[25]

General Kirby Smith moved his headquarters to Houston, Texas, on May 18, leaving Lieutenant General Buckner in charge at Shreveport. Smith's purpose, apparently, was to concentrate the entire strength of the Trans-Mississippi Department in Texas. But soon after his arrival in Houston he discovered that he was a general without an army. On May 30 Smith wrote to Lieutenant Colonel Sprague of the United States Army:

When I gave you, at Shreveport, a memorandum which I hoped might be the basis of negotiations with the United States Government, I commanded an army of over 50,000 men and a department rich in resources. I am now without either. The army in Texas disbanded before my arrival here. From one extremity of the department to the other the troops, with unexampled unanimity of action, have dissolved all military organization, seized the public property, and scattered to their homes. . . . The department is now open to occupation by your Government.[26]

Evidently there was nothing left for the commanding officers to do but to make peace. In fact, Confederate general officers in Louisiana opened negotiations for surrender soon

[25] Dorsey, *Recollections of Henry Watkins Allen*, 294–95. See Tunnard, *History of the Third Regiment Louisiana Infantry*, 337, for the plundering in Shreveport on Sunday, May 21. Tunnard said the scene "beggared description."

[26] *Official Records*, Ser. I, Vol. XLVIII, Pt. I, 193–94; Noll, *General Kirby-Smith*, 261–62. Kirby Smith, however, added a postscript to his letter saying that he had learned that "the Missouri and a portion of the Arkansas troops still retain their organization."

after General Smith's departure for Houston, and Smith appointed emissaries for the purpose about the same time. Major General Harry Hays, commanding the Military District of West Louisiana, authorized Brigadier General Brent, Colonel Alcibiades De Blanc, and Colonel Ross E. Burke to agree to terms of peace. These three officers went to Baton Rouge and conferred with Major General Francis J. Herron of the Federal army on May 23. Also, Lieutenant General Buckner, Major General Price, and Brigadier General Brent were authorized by General Smith to make arrangements for the surrender of the Confederate forces in the Trans-Mississippi Department. They went to New Orleans and conferred with Major General Canby on May 25.[27]

The usual date given by historians for the end of hostilities in Louisiana and in the trans-Mississippi territory is May 26, 1865. On that date, in New Orleans, Buckner, in behalf of General Kirby Smith, signed the terms of surrender of the Confederate forces west of the Mississippi River. The terms were the same as those extended by General Grant to General Lee at Appomattox, namely, that the Confederate officers and soldiers were to be paroled until duly exchanged or released from the obligation of parole by authority of the United States; that Confederate property such as artillery, small arms, ammunition, gunboats and transports, except the sidearms and private horses and baggage of Confederate officers and men, should be surrendered to the United States; that officers and men paroled would be allowed to return to their homes, not to be disturbed by the authorities of the United States as long as they continued to observe the conditions of their parole and the laws in force where they resided.[28]

Two events of historic importance occurred on June 2.

[27] *Official Records*, Ser. I, Vol. XLVIII, Pt. II, 562–63, 591; Stickles, *Simon Bolivar Buckner, Borderland Knight*, 269–72.

[28] The peace terms are found in *Official Records*, Ser. I, Vol. XLVIII, Pt. II, 600–01.

The End of the War

Kirby Smith signed the articles of surrender on board the United States steamer *Fort Jackson,* off Galveston harbor. This might be considered as the end of the Civil War, since General Smith was the last of the departmental commanders to accept the Federal peace terms.

The other event was of more immediate concern to Louisiana. Henry Watkins Allen, perhaps the greatest governor in Confederate history, surrendered the cares of office and bade his people of Louisiana farewell in a communication addressed to them. It was an eloquent message and is evidence of the noble character of the man who placed duty to his state above personal ambition or gain, served with distinction on the battlefield and in the governor's chair, and, having lost the struggle, counseled his people to accept the results courageously and gracefully. Governor Allen said, in part:

Fellow citizens:—I have thought it my duty to address you a few words in parting from you, perhaps forever. My administration as Governor of Louisiana closes this day. The war is over, the contest is ended, the soldiers are disbanded and gone to their homes, and now there is in Louisiana no opposition whatever to the Constitution and the laws of the United States. Until order shall be established, and society with all its safeguards fully restored, I would advise that you form yourselves into companies and squads for the purpose of protecting your families from outrage and insult, and your property from spoliation. A few bad men can do much mischief and destroy much property. Within a short while the United States authorities will no doubt send you an armed force to any part of the State where you may require it for your protection.

My countrymen, we have for four long years waged a war, which we deemed to be just in the sight of high heaven. We have not been the best, the wisest, nor the bravest people in the world, but we have suffered more and borne our sufferings with greater fortitude than any people on the face of God's green earth. Now let us show to the world that as we have fought like men—like men we can make peace. Let there be no acts of violence, no heart burnings, no intemperate language, but with manly dignity submit to the inevitable course of events. Neither let there be any repinings after lost property. Let there be no crimination or recrimination—no murmurs. It will do no good, but may do much harm. You who, like myself, have lost all (and oh, how many there are!) must begin life anew. Let us not talk of despair, nor whine about our misfortunes, but with strong arms and stout hearts adapt ourselves to the circumstances which surround us.

. . . .

Refugees, return to your homes. Repair, improve and plant. Go to work with a hearty good will, and let your actions show that you are able and willing to adapt yourselves to the new order of things. We want no Venice here, where the denizens of an unhappy State shall ever meditate with moody brow, and plot the overthrow of the government, and where all shall be dark and dreary—cold and suspicious. But rather let confidence be restored. If required, let each and every one go forward cheerfully and take the oath of allegiance to that country in which they expect in future to live and there pursue their respective avocations with redoubled energy as good, true, and substantial citizens.

I go into exile not as did the ancient Roman, to lead back foreign armies against my native land—but rather to avoid persecution, and the crown of martyrdom. I go to seek repose for my shattered limbs. It is my prayer to God that this country may be blessed with permanent peace, and that real prosperity, general happiness, and lasting contentment may unite all who have elected to live under the flag of a common country. If possible forget the past. Look forward to the future. Act with candor and discretion, and you will live to bless him who in parting gives you this last advice.[29]

With the surrender of Kirby Smith and the retirement of Allen, J. Madison Wells became governor of all of Louisiana, and his position was recognized by President Andrew John-

[29] Alexandria *Louisiana Democrat*, June 14, 1865; also quoted in full by Dorsey, in *Recollections of Henry Watkins Allen*, 298–300. Governor Allen went to Mexico, where he died on April 22, 1866.

son. From his executive offices in New Orleans Governor Wells, on June 10, issued a proclamation to the people of the thirty-five parishes which had been within the Confederate military lines, extending to them congratulations on being restored to the protection of the United States flag, recommending that the bitterness of the past be forgotten and that all look to the future, and advising that they go to work and organize civil governments in the parishes.[30]

It should be observed in closing that neither the retiring Confederate governor, Allen, nor the Union governor, Wells, indulged in any bitterness, recrimination, or vindictiveness. Peace, general happiness, forgiveness, and fraternity were their common aspirations. Their spirit in 1865 was probably representative of the spirit of the people of Louisiana and suggests what might have been had Louisiana been allowed to work out her own destiny. But there were others like Charles Sumner and Thaddeus Stevens who were to control that destiny, and, as our story ends, Louisiana was passing from the tragedies of war to what an eminent American author has styled the Tragic Era.

[30] Alexandria *Louisiana Democrat,* June 21, 1865; *Annual Cyclopaedia,* V (1865), 510–11.

Bibliography

PRIMARY SOURCES

Manuscript Collections

Banks (Nathaniel P.) Papers.
Essex Institute, Salem, Massachusetts. Microfilm copy of the correspondence for 1862–1865 in the University of Texas Archives used in this study.

Confederate States Army Collection (B), 1852–1865.
Louisiana State University Department of Archives.

Consolidated Association of Planters of Louisiana Collection, 1791–1912.
Louisiana State University Department of Archives.

Denison (George S.) Papers.
Library of Congress. Microfilm copy in the University of Texas Archives.

Egan (Lavinia) Collection.
Mt. Lebanon, Louisiana. Miss Egan is a granddaughter of Dr. Bartholomew Egan, superintendent of the state laboratory at Mt. Lebanon, 1864–1865.

Ellis (E. John, Thomas C. W., and Family) Collection, 1829–1936.
Louisiana State University Department of Archives.

Garland (J. D.) Papers, 1863–1870.
Originals in possession of Mrs. J. B. Wright, Monticello, Arkansas. Typed copy in the Louisiana State University Department of Archives.

Good Hope Plantation Collection (A), 1864–1867.
Louisiana State University Department of Archives.

Bibliography

Gras-Lauzin (Family) Papers, 1783–1864.
Louisiana State University Department of Archives.

Landry (Severin, and Family) Collection, 1838–1887.
Louisiana State University Department of Archives.

Liddell (St. John R., and Family) Collection, 1792–1891.
Louisiana State University Department of Archives.

Mandeville (Henry D., and Family) Collection, 1815–1915.
Louisiana State University Department of Archives.

Moore (Thomas O.) Papers, 1832–1877.
Louisiana State University Department of Archives.

Palfrey (William T. and George D.) Collection, 1832–1918.
Louisiana State University Department of Archives.

Pugh (Alexander F., and Family) Collection (A), 1852–1865.
MS. Diary used in this study. Louisiana State University Department of Archives.

Roberts (Abishai W.) Collection, 1837–1916.
Louisiana State University Department of Archives.

Robinson (Harai) Papers, 1861–1889.
Louisiana State University Department of Archives.

Solomon (Clara E.) Diary, 1861–1862.
Louisiana State University Department of Archives.

Tunnard (William H.) Diary, January 1, 1864–December 1, 1864.
Possessed by Mrs. H. T. Gladney, Tunnard's granddaughter, Shreveport, Louisiana.

Weeks (David, and Family) Collection, 1782–1894.
The Weeks Hall Memorial Collection. Louisiana State University Department of Archives.

Public Documents

A. MANUSCRIPTS

Contingent Fund, State of Louisiana, 1860–1865.
Records of the War Department, Confederate Records, Chapter 8, Vol. 116. The National Archives, Washington. Microfilm copy possessed by the writer.

Louisiana in the Confederacy

Contracts of the State of Louisiana.
> Records of the War Department, Confederate Records, Chapter 8, Vol. 134. The National Archives, Washington. Microfilm copy possessed by the writer.

Executive Orders and Proclamations of the Governors of Louisiana, 1860–1865.
> Records of the War Department, Confederate Records, Chapter 8, Vol. 132. The National Archives, Washington. Microfilm copy possessed by the writer.

Journal, Louisiana House of Representatives, Sixth Legislature, 1861–1862.
> Louisiana State University Department of Archives. This journal was never published.

Letters Received, Executive Department, State of Louisiana, 1860–1865.
> Records of the War Department, Confederate Records, Chapter 8, Vol. 131. The National Archives, Washington. Microfilm copy possessed by the writer. Records show dates of letters, names of writers, and brief summaries of contents—sometimes only the subject of the correspondence.

Letters Received, Executive Department, State of Louisiana, July, 1863–May, 1865.
> Records of the War Department, Confederate Records, Chapter 8, Vol. 139. The National Archives, Washington. Microfilm copy possessed by the writer. Records show dates of letters, names of writers, brief statement of contents or of subject matter.

Letter Books, 1860–1862, Mayor's Office, New Orleans.
> City Hall Archives, New Orleans, Louisiana.

Treasurer's Office Records, State of Louisiana, 1859–1865.
> Records of the War Department, Confederate Records, Chapter 8, Vol. 125. The National Archives, Washington. Microfilm copy possessed by the writer.

Volunteer Relief Committee Account Book, 1862, 1st District, New Orleans.
> City Hall Archives, New Orleans, Louisiana.

Bibliography

B. PUBLISHED RECORDS

Acts Passed by the First Legislature of the State of Louisiana, 1853.
> New Orleans, 1853. Library, University of Texas. This was the first Legislature under the new constitution of 1852.

Acts Passed by the Fifth Legislature of the State of Louisiana, Second Session, 1861.
> Baton Rouge, 1861. This volume contains also the acts of the special session of December, 1860. Library, University of Texas.

Acts Passed by the Sixth Legislature of the State of Louisiana, First Session, 1861–1862.
> Baton Rouge, 1862. Library, University of Texas.

Acts Passed by the Twenty-seventh Legislature of the State of Louisiana, Extra Session, Opelousas, December, 1862, January, 1863.
> Natchitoches, 1864. Library, University of Texas

Acts Passed by the Sixth Legislature of the State of Louisiana, Extra Session, 1863.
> Shreveport, 1863. Library, University of Texas.

Acts Passed by the Seventh Legislature of the State of Louisiana, First Session, 1864.
> Shreveport, 1864. Howard Memorial Library, New Orleans.

Acts Passed by the General Assembly of the State of Louisiana, First and Second Session, 1864–1865.
> New Orleans, 1865. Library, University of Texas. This was the "Union" Legislature in New Orleans.

Acts Passed by the Seventh Legislature of the State of Louisiana, Second Session, 1865.
> Shreveport, 1865. Library, University of Texas.

Annual Message of Governor Thomas O. Moore to the Twenty-eighth General Assembly, January, 1864.
> Shreveport, 1864. Copy in the Confederate Memorial Museum, New Orleans.

Louisiana in the Confederacy

Annual Message of Governor Henry Watkins Allen to the Legislature of the State of Louisiana, January, 1865.
> Shreveport, 1865. Copy in the Confederate Memorial Museum, New Orleans.

Congressional Globe, Thirty-seventh and Thirty-eighth Congresses, 1861–1865.

Correspondence of the Treasury Department of the Confederate States of America, 1861–1865.
> Compiled by Raphael P. Thian. Washington, 1879.
> Microfilm copy, University of Texas Archives.

Documents of the First Session of the Fifth Legislature of the State of Louisiana, 1860.
> Baton Rouge, 1860. Library, University of Texas.

Documents of the Second Session of the Fifth Legislature of the State of Louisiana, 1861.
> Baton Rouge, 1861. Library, University of Texas.

Executive Documents Printed by order of the House of Representatives, During the First Session of the Thirty-sixth Congress, 1859–1860.
> Washington, 1860.

Iberville Parish Police Jury Minutes, 1850–1862 in *Transcription of Parish Records of Louisiana,* No. 24, Series I, prepared by The Historical Records Survey, Work Projects Administration, University, Louisiana, 1940.

Journal of the Convention to Form a New Constitution for the State of Louisiana, 1852.
> New Orleans, 1852. Library, University of Texas.

Official Journal of the Proceedings of the Convention of the State of Louisiana, 1861.
> New Orleans, 1861. Library, University of Texas.

Official Journal of the Proceedings of the Convention for the Revision and Amendment of the Constitution of the State of Louisiana, 1864.
> New Orleans, 1864. Library, University of Texas.

Bibliography

Official Journals of the House and Senate of Seventh Legislature of Louisiana, Session of 1864.
> Shreveport, 1864. Library, University of Texas.

Official Journals of the Senate and House of Representatives of the State of Louisiana, Seventh Legislature, Second Session, 1865.
> Shreveport, 1865. Copy owned by Professor Charles W. Ramsdell, University of Texas.

Official Records of the Union and Confederate Navies in the War of the Rebellion, 31 vols.
> Washington, 1895–1927.

Official Report Relative to the Conduct of Federal Troops in Western Louisiana During the Invasions of 1863 and 1864. Compiled From Sworn Testimony Under Direction of Governor Henry W. Allen.
> Shreveport, 1865. Copy in Louisiana State University Library. Reprinted by Otto Claitor, Baton Rouge, 1939.

Public Laws of the Confederate States of America, First and Second Congresses.
> Richmond, 1862–1864.

Reports of the Secretary of the Treasury of the Confederate States of America, 1861–1865.
> Compiled by Raphael P. Thian. Washington, 1878. Microfilm copy, University of Texas Archives.

Richardson, James D., *A Compilation of the Messages and Papers of the Presidents,* 10 vols.
> Washington, 1896–1899.

The Statutes at Large of the Provisional Government of the Confederate States of America, February 8, 1861–February 18, 1862.
> Richmond, 1864.

United States Census, 1810–1860.
> Government Printing Office, Washington.

The War of the Rebellion: A Compilation of the Official Records of the Union and Confederate Armies, 129 vols.
> Washington, 1880–1902.

Louisiana in the Confederacy

Newspapers

A. NEW ORLEANS NEWSPAPERS

Daily Crescent.

Daily Delta.

Daily Picayune.

Price-Current, Commercial Intelligencer and Merchant's Transcript.

Daily True Delta.

> For all New Orleans papers, the files of the Library of the University of Texas and the Howard Memorial Library, New Orleans, were used.

B. OTHER LOUISIANA NEWSPAPERS

Bossier Banner (Bellevue).

> A weekly. Files for July 1, 1859, to June 22, 1860, at the *Bossier Banner,* Benton, Louisiana.

Daily Gazette and Comet (Baton Rouge).

> Files for January 3, 1860, to July 27, 1860, in the Louisiana State University Library.

Louisiana Democrat (Alexandria).

> A weekly. A few copies for the period of the war and a complete file for June 14 to August 2, 1865, in the Public Library, Alexandria, Louisiana.

Shreveport News.

> The name of this paper changed to *Semi-Weekly News* and to *Weekly News* during the war. A complete file for April 13, 1861, to the end of the war, in the Louisiana State University Library.

The South-Western (Shreveport).

> A weekly. Fairly complete files for the war period in the Library of the University of Texas.

Weekly Gazette and Comet (Baton Rouge).

> Files for March 4, 1860, to May 16, 1862, and for August, 1863, to June, 1865, in the Louisiana State University Library.

320

Bibliography

Other Primary Sources

The American Annual Cyclopaedia and Register of Important Events, 1861–1902, generally known as *Annual Cyclopaedia,* 42 vols.
New York, 1862–1903.

Bacon, Edward, *Among the Cotton Thieves.*
Detroit, 1867.

Barker, Jacob, *The Rebellion: Its Consequences, and the Congressional Committee, Denominated the Reconstruction Committee, with Their Action.*
New Orleans, 1866.

Blessington, Joseph P., *The Campaigns of Walker's Texas Division.*
New York, 1875.

Butler, Benjamin F., *Private and Official Correspondence of Gen. Benjamin F. Butler During the Period of the Civil War,* 5 vols.
Norwood, Mass., 1917. Vols. I and II used in this study.

Chase, Salmon P., *Diary and Correspondence of Salmon P. Chase,* in Vol. II of *Annual Report of the American Historical Association, 1902.*
Washington, 1903.

Cox, Samuel S., *Three Decades of Federal Legislation.*
Providence, R. I., 1885.

Davis, Jefferson, *The Rise and Fall of the Confederate Government,* 2 vols.
New York, 1881.

Dawson, Sarah Morgan, *A Confederate Girl's Diary.*
Boston, 1913.

De Bow, J. D. B. (ed.), *De Bow's Review and Industrial Resources, Statistics, Etc.*
New Orleans and Charleston, 1846–1880.

Dorsey, Sarah A., *Recollections of Henry Watkins Allen.*
New York, 1866.

Louisiana in the Confederacy

Dumond, Dwight Lowell (ed.), *Southern Editorials On Secession.*
New York, 1931.

Fleming, Walter L. (ed.), *General W. T. Sherman As College President.*
Cleveland, 1912.

Flinn, Frank M., *Campaigning With Banks in Louisiana, '63 and '64, and With Sheridan in the Shenandoah Valley in '64 and '65.*
Boston, 1889.

Fremantle, Arthur James Lyon, *Three Months in the Southern States, April–June, 1863.*
New York, 1864.

Gordon, George H., *A War Diary of Events in the War of the Great Rebellion, 1863–1865.*
Boston, 1882.

Hepworth, George H., *The Whip, Hoe, and Sword; or, The Gulf Department in '63.*
Boston, 1864.

Hoffman, Wickham, *Camp Court and Siege; a Narrative of Personal Adventure and Observation During Two Wars: 1861–1865; 1870–1871.*
New York, 1877.

Jones, John B., *A Rebel War Clerk's Diary at the Confederate States Capital.* New and enlarged edition, edited by Howard Swiggett, 2 vols.
New York, 1935.

Nicolay, John G., and Hay, John (eds.), *Complete Works of Abraham Lincoln.* New and enlarged edition, 12 vols.
New York, 1905.

Olmsted, Frederick Law, *A Journey in the Seaboard Slave States, with Remarks on Their Economy.*
New York, 1861.

Bibliography

Peabody, Charles A., *The United States Provisional Court for the State of Louisiana, 1862–1865,* in *Annual Report of the American Historical Association for the year 1892.*
  Washington, 1893.

Ripley, Eliza McHatton, *From Flag to Flag; a Woman's Adventures and Experiences in the South During the War, in Mexico, and in Cuba.*
  New York, 1889.

Rowland, Kate Mason, and Croxall, Mrs. Morris L. (eds.), *The Journal of Julia Le Grand, New Orleans, 1862–1863.*
  Richmond, 1911.

Russell, William Howard, *My Diary North and South.*
  Boston, 1863.

Sherman, W. T., *Memoirs of General W. T. Sherman.* Fourth edition, 2 vols.
  New York, 1891.

Smith, Gustavus W., *Confederate War Papers.*
  New York, 1884.

Southwood, Marion, *"Beauty and Booty," The Watchword of New Orleans.*
  New York, 1867.

Taylor, Richard, *Destruction and Reconstruction: Personal Experiences of The Late War.*
  New York, 1879.

Tunnard, William H., *A Southern Record. The History of the Third Regiment Louisiana Infantry.*
  Baton Rouge, 1866.

Van Alstyne, Lawrence, *Diary of An Enlisted Man.*
  New Haven, 1910.

Velazquez, Madame Loreta Janeta, *The Woman in Battle.*
  Richmond, 1876.

Louisiana in the Confederacy

SECONDARY WORKS

Books

Booth, Andrew B. (ed.), *Records of Louisiana Confederate Soldiers and Louisiana Confederate Commands,* 3 vols.
New Orleans, 1920.

Butler, Pierce, *Judah P. Benjamin.*
Philadelphia, 1907.

Cable, George W., *The Creoles of Louisiana.*
New York, 1910.

Caldwell, Stephen A., *A Banking History of Louisiana.*
Baton Rouge, 1935.

Callahan, James Morton, *The Diplomatic History of the Southern Confederacy.*
Baltimore, 1901.

Caskey, Willie Malvin, *Secession and Restoration of Louisiana.*
University, La., 1938.

Chambers, Henry Edward, *A History of Louisiana,* 3 vols.
New York, 1925.

Cole, Arthur Charles, *The Irrepressible Conflict, 1850–1865.*
New York, 1934, in Vol. VII of *A History of American Life,* edited by A. M. Schlesinger and D. R. Fox.

Dictionary of American Biography, 20 vols. and index.
New York, 1929–1937.

Dumond, Dwight Lowell, *The Secession Movement, 1860–1861.*
New York, 1931.

Evans, Clement A. (ed.), *Confederate Military History,* 12 vols.
Atlanta, 1899.

Fay, Edwin Whitfield, *The History of Education in Louisiana.*
Washington, 1898.

Ficklen, John Rose, *History of Reconstruction in Louisiana, (Through 1868).*
Baltimore, 1910.

Bibliography

Fite, Emerson David, *The Presidential Campaign of 1860.*
New York, 1911.

Fleming, Walter L., *Louisiana State University, 1860–1896.*
Baton Rouge, 1936.

Gayarré, Charles, *History of Louisiana,* 4 vols.
New York, 1854–1866.

Hardin, J. Fair, *Northwestern Louisiana, A History of the Watershed of the Red River, 1714–1937,* 3 vols.
Louisville, 1937.

Hesseltine, William B., *A History of the South.*
New York, 1936.

King, Grace, *New Orleans, The Place and the People.*
New York, 1904.

Livermore, Thomas L., *Numbers and Losses in the Civil War in America, 1861–1865.*
Boston, 1900.

Lonn, Ella, *Desertions During the Civil War.*
New York, 1928.

——, *Foreigners in the Confederacy.*
Chapel Hill, 1940.

——, *Salt as a Factor in the Confederacy.*
New York, 1933.

Mahan, Alfred Thayer, *The Gulf and Inland Waters.*
New York, 1883.

Martin, François Xavier, *The History of Louisiana, From the Earliest Period.* 2 vols.
New Orleans, 1882.

Moore, Albert Burton, *Conscription and Conflict in the Confederacy.*
New York, 1924.

Noll, Arthur Howard, *General Kirby-Smith.*
Sewanee, Tenn., 1907.

O'Pry, Maude Hearn, *Chronicles of Shreveport.*
Shreveport, 1928.

Louisiana in the Confederacy

Owsley, Frank Lawrence, *King Cotton Diplomacy; Foreign Relations of the Confederate States of America.*
Chicago, 1931.

——, *State Rights in the Confederacy.*
Chicago, 1925.

Parton, James, *General Butler in New Orleans.*
New York, 1864.

Paxton, W. E., *A History of the Baptists of Louisiana.*
St. Louis, 1888.

Phelps, Albert, *Louisiana; A Record of Expansion.*
Boston, 1905.

Reed, Emily Hazen, *Life of A. P. Dostie; or, The Conflict of New Orleans.*
New York, 1868.

Rhodes, James Ford, *History of the Civil War, 1861–1865.*
New York, 1917.

——, *History of the United States from the Compromise of 1850 to the McKinley-Bryan Campaign of 1896.* New edition, 8 vols.
New York, 1920.

Rightor, Henry (ed.), *Standard History of New Orleans.*
Chicago, 1900.

Robertson, James Alexander, *Louisiana Under the Rule of Spain, France, and the United States, 1785–1807.* 2 vols.
Cleveland, 1911.

Rowell, Chester H., *A Historical and Legal Digest of All the Contested Election Cases in the House of Representatives of the United States, 1789–1901.*
Washington, 1901.

Schouler, James, *History of the United States of America Under the Constitution.* Revised edition, 6 vols.
New York, 1894–1899.

Schwab, John Christopher, *The Confederate States of America; 1861–1865.*
New York, 1901.

Bibliography

Sears, Louis Martin, *John Slidell.*
Durham, N. C., 1925.

Shotwell, Walter Gaston, *The Civil War in America,* 2 vols.
London, 1923.

Shugg, Roger W., *Origins of Class Struggle in Louisiana.*
University, La., 1939.

The South in the Building of the Nation, 12 vols. and index.
Richmond, 1909–1913.

Spears, John Randolph, *David G. Farragut.*
Philadelphia, 1905.

Stickles, Arndt M., *Simon Bolivar Buckner, Borderland Knight.*
Chapel Hill, 1940.

Thwaites, Reuben Gold, *France in America, 1497–1763.*
New York, 1905.

Periodicals

Calhoun, Robert Dabney, "The John Perkins Family of Northeast Louisiana," in *Louisiana Historical Quarterly,* XIX (1936).

Coulter, E. Merton, "Commercial Intercourse with the Confederacy in the Mississippi Valley, 1861–1865," in *Mississippi Valley Historical Review,* V (1919).

Greer, James K., "Louisiana Politics, 1845–1860," in *Louisiana Historical Quarterly,* XII, XIII (1929, 1930).
This has also been published in book form.

Hardin, J. Fair, "An Outline of Shreveport and Caddo Parish History," in *Louisiana Historical Quarterly,* XVIII (1935).

Kendall, Lane Carter, "The Interregnum in Louisiana in 1861," in *Louisiana Historical Quarterly,* XVI, XVII (1933, 1934).

Landers, Colonel H. L., "Wet Sand and Cotton—Banks' Red River Campaign," in *Louisiana Historical Quarterly,* XIX (1936).

McLure, Mary Lilla, "The Election of 1860 in Louisiana," in *Louisiana Historical Quarterly,* IX (1926).

Louisiana in the Confederacy

Owsley, Frank L., "Local Defense and the Overthrow of the Confederacy: A Study in State Rights," in *Mississippi Valley Historical Review,* XI (1925).

Prichard, Walter, "The Effects of the Civil War on the Louisiana Sugar Industry," in *Journal of Southern History,* V (1939).

Ramsdell, Charles W., "The Confederate Government and the Railroads," in *American Historical Review,* XXII (1916–1917).

Roberts, A. Sellew, "The Federal Government and Confederate Cotton," in *American Historical Review,* XXXII (1926–1927).

Robertson, J. C., "Henry Watkins Allen," in *Contemporary Review,* VIII (1866).

Russ, William A., Jr., "Disfranchisement in Louisiana (1862–1870)," in *Louisiana Historical Quarterly,* XVIII (1935).

Shugg, Roger Wallace, "A Suppressed Co-operationist Protest Against Secession," in *Louisiana Historical Quarterly,* XIX (1936).

Trexler, H. A., "The Confederate Navy Department and the Fall of New Orleans," in *Southwest Review,* XIX (1933–1934).

White, M. J., "Louisiana and the Secession Movement of the Early Fifties," in *Proceedings of the Mississippi Valley Historical Association For the Year 1914–1915,* VIII.

Whittington, G. P., "Concerning the Loyalty of Slaves in North Louisiana," in *Louisiana Historical Quarterly,* XIV (1931).

——, "Papers of Thomas O. Moore," in *Louisiana Historical Quarterly,* XIII (1930).

——, "Rapides Parish, Louisiana—A History," in *Louisiana Historical Quarterly,* XV–XVIII (1932–1935).

Wiley, B. I., "Vicissitudes of Early Reconstruction Farming in the Lower Mississippi Valley," in *Journal of Southern History,* III (1937).

Winston, James E., "Notes on the Economic History of New Orleans, 1803–1836," in *Mississippi Valley Historical Review,* XI (1924–1925).

Bibliography

Unpublished Secondary Works

Barker, Olden Lee, "An Historical Account of Red River as an Inland Water-Way."
  M.A. Thesis, University of Colorado, 1929. Copy in possession of Mr. J. Fair Hardin, Shreveport, Louisiana.

Chandler, Luther Edward, "The Career of Henry Watkins Allen."
  Ph.D. Dissertation, Louisiana State University, 1940.

——, "The Regime of General Butler in New Orleans."
  M.A. Thesis, University of Texas, 1930.

Egan, Lavinia, "The History of the Egan Family."
  MS. in possession of Miss Egan at Mt. Lebanon, Louisiana.

——, "The Salines of Bienville Parish."
  MS. in possession of Miss Egan at Mt. Lebanon, Louisiana.

Fontenot, Elfa Lavonia, "Social and Economic Life in Louisiana 1860–1865 as Recorded by Contemporaries."
  M.A. Thesis, Louisiana State University, 1933.

Landry, Ernest Adam, "The History of Forts Jackson and St. Philip with Special Emphasis on the Civil War Period."
  M.A. Thesis, Louisiana State University, 1938.

Leland, Edwin Albert, "Organization and Administration of the Louisiana Army During the Civil War."
  M.A. Thesis, Louisiana State University, 1938.

Ware, Sarah Frances, "General Banks's Red River Campaign of 1864."
  M.A. Thesis, University of Texas, 1931.

Index

Index

Index

Index

Index

Index

Index

Index

Index

Index

Index